KILLING KENNEDY

KILLING KENNEDY

Exposing the Plot, the Cover-Up, and the Consequences

JACK ROTH

FOREWORD BY CYRIL H. WECHT, MD, JD

Skyhorse Publishing

Skyhorse Publishing books may be purchased in bulk at special discounts for
sales promotion, corporate gifts, fund-raising, or educational purposes. Special
editions can also be created to specifications. For details, contact the Special Sales
Department, Skyhorse Publishing, 307 West 36th Street, 11th Floor, New York,
NY 10018 or info@skyhorsepublishing.com.

Skyhorse® and Skyhorse Publishing® are registered trademarks of Skyhorse
Publishing, Inc.®, a Delaware corporation.

Visit our website at www.skyhorsepublishing.com.

10 9 8 7 6 5 4 3 2

Library of Congress Cataloging-in-Publication Data is available on file.

Hardcover ISBN: 978-1-5107-7543-5
eBook ISBN: 978-1-5107-7545-9

Cover design by Brian Peterson

Printed in the United States of America

For those who seek a greater truth.

The very word "secrecy" is repugnant in a free and open society; and we are as a people inherently and historically opposed to secret societies, to secret oaths and to secret proceedings. . . . Our way of life is under attack. Those who make themselves our enemy are advancing around the globe . . . no war ever posed a greater threat to our security. If you are awaiting a finding of "clear and present danger," then I can only say that the danger has never been more clear and its presence has never been more imminent. . . . For we are opposed around the world by a monolithic and ruthless conspiracy that relies primarily on covert means for expanding its sphere of influence—on infiltration instead of invasion, on subversion instead of elections, on intimidation instead of free choice, on guerrillas by night instead of armies by day. It is a system which has conscripted vast human and material resources into the building of a tightly knit, highly efficient machine that combines military, diplomatic, intelligence, economic, scientific, and political operations. Its preparations are concealed, not published. Its mistakes are buried, not headlined. Its dissenters are silenced, not praised. No expenditure is questioned, no rumor is printed, no secret is revealed.

President John F. Kennedy
Address to the American Newspaper Publishers
Waldorf Astoria Hotel, New York, April 27, 1961

President John F. Kennedy. (Source: Bettmann via Getty Images)

CONTENTS

ACKNOWLEDGMENTS

First and foremost, I would like to thank my friend Miguel Mendonça, an extraordinary writer and true Renaissance man, whose invaluable insight into history and human nature helped me determine what kind of book was still worth writing about this topic fifty-eight years after the fact. I will never forget our engrossing—and epically long—conversations about the JFK assassination. His involvement, especially early in the process, set the tone for what was to become a fun and memorable journey. I would also like to thank Mike Candelaria, a great friend and editor whose understanding of storytelling allowed me to confidently bounce every chapter off him and get the feedback I needed regarding the tone, flow, and readability of what were all very complex and extensive interviews. Thanks also to Lorien Fenton, who graciously shared her contacts in the JFK assassination community and allowed me to get my foot in the door with many of the interviewees in this book. To Peter Janney, thank you not only for sharing your incredible insight into the life and death of Mary Pinchot Meyer, but also for your generosity in helping me get this book published and out to the masses. Thank you to all the individuals I interviewed in this book. Your courage, commitment, and desire to seek the truth has truly inspired me, and I will be forever grateful for your time and willingness to tell your stories. And, finally, a heartfelt thank you to my wife, Lisa, and my son, Nathaniel, who have always supported me regardless of how unconventional my projects and endeavors might be. Their unwavering support emboldens me to be "on purpose" in life and seek the truth so that they may experience a better world.

FOREWORD

The author of *Killing Kennedy*, Jack Roth, makes it clear, in no uncertain terms, that John F. Kennedy's assassination matters as much today as it did on Friday, November 22, 1963, because the path the world took following that fateful day instantly deviated from peace and prosperity, shifting toward conspiracy, cover-up and corruption—themes that remain ever-present today.

Roth deftly uses a question/answer format to present this historical event through the eyes of myriad individuals who add color, insight, perspective, and curiosity that hasn't existed in previous books on the subject. It is profoundly fresh and unique, and I commend the author for taking a less-defined path versus a well-worn one when exploring JFK's assassination.

While the book doesn't attempt to exonerate Lee Harvey Oswald, it does explore the human side of a person who very well may have been in the right place at the right time as far as a government cover-up was concerned. Through first-person accounts, Roth helps us better understand the man who was manipulated by the very people to whom he was loyal.

Just when government operatives and caretakers of the lie think—and hope—the relevancy of the JFK assassination is fading into obscurity, *Killing Kennedy* appears, shedding new light, posing new questions, and, most importantly, poking the hornet's nest at just the right time.

As we forlornly approach the sixty-year anniversary of Camelot's sudden and sad demise, it's hard not to wonder what a two-term

Kennedy administration would've delivered. We live in a world shaped by an event so horrific that every citizen—to this day—should demand answers.

Only by acknowledging our past can we hope to avoid the errors of our ways, and that means holding those involved in the conspiracy, the cover-up, and the corruption liable for their dirty deeds. This book provides new insight that could very well move the conversation in the direction of accountability.

It is fascinating to note that the assassination of President Kennedy remains such a point of controversy fifty-nine years later. As we know from history, other US presidents have been assassinated, and there have been unsuccessful attempts to assassinate others. However, with the passage of time, each of those cases came to be accepted as a matter of history by the American public.

Why is the JFK assassination different? Why, after almost six decades, do approximately 60 to 75 percent of Americans continue to reject the conclusions of the Warren Commission, which was established by President Johnson to review the JFK assassination and present its findings to the American public? How many issues in the history of American politics have consistently been rejected by a majority of American voters? Why can we not allow this great tragedy to simply fade away?

If this horrible event had happened in the era of modern-day high technology, I believe the national news media would've pounced on the story like famished hyenas. Imagine the number of cell phones that would've captured still photographs and videos of the presidential motorcade at Dealey Plaza in Dallas that day, from a dizzying array of distinct vantage points, and with image clarity unattainable in the early 1960s. There would've been a drumbeat of blanket, round-the-clock news coverage on cable television, not to mention the vast number of uncensored theories that would no doubt be pinging around the blogosphere.

The federal government wouldn't be able to control something like the Kennedy assassination investigation if it were to happen today. Putting it all together, a passive, politically ignorant public, ambivalent criminal justice professionals and legislators, and journalistic pusillanimity on the part of our major news media are responsible for the way in which the Warren

Commission Report has continued to be accepted and promulgated by the federal government.

The government took advantage of our collective shock as a nation. In the past, the news media knew things we had never learned about, high-level shenanigans such as mistresses in the White House. It's true the media "safety net" for government officials was ultimately torn down by the truth revealed about the Vietnam War and the Watergate scandal and finally fell through under the weight of the Bill Clinton-Monica Lewinsky affair. Today, news media may have reached a new level of obnoxiousness, but it's a different world, especially for the rich and powerful. Nothing will stay secret for long.

Who was responsible for this assassination? In a nutshell, it's the theory of the serious Warren Commission Report critics/researchers that what happened to President Kennedy on that sunny autumn afternoon in Dallas was an act so precise and profound it couldn't have been the work of a lone gunman. The assassination of President Kennedy was a coup d'état, the overthrow of the government. The only people who could've pulled this off were either active or former top-level US military and CIA personnel. It could only have been orchestrated by a host of very secretive, powerful people.

As the author asks: Why is it important to continue to pursue the truth about who killed JFK? Why does this question still matter today?

The simple answer is this: Our country was established upon a foundation of democratic principles. Our position of international power and respect can only remain standing upon pillars of truth.

In the post-World War II years, the CIA, which developed from the Office of Strategic Studies (OSS), became a nation unto itself. It acted as its own government, deciding what was good for America. Any nation whose policies were deemed to be inimical to the United States was dealt with by the CIA through political assassinations, political overthrows of governments, and other furtive means. The CIA was answerable to nobody.

Accordingly, when JFK became president and undertook to make changes of national and international policy that were anathema to the modus operandi and raison d'être of the CIA, he posed a threat to this secretive organization. Following the Bay of Pigs debacle, Kennedy vowed to destroy the CIA. Quite obviously, this presented a serious challenge to that organization.

It must be kept in mind that the people who organized and controlled the CIA, as well as many of the top military personnel in our country, saw America going to hell in a basket under Kennedy's rule. They were looking at five more years of JFK, very likely to be followed by eight years of Robert F. Kennedy, and thirteen years is a lifetime in the sociopolitical development of a country. There was no way they could beat the Kennedys at the polls. There was only one way to get America back on course, as perceived in their eyes. That was by the elimination of John F. Kennedy and five years later the assassination of Robert F. Kennedy.

If this nation is to continue as a respected democracy, we cannot allow actions such as the assassination of a president to go unchallenged.

The continuing cover-up of thousands of pages of documents compiled by the Warren Commission is unacceptable. President Trump and, more recently, President Biden, have withheld the release, which was to have occurred in 2019. This has nothing to do with our national security today. It's absolutely absurd for Trump and Biden to have used this argument to justify the continuing sequestration of all the Warren Commission Report documents.

If the United States is to continue to be a leader in the free world, it's essential our federal government maintain its credibility among American citizens and internationally. To cover up a heinous crime of any individual is morally, ethically, and legally unjustifiable. To do so when it involves an assassination of a president is truly incredible.

I'm confident, and thankful, this book will help keep the JFK assassination relevant and compel readers to ask the important questions . . . and demand truthful answers from our leaders.

—Cyril H. Wecht, MD, JD
Forensic Pathologist and Medicolegal Consultant
December 17, 2021

PREFACE

As a Gen Xer, I have a unique perspective on the United States. I was born in Brooklyn, New York, in 1965, so my earliest and most impressionable memories occurred in the late 1960s and early 1970s—one of the most volatile periods in US history. The Vietnam War, the counterculture movement, the Civil Rights Movement, the Cold War, the Space Race, and political shenanigans (Watergate) all interweaved to create the rather colorful tapestry of my youthful memories.

I was born two years after the John F. Kennedy assassination (1963) and was too young to be directly affected by the Martin Luther King Jr. and Robert Kennedy assassinations (1968). What I *was* affected by were their ripple effects. The world I grew up in was one in which disenchantment reigned and the institutions my parents and grandparents trusted implicitly could no longer be relied upon for having our best interests in mind. I specifically remember watching downtrodden Vietnam veterans, walking around in a half-dazed state as if betrayed by those they trusted and left alone to deal with the wounds (both physical and psychological) they received in Southeast Asia.

I remember feeling like my country was frayed, having recently lost its innocence and left exposed by the wrongdoings of its leaders. The feeling was palpable . . . thus a specific paradigm of the world was etched on my young brain.

By 1976, however, I was living the unincumbered life of an eleven-year-old American boy enthralled with Bicentennial celebrations, the movie *Rocky*, and Nadia Comaneci at the 1976 Summer Olympics. I was a happy-go-lucky kid, but it was around this time I saw something on TV about the JFK assassination and how Jack Ruby shot Lee Harvey Oswald—the only suspect in custody—in the basement of the Dallas police station two days after the assassination. And I remember, after analyzing the events surrounding that shocking development, my logical mind screaming, "Foul play!"

The fact that Ruby (a nightclub owner with ties to the mob) gained such easy access to the police station that day and was able to walk right up to Oswald and shoot him at point-blank range left no doubt in my mind something was rotten in the state of the United States. No trial for Oswald. No opportunity for Oswald—who, after being taken into custody, asserted very plainly that he was a patsy—to tell his side of the story. The "presumed" murderer of President Kennedy had been conveniently silenced forever.

Ruby himself hinted at the conspiracy while in custody, stating, "Everything pertaining to what's happening has never come to the surface. The world will never know the true facts of what occurred, my motives. The people who had so much to gain and had such an ulterior motive for putting me in the position I'm in will never let the true facts come above board to the world."

The entire affair didn't sit well with me, but my mind quickly set its attention on other, more age-appropriate concerns, such as being a seventh grader, playing baseball, and crushing on girls. Life went on, and then, in 1991, at the age of 26, the lights went on for good, thanks to Oliver Stone and his award-winning film *JFK*. I remember being in the theater with my father, watching intently and feeling alternately twinges of anger and sadness. I left the theater in a state of shock, feeling totally betrayed by my own country and knowing—at that moment intuitively and later intellectually after conducting years of research—the official narrative of the Kennedy assassination was a lie.

That evening, I remember sitting with my parents in our living room, talking about how impactful the movie was. My father felt the same way I did, which was that Ruby killing Oswald was more than enough to convince him there was a conspiracy. (He also mentioned the rather ludicrous

Magic Bullet Theory and how he never liked Gerald Ford or trusted Richard Nixon.) My mother specifically recalled a popular journalist and television game-show panelist named Dorothy Kilgallen, who died under mysterious circumstances in 1965. My mother shared that the scuttlebutt back then, and in which she believed, was Kilgallen was murdered because she was investigating the Kennedy assassination and knew too much. Both of my parents added they were profoundly affected by the assassination and would never forget that day as long as they lived.

The conversation with my parents that night, in addition to the world's visceral response to the movie, convinced me that regardless of who killed President Kennedy and why, the ripple effects of the assassination were still being felt not only by Americans, but also by the global community. I also came to the realization the Kennedy assassination was as monumental as the American Civil War. Historians often distinguish between the United States *before* the Civil War and the United States *after* the Civil War, and between the United States *before* the Kennedy assassination and the United States *after* the Kennedy assassination. These two defining events radically changed the course of our history, which is why they will always matter.

When the idea of writing a book about the JFK assassination first crossed my mind, a good friend (also a writer) asked me an important question: What book can you write about the JFK assassination that hasn't already been written and is different from the thousands of other books already published? It was a sobering question and one that forced me to ask what I could contribute that would be fresh. Hours of deep conversation ensued, during which we talked about specific aspects of the assassination and how another book on the topic could be relevant and unique.

Phrases such as "the cost of conspiracy," "perpetual ripple effects," "why it still matters," "a people's history," and "present-day relevance" kept coming up repeatedly. A clear theme was evolving around the idea of the ripple effects of the assassination still being felt today, which is why it still matters fifty-eight years later. Also, the notion of the United States as a beacon of democracy was forever shattered on November 22, 1963, strongly implying there is a serious cost associated with malevolent behavior, conspiracy, and corruption, especially at the highest levels of government and power. Additionally, we must examine our history and learn from our past mistakes, which is why sparking interest in young people is critically important.

The more I thought about it, I also realized that providing context about Lee Harvey Oswald as a human being, and not simply as either a lone-nut assassin or patsy, was something readers would benefit from now and in the future. I set out to speak to individuals who could provide uncommon perspectives on Oswald, thus offering readers an opportunity to know Oswald in different ways. My goal was to gain insight into who Oswald was as a person, what his connection was to the US Intelligence Community, and whether he was "sheep-dipped" to be a patsy.

Interviewing people with distinct perspectives on the assassination (based on either their research or personal experiences) supports the book's goal of offering a comprehensive "people's history" of the event. As such, I endeavored to interview assassination researchers; eyewitnesses to the assassination or related events; sons and daughters of US intelligence operatives who played a role in the assassination or related events; scholars and academics with disciplines in psychology, philosophy, history, and social science; journalists; filmmakers; and those still working to keep the story alive.

With a clear path for this book now laid out in front of me, I was still faced with a rather challenging dilemma involving what I call the three Cs: conspiracy, cover-up, and corruption. Considering recent political events, I wanted to avoid authoring something that would scream "conspiracy theory" and label me a "conspiracy theorist." The word "conspiracy" and phrase "conspiracy theorist" have been muddied and sullied to the point where the very mention of them causes people to roll their eyes. As a result, I concluded it was my responsibility to clear up any misconceptions about the nature of conspiracies and put the Kennedy assassination in its proper place among them. Read: Not all conspiracies are created equal.

Simply stated, if the Kennedy assassination involved more than one assassin, or planning by more than one person, it was a conspiracy. As defined, a conspiracy is *an evil, unlawful, treacherous or surreptitious plan formulated in secret by two or more persons*. Therefore, we must come to the logical conclusion that many people conspire every day (at all levels of power and responsibility) to reach desired outcomes. Whether two coworkers conspire to make another coworker look bad, four thieves conspire to rob a bank, or a foreign government conspires to unlawfully subjugate its citizens, a conspiracy has occurred. Conspiracy is not rare; it is a natural byproduct of human nature.

I want to share two more definitions for the benefit of readers: cover-up and corruption. A cover-up is *any action, stratagem, or other means of concealing or preventing investigation or exposure.* If a young boy steals a cookie from a cookie jar, then cleans up the crumbs on the kitchen counter and denies ever being in the kitchen, he is engaging in a cover-up. On a much larger scale and in the case of the Kennedy assassination, the cover-up would have occurred *after* the assassination took place to prevent any conspiracy from coming to light. You will read a great deal about the many aspects of this particular cover-up in this book.

Corruption is *a form of dishonesty or criminal offense undertaken by a person or organization entrusted with a position of authority, to acquire illicit benefit or abuse power for one's private gain.* History has clearly shown that in the United States, corruption abounds at all levels of government and in the private sector. A local judge receives a bribe to ensure a defendant is found innocent; a CEO embezzles money from his business to pay off a gambling debt; and more specifically: In 1954, the CIA sponsors a coup to dispose of the democratically elected president of Guatemala to protect the profits of the United Fruit Company. These are all forms of corruption.

In this book, the three Cs come up repeatedly in almost every interview, strongly indicating that current perspectives on US politics and institutional behavior in the 1960s (and up to the present day) are far from flattering.

An important fact pertaining to the three Cs is there are many conspiracy theories that turned out to be true. Examples include: the CIA secretly gave LSD to unsuspecting individuals to test mind control (Project MKUltra); the Gulf of Tonkin attack never happened; the Tuskegee Study of Untreated Syphilis in the Negro Male was sanctioned by the US government, resulting in the deaths of more than 128 black men from syphilis and related causes; tobacco companies hid evidence that smoking is deadly; the US government employed Nazi scientists after World War II

(Operation Paperclip); the CIA developed a heart attack gun; the CIA spied on and controlled the American media (Operation Mockingbird); contaminated polio vaccines spread a cancer-causing virus; and the US government planned to commit domestic terrorism and blame Cuba (Operation Northwoods). In each of these examples, the parties involved in the conspiracy denied any involvement in the plan and attempted to cover it up.

I knew at the outset of this project I would gain a much deeper understanding of not only the Kennedy assassination, but also of the unique period in US history during which this crime was committed. In 1963, the Cold War dictated US government policy, and our intelligence agencies ran amok with zero accountability to ensure Communism was thwarted. The CIA, along with other extremely powerful agencies and individuals, were given carte blanche to play God, mandates and laws be damned. Assassinations of foreign heads of state and CIA-sanctioned military coups in foreign countries were commonplace, as was the Cold Warrior mind-set, which dictated that any means to an end, including nuclear war, was justified to defeat the Red Menace.

On December 22, 1963, exactly one month after JFK's murder, former President Harry Truman said, "I never had any thought that when I set up the CIA that it would be injected into peacetime cloak and dagger operations. . . . There is something about the way the CIA has been functioning that is casting a shadow over our historic position, and I feel that we need to correct it."

The reality is, many factors came into play to seal the fate of President Kennedy, including the Bay of Pigs fiasco and his desire to "splinter the CIA into a thousand pieces and scatter it into the winds." When people ask me who killed Kennedy, I reply, "The Cold War." My hope is that readers also gain a more nuanced understanding of how the prevailing mentality of those times led to Kennedy's death.

Based on my own research, I have formed my own opinions regarding the assassination, although I will readily admit I will probably never know exactly what happened because, simply stated, I was not there. But as a writer and journalist, I wanted to approach the interviews for this book in an objective manner, while also taking a more conversational and relaxed approach with the interviewees, who, in some cases, would be sharing very personal and emotional memories with me. I prepared a few "fixed" questions I would ask everyone based on the book's overriding themes, and then I came up with several more fluid questions depending on the interviewee's specific discipline or experiences.

In essence, I would follow the lead of the interviewees. By doing so, I attempted to create a tome of comprehensive insights on the assassination that would ultimately represent a springboard for readers on which they could jump off in any direction they desire. The goal of the book is to entertain and inform readers, but also to inspire them to learn more, think critically and draw their own conclusions as free-thinking individuals.

It is my deepest desire this book brings to light the fact that regardless of who killed President Kennedy and why, it is our responsibility as citizens living in a free society to call out and hold responsible all conspirators; corrupt, narcissistic leaders; privileged elitists bent on control; and those who would cover up the truth for personal gain. It is also our responsibility to recognize the victims and collateral damage associated with conspiracy and corruption. In the case of the Kennedy assassination, the collateral damage was, and continues to be, vast and immeasurable.

We also have a responsibility to recognize those who have dedicated their lives to searching for the truth to make *everyone's* lives better. I'm amazed at the dedication of the researchers who continually risk their reputations to dare question the validity of official narratives, and I admire their courage and determination.

And finally, we have a responsibility to look at the Kennedy assassination with fresh eyes, with the eyes of those who have not been indoctrinated by Cold War rhetoric and blinded by the dangerous lure of nationalism. John F. Kennedy was far from a perfect man, but he was a thoughtful, empathetic leader who stood for hope, progress, and peace. And Lee Harvey Oswald was not a nut case bent on achieving infamy; he was a highly intelligent man who, according to those who really knew him, admired John F. Kennedy. People are complicated, and nothing is ever "black and white." Such is the case with the Kennedy assassination.

The truth is important, and unfortunately, in some cases, it does not come freely or easily. The late Carl Sagan noted, "One of the saddest lessons of history is this: If we've been bamboozled long enough, we tend to reject any evidence of the bamboozle. We're no longer interested in finding out the truth. The bamboozle has captured us. It's simply too painful to acknowledge, even to ourselves, that we've been taken. Once you give a charlatan power over you, you almost never get it back."

We must steadfastly seek to uncover and ultimately demand the truth in all things. Nobody has ever been tried or punished for the murder of the 35th president of the United States. Lee Harvey Oswald never had a chance to tell his story or have his day in court. We should all see this as a travesty of justice. My hope is this material triggers something in readers and inspires them to dig further. Democracy and freedom depend on all of us doing so. As Kennedy himself once said, "One person can make a difference, and everyone should try."

—Jack Roth
October 7, 2021

PART 1

THE RESEARCHERS

At a certain point in his presidency, John Kennedy turned a corner, and he didn't look back. I believe that decisive turn toward his final purpose in life, resulting in his death, happened in the darkness of the Cuban Missile Crisis. Although Kennedy was already in conflict with his national security managers, the missile crisis was the breaking point. At that most critical moment for us all, he turned from any remaining control that his security managers had over him toward a deeper ethic, a deeper vision in which the fate of the earth became his priority. Without losing sight of our own best hopes in this country, he began to home in, with his new partner, Nikita Khrushchev, on the hope of peace for everyone on this earth—Russians, Americans, Cubans, Vietnamese, Indonesians, everyone on this earth—no exceptions. He made that commitment to life at the cost of his own. What a transforming story that is.

—James Douglass, author and researcher
From his keynote address at the 2009 Coalition on Political
Assassinations Conference in Dallas

CHAPTER 1

DAVID MANTIK

David W. Mantik, MD, PhD, received his doctorate in physics from the University of Wisconsin and was a member of the physics faculty (as assistant professor) at the university before leaving for medical school. He completed his internship and residency in radiation oncology at LAC/USC Medical Center in Los Angeles. He also completed fellowships in physics at the University of Illinois and in biophysics at Stanford University, as well as a junior faculty clinical fellowship with the American Cancer Society. Mantik has carried out extensive research into the assassination of John F. Kennedy, including detailed studies of Kennedy autopsy X-rays and the Zapruder film. In 1993, after examining the autopsy X-rays at the National Archives, Mantik disclosed they had been altered. He also stated there were three shots that struck Kennedy's head and that the magic bullet theory was anatomically impossible. Learn more about his research by going to his website, themantikview.com.

Where were you when the assassination occurred, and what was your reaction?

I was working on my PhD in physics at the University of Wisconsin, Madison. It was lunchtime, the same time as in Dallas. We didn't have a TV in our lunchroom, but we had a radio on. So, as soon as the events transpired, we listened to them on the radio. The whole weekend was one of mourning for most of us. We went on with our research that afternoon, but I remember gathering with friends that evening and commiserating with them about this disaster. It was totally shocking. It just came out of nowhere.

It was clear this was deliberate as soon as we heard the news. It would take quite a marksman to do this, even if you were just listening over the radio. So, we knew there was something nefarious going on, but we didn't really have any idea who was behind it.

I missed the moment Oswald was shot on live television, but I heard about it shortly after. I did get a chance to watch the replays on television that same day. I was at Memorial Union on the University of Wisconsin campus. It was stunning. Immediately, you start thinking, "Wow. What's going on here? This isn't normal behavior." But final conclusions had to wait.

What triggered your involvement in this work?
The movie *JFK* by Oliver Stone really sent me down this path. My wife wanted to see the movie, and I said, "So do I, but I don't want to be brainwashed by Oliver, so let me do a little research first, and then we'll see the movie." What I discovered was amazing. There was so much uncertain material in the public eye and so much work that hadn't been done by historians. I was simply astonished. A few months later we finally saw the movie, and I wasn't surprised at all.

The other trigger was the Journal of the American Medical Association (JAMA). I was a member, so I received the journal regularly, and I was horrified at the interviews they did with James Humes and Thornton Boswell, the autopsy pathologists. I predicted in advance they wouldn't describe the throat wound because that would give the game away. And of course, I was right. They never described it in either of the two articles they did. They totally evaded the issue. I was so horrified by this I told the AMA to drop my membership.

What caught my attention in this case was the X-rays. It was said there was no evidence of a blowout to the back of Kennedy's head, which was what was reported by virtually all the witnesses at Parkland Hospital. As we later learned, this was echoed by the witnesses at Bethesda Naval Hospital, where the autopsy was performed. They agreed with one another, but it was also asserted there was no visible hole in the back of the head on the X-rays. In addition, there was no evidence for a large bullet fragment on the skull X-rays at the autopsy, but during the Clark Panel examination in 1968,[1] this was found to be false. There was a blatant disagreement between the autopsy personnel and the Clark Panel experts. On the extant X-rays in the National Archives, there's a large cross section of a bullet within JFK's right orbit.

I was able to view these images in David Lifton's book, *Best Evidence*, as the X-rays had become public by that time. I was focused on that nearly circular 6.5 mm object on the anterior-posterior X-ray, which looked white on the prints in the book. I wondered how it could be there and yet apparently not be visible to anyone at the autopsy. Not only did they not report it, but probably dozens of other people in the autopsy room saw the X-rays that night. They were posted publicly in the morgue, and nobody asked a single question about that, which was totally incomprehensible to me.

To really make the point, when I was looking at these images in Lifton's book at breakfast one morning, I realized how obvious it was. My seven-year-old son and five-year-old daughter were having breakfast with me, so I asked each of them in turn to see if they could spot the bullet in the image. They both found it almost immediately. Neither of them had any training in radiology, but they could do better than all the autopsy personnel, including the radiologist, John Ebersole, who was at the autopsy. This made no sense to me.

What happened next?

After reading Lifton's book, I wanted to visit the National Archives to examine the X-rays in person. I wrote a letter to Burke Marshall, who was the Kennedy family attorney, and it took him about a year to approve my request. I have no idea why it took so long. I went armed with everything, virtually all my equipment I thought might be useful. It was quite an experience. You can't look at any of the JFK autopsy material without one, if not two, personnel from the Archives lurking over your shoulder, making sure you don't destroy any of the evidence.

It was extremely rewarding for me. I took the optical densitometer so I could take measurements of various sites on the X-rays, and especially on the 6.5 mm object within JFK's right orbit. I prepared in advance a very detailed screw mechanism so I could take measurements at 1/10th of 1 mm intervals across this object, in multiple directions, which is very precise. I made hundreds of measurements on this object and other parts of the X-rays, as well.

What did you discover?
It was immediately obvious this object was added to the original X-ray via a second exposure[2] because I could compare the optical density of the object with the optical density measurements on JFK's dental amalgams, which were mercury silver. This object, based on the measurements, had to be several centimeters long from front to back in that right orbit. And that makes no sense because the dental amalgams, which you can see in the House Select Committee on Assassinations report, and which I could measure on the X-rays, were indicating they were not as thick as this object. JFK had three or four teeth with dental amalgams on each side of his mandible, so this object in the right orbit was longer from front to back than all these amalgams lined up in a row. And that's crazy because on the lateral X-ray you can see that this object, supposedly within the right orbit, can only be a few millimeters at the most in length. So, there was a gross inconsistency that was obvious right away.

What have you concluded about the assassination based on your research?
I concluded the Warren Commission wasn't really interested in the truth. That's the bottom line.

The autopsy pathologist stated quite clearly there was a shot to the right rear of the head, near the external occipital protuberance. I agree with that. And there must be at least one more shot to the head, most likely from the front, entering the hairline in the right forehead, because there's a metallic trail of debris across the top of the skull. So, whether you argue it's from the front or back, there must be a second shot to the head. And that's immediately a problem because, according to the Zapruder film, there wasn't enough time to get off what would be a fourth shot. It's also clear this second shot came from the front, as well, because there are tiny metal fragments in the forehead area.

So, we've got a shot from the front, entering at the hairline in the right forehead, and that trail of debris goes posteriorly, but it's at the top of the skull. Then we have a shot from the right rear of the head, near the external occipital protuberance, which is a second shot. We have a lot of eyewitnesses who saw this, and we have personnel who saw autopsy photographs very early in the game who saw that shot.

I also know from visual inspection and from my optical density measurements the bone is missing there, so everything fits together perfectly with that scenario. But there had to be a third shot to the head because the shot that came in at the right forehead seems to have petered out. The metallic trail of debris ends before it gets to the back of the head, and witnesses clearly described a large hole, perhaps grapefruit-size, at the right rear of the head. This forehead shot didn't do that. It's in the wrong location, it's too high, and it peters out too quickly, yet we have many other eyewitnesses who saw a shot enter just in front of the right ear, near the top.

James Jenkins, who was assisting Humes and Boswell that night, described a hole in the skull at that point, and he was literally inches away from it. A shot coming in at a tangential angle would be just right to produce the large hole at the rear of the skull, and this is the shot that led to the debris that hit the motorcycle police to the rear of the presidential limo.

I didn't arrive at this conclusion of three headshots right away. This scenario evolved over the years as I slowly integrated all the data, including eyewitness testimonies. So, we're left with three shots to the head, which is uncanny. If you don't put all three shots in there, you're left with no explanations for certain observations or results you can see on the X-rays. It's just an incomplete picture.

What did you discover during your follow-up visit to the National Archives in 2001?

It proved to be an extremely useful visit, as I made one very important new observation. On one of the lateral X-rays of JFK's skull, there's a T-shaped inscription. It's like somebody scraped the emulsion. It's lying on its side, just below the mandible. By itself it has no significance or meaning, and we shouldn't focus on that. But what I wondered about was something else, from a radiologist point of view. It prompted a very simple question. Since this could only have been formed by scraping the emulsion off the X-ray film, I wondered if the emulsion was truly missing on that X-ray. And to my amazement, when I looked at the film, the emulsion wasn't missing.

This was the one occasion when Steve Tilley, the caretaker of the JFK Collection, took the X-ray film out of its transparent plastic sheet so I could look directly at the surface on both sides. We looked at the surface with glancing light so I could easily detect whether emulsion was missing, but in this case, it was like a smoothly glazed skating rink. It was extremely smooth on both sides. There was no emulsion missing, and yet this thing could only have been made by scraping the emulsion off.

So, the bottom line is this: This is a copy film. There's no other alternative that works here. Somebody copied the original X-ray, thus saving the

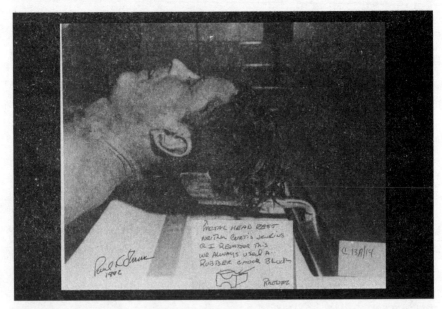

An autopsy photograph of the body of President Kennedy at Bethesda Naval Hospital in Bethesda, Maryland. (Photo by Pascal Le Segretain/Sygma via Getty Images)

T-shaped inscription. But on the copy film, the emulsion wasn't missing. Nobody scraped it off the copy film; they scraped it off the original. I could conclude, therefore, that this wasn't the original film. It can't possibly be. This is basically a photograph of the original film made in a darkroom.

These obviously have been altered by time. If you look at the edges of these films, the emulsion is peeling up, as it does over decades. I looked at them carefully through the microscope, as well. Everything fits with these being fifty-plus-year-old films, so no problem there. As far as the alterations, of course, the 6.5 mm object within JFK's right orbit is an alteration, but I knew this from earlier visits.

What was your biggest eureka moment as a JFK assassination researcher?
I was back home thinking about these X-rays and the so-called "Harper fragment" and wondering where it possibly could've come from. This was a piece of JFK's skull found in Dealey Plaza by Billy Harper, a premed student at the time, so it was named after him. I realized, while looking at the X-ray taken from the front of the skull, there was bone missing at the back of the skull. I hadn't quite realized how easily the Harper fragment could fit in there because there's a lot of bone the X-ray beam encounters in going from front to back. I realized the fragment could fit right in there, at the back of the skull.

I was able to confirm, in subsequent visits to the Archives, that the fragment fits very clearly into the back of the skull. I was also able to confirm it by another totally separate route. I measured the optical density on the lateral X-ray of the back of the head. As you go down the back of the head on the X-ray, you can measure the optical density from top to bottom. If there's a sudden disruption in the continuity of the numbers, you know bone is missing, and that's exactly what I found.

So, I could place the fragment precisely at the back of the head, but it really required these detailed measurements to confirm it. And this is important because the fact the Harper fragment came from the back of the skull is only possible with a shot from the front. And specifically, it would've happened because of the shot near the right ear, not from the forehead.

Harper took it to his uncle, who was a pathologist in Dallas. Three pathologists at the hospital examined it, and all of them agreed it was from the back of the head, totally consistent with what I concluded. In the early '90s, we interviewed one of these pathologists on a radio show in Palm Springs, and he confirmed this was the case. He never changed his mind about it. He also described lead light debris on one edge, and this is probably where the posterior bullet came into the skull and deposited some lead on the surface of the fragment.

Were there any low points along your journey?
A JFK researcher attacked me and told the public I was lying. That wasn't very nice. I was raised by a devoutly religious mother who drummed one lesson into my head, and that was never lie. This has stayed with me all my life. This researcher is a believer in conspiracy in this case, but he has his own opinions about what happened. He disagrees with my findings, which is fine, but he accused me of lying, which is extreme.

I grew up a very dedicated American, believing in my government, thinking the United States knew what to do and what was right. Those beliefs stayed with me for a very long time, and it wasn't until I encountered the JFK fiasco I began to seriously question many other areas of American public life.

In view of what I told you about my mother, my focus always has been on finding out the truth, which does come at some personal cost. Not everybody is happy to hear the truth. One must be careful, even with one's friends, when you declare the government has been lying about one issue or another.

What have been the ripple effects of the assassination?
Immediately after the assassination, the Europeans seemed to know what was going on. If you read their early books, they were quite convinced this was a domestic conspiracy. It was only in America we didn't seem to know that. For us it had to be a lone-nut communist, but the Europeans knew better. It made us look bad on the national scene to be so narrow-minded and so focused on Oswald. There was a price to be paid there. We were looked down on as being rather simple about this.

In your opinion, was Lee Harvey Oswald a patsy?
Yes. He said that, and I believe that's the case. He must've known something about this whole scenario to even think of uttering that phrase. How
many other so-called assassins have ever uttered a phrase like that? "I'm
just a patsy." Can you think of any in history who have said that? The
bottom line is there were too many shots to fit into the Zapruder film and
the time required to fire the Mannlicher-Carcano rifle, so it doesn't make
any sense at all.

When I look at the case, the entire range of emotions comes to the surface for me. I'm angry, very disappointed in the government investigation,
and at some level furious that this kind of misbehavior could occur using
our own tax dollars. We don't contribute money to Washington, DC, to
have something like this happen.

Why does the JFK assassination still matter all these years later?
For me, it cracked open the door to government misbehavior in general.
I think this has been the case for many other researchers, as well. We
may have suspected at some level the government wasn't always telling
the truth, and we're vaguely aware of that, but when you see how blatantly they were willing to cover up and overtly lie about the assassination,
it really opens your eyes, and you wonder, "What can you trust in the
end?" And of course, in view of the decades that have passed since, those
questions become ever larger, in boldface. And you wonder, "Where's the
truth? How can you even find it today?"

This case reveals what human beings will do under pressure or when
their deep beliefs are challenged. This is the most important lesson I've
learned through this case. It's not simply that there was a conspiracy and
the government didn't want us to know; it taught me what human beings
are really like. Because once you know what the truth is, you have a good
measuring stick to assess other people's responses, their logical abilities,
their emotional status, and their personal biases. And most human beings
fall pretty darn short of being perfect on that scale.

The work of American social psychologist Stanley Milgram was published in 1963, just months before the assassination. Milgram found that
most human beings, under a little duress from people of authority, will go

to amazing lengths to follow orders. We knew this from the Nazis, didn't we? This is just natural human behavior. There's nothing new here, but the JFK assassination just reaffirmed all these issues so indelibly in my mind.

Human beings are generally friendly and happy to work with you, that is, until their beliefs are oppressed, or unless there's an authority figure telling them what to do. Of course, Humes and Boswell were the prime examples of this. They were in the military. Humes was a Catholic. Is there authority in the Catholic church and the military? He just couldn't tell the truth about what he really found, but he tried very hard to do it. Over the years, I've picked up subtle hints he was trying to share what he could, but he was so limited in what he could say.

We should also remember the CIA was formed in the late 1940s, and the unaccountability of the intelligence agencies is clearly behind all of this. If you don't have accountability, human behavior can go awry quickly. We've seen this in spades in this case. So, I think our country, our democracy, changed dramatically when the intelligence agencies came on the scene in the post-World War II era.

What would you want younger generations to understand about the JFK assassination?
I would like the history books to tell the truth. We've emphasized truth a great deal in this conversation today, but I think history books should tell the truth, too. Why don't we just tell our students our president was killed by domestic conspiracy? Because he was. I remember going to my daughter's fifth- or sixth-grade class. Coincidentally, when I was there, one of her classmates gave a talk on the JFK assassination, and she said, quite overtly, that Oswald did it. And I thought, "Oh my god. Really?" So, at least the history books should tell the truth; we shouldn't routinely be lying to our children.

And the media are captured by the corporate mind-set. People who try to tell the truth in this case can't because the people at the top won't let them. In fact, I have a good example of this. I did a long series of video interviews with Fox News once. The two fellows who were doing this were really excited about it, and I was hopeful something would happen, but the CEO of Fox News at the time, Roger Ailes, caught wind of it, and that was the end of those interviews ever airing.

If you could get the answer to one question in the case, what would it be?

At this stage of my research, I'm most curious about who pulled the triggers and who told them to. What was the chain of command there? I think we're getting a little more information about that now. This isn't my area of expertise, so I'm not going to make any specific comments, but I'd be delighted for other researchers to give us more information about the chain of command.

And I wonder, given his role in the case, how did William Harvey[3] justify his membership on the governing board of his church? He was one of the top counterintelligence officials in the CIA. He worked very closely with James Jesus Angleton and was responsible for building the tunnel in Berlin during the height of the Cold War. He's one of the top men in the CIA going way back, and most researchers suspect he either knew about the conspiracy or may even have been one of the primary planners of the assassination.

So, I found it interesting he was so devout in his church work, the Lutheran church in Ohio, after he retired. Given my own background in the Pentecostal church, I couldn't put those two things together. I couldn't live with myself if I had any guilt at all from the Kennedy assassination, so that's a real conundrum to me.

What is your biggest motivation at this point to continue your work?

I don't think there's much more I can do on the medical side. I've been to the National Archives nine times and focused on integrating those findings with the research in collaboration with witnesses and other experts. My optical density measurements have been verified to a degree. The gatekeepers are now very stingy about letting people back into the Archives. In fact, the tenth time I asked for permission to visit, I was flatly refused. The reason they offered was I had been there nine times, and that was enough. They felt I should've seen everything I needed to see during those visits.

If we had been allowed to see the original autopsy photographs and X-rays unaltered, everyone, even nonmedical people, would've known there were shots from the front, and the official story would've been torn apart immediately. So, they had to cover this up if they wanted to go with the Oswald narrative. They really had no choice, and they went to extreme lengths to do it. They did some stupid things in the alterations, from my perspective.

On the autopsy photos, the back of JFK's head is intact, and there's virtually no blood. It looks like somebody had just washed his hair, and there's no hole in the back of his head whatsoever. Sixteen Parkland physicians were shown these autopsy photos and asked, "Is this what you remember?" And all sixteen of them said, "No. That's not what I remember." It's absurd when you really look at it.

Is there anything else you wish to add?
I wish you the best with your work. You must carry the flame forward now. You and other researchers like yourself must do this because I've done my bit. If there were more I could do, I would do it, but I think I've pretty much reached the end of the road as far as the medical evidence is concerned. So, my best wishes to you.

CHAPTER 2

LARRY RIVERA

Larry Rivera was born the son of a career military man who served as a CID officer in the Army (criminal investigations). He is a Certified Network Engineer who has made a lifelong study of the JFK assassination, making his first trip to Dealey Plaza in 1991. He is the author of *The JFK Horsemen*, in which he presents compelling evidence—using modern-day digital computer technology and forensic digital overlays—that places Lee Harvey Oswald standing in the Texas School Book Depository front doorway while the assassination took place. Through this type of digital overlay analysis, he also determined the backyard photos of Lee Harvey Oswald holding the rifle used to shoot Kennedy were cleverly manufactured to frame him. Rivera is also considered a leading expert on the JFK motorcycle escort officers.

What triggered your involvement in JFK assassination research?
We lived in Germany at the time of the assassination because my dad was stationed there at the time. I was six years old, and I remember that night my dad had the graveyard shift but hadn't left for work yet. My mother came in and told us after a neighbor told her. The expression on my father's face . . . his reaction to hearing the news . . . was overwhelming to me. It was a mixture of shock and sadness.

From there I maintained an interest in the case. As I grew up, I read magazines that discussed it. When I went to college, the House Select

Committee on Assassinations[1] was looking into the assassinations of JFK and Martin Luther King Jr., so I read what little came out in the newspapers about that. I eventually left college and started to work, but I continued to read many of the books that were coming out.

In the early 1990s, I happened to be in Dallas for an IT certification. I made a point of going to Dealey Plaza, and my first impression was how small it was and how mystical it seemed. It's so small in comparison to what you see in videos and movies. Some people who profess some type of knowledge about the case, believe it or not, have never been to Dealey Plaza. If you're going to investigate this case, you should go there, look at the angles, and study the place.

On the 25th anniversary of the assassination, 1988, a lot of shows were produced. I believe that's the first time they showed the Nigel Turner documentary series *The Men Who Killed Kennedy*. His contributions were so fantastic that the deep state[2] had to take measures to make sure those episodes, especially the last ones, were never aired again. Fortunately, they're on YouTube, and you can download them there.

How did your interest grow from there?
I started studying the contributions of early researchers, including Sylvia Meagher, Harold Weisberg, Mark Lane, and Vincent Salandria. These are people who risked their lives to investigate this when the case was still fresh. There was a woman named Shirley Martin who decided to start interviewing witnesses almost immediately after the assassination, and a few years later her oldest daughter, Victoria, who had accompanied her mother to Dallas to interview witnesses, was killed when another car sideswiped her Volkswagen Beetle. Shirley gave up her research after that. I got to know her son, Steve, whom I interviewed for my book.

I also must credit J. Gary Shaw, who wrote the outstanding book *Cover-Up* in 1976. I wrote him and asked for some resources and contacts in the research community, and he suggested contacting Jerry Rose, who published the now defunct *The Third Decade*, which became *The Fourth Decade*, a journal that published six times a year. Before the Internet, that's when researchers published their papers and investigations. I devoured all that and kept buying books. After the movie *JFK* came out, I started obtaining documents. I'm a firm believer in using primary source material and not just reading a book and interpreting somebody else's interpretation. I like to read the documents they cite and form my own opinion.

Now that we're seeing this deluge of new declassified documents coming out, for those of us who have been on the case for so long, they're a treasure trove. You just have to get in there, roll up your sleeves, and read, collate, classify, and see where these new pieces of the puzzle fit. Then you must step back and look at the big picture again with a different frame of mind.

What do these new declassified documents reveal?
They tell us a lot about what happened in Mexico City. For example, one of the most important chapters of my new book is on Sylvia Duran, the secretary at the Cuban Consulate. She supposedly had these encounters with a "Lee Harvey Oswald" who was there to obtain a transit visa to go to Cuba, then on to the Soviet Union, after supposedly making his escape after the assassination. When you look at that in terms of a timeline, you ask how he could go in late September or early October to get this visa, but he wasn't escaping until late November. There's no cohesiveness there, and it doesn't even say he's coming with his wife and kids. It doesn't make any sense at all.

Another thing we've learned is three of Mexico's most important presidents, from 1958 to 1976, three consecutive presidents on six-year terms, were active CIA agents with their own cryptonyms. Winston Scott was the CIA Chief of Station in Mexico City and was the architect of the espionage operation, wiretapping, and photographing of the Cuban and Soviet embassies, which were done in league with the Mexican government. The Mexicans provided the manpower, and the Americans provided the technology. Journalist Jefferson Morley called Mexico City the "Casablanca of the Cold War" through its connections to competing capitalist and communist governments and agendas.

Looking at the cables coming out of Mexico City, former Canadian diplomat Peter Dale Scott has determined they don't make any sense if you construct a timeline. It looks more like a CIA operation, post-assassination, where they're trying to create the document trail saying this is Lee

Harvey Oswald walking into the Cuban consulate applying for visas. If it *did* happen, it was an imposter. They're backdating documents and cables to create a paper trail they could use to prove Oswald went to Mexico City.

This was something that came out of the Lopez Report, which was classified until 1992, when it became one of the first documents released through the Assassination Records Review Board,[3] which was set up because of the movie *JFK*. The Lopez Report was a 400-page report written by House Select Committee on Assassinations staffers Edwin Lopez and Dan Hardway, who went to Mexico City to investigate. They interviewed Sylvia Duran and concluded there was no hard evidence that the Lee Harvey Oswald killed in Dallas was ever in Mexico City. Now, with the other documents coming out, we're starting to get more corroborating evidence on that. We now have the full organization chart and the identifications of the people who were involved in everything going on in Mexico City.

I have a list of ten instances of new information that, if you know how to apply it, gives you a new perspective on the case. First, it was a coup d'état involving many different players. It was all about Cuba. There's a lot of compelling evidence on LBJ's complicity, but it also involved the CIA and the military-industrial complex. J. Edgar Hoover provided the cover-up mechanism, which starts with control of the body and the autopsy. Nobody could control that except the military, so they had to be involved. You have Chief Justice Earl Warren, who was involved in the cover-up, and of course Gerald Ford, who was the one who changed the position of Kennedy's back to better fit the craziness of the single-bullet theory put forth by Arlen Specter.[4] I don't know how anybody can believe that crock, but that's a whole different story.

When did you first see the Warren Commission Report?
When I was in high school, I saw the 888-page paperback version of the Warren Commission Report. I couldn't stop laughing because this was what was presented to the American public at the time. They didn't release the 26 volumes with all the evidence and the hearings until later. You had to pay $79 for a set of those books, and they didn't even have an index. It was Sylvia Meagher who created the first index.

So, a few of the early researchers read them and said, "Wait a minute, there's something really fishy going on here because so much of what's in the twenty-six volumes isn't in the 888-page report." The report is just a fantasy. When you read the interviews in the volumes, you discover all the leads that *weren't* followed. It was all done on purpose, obviously.

Then you have the individuals who weren't brought in to testify. The most egregious example has to be the four motorcycle cops, especially the two on the right side of the limo, James Chaney and Douglas Jackson. The two on the other side were Bobby Hargis and B.J. Martin, and their testimony covered a total of seven pages combined. Hargis was right there and got splattered with blood and bone from the headshot. He thought he had been shot himself. The way the Commission handled this in the inquiry tells you something was obviously very wrong.

President Kennedy's motorcade passes the Texas School Book Depository prior to the assassination. Is the man in the doorway of the Depository Lee Harvey Oswald? (Photo by © CORBIS/Corbis via Getty Images)

You've done some careful photographic analysis as part of your research. What have you concluded from that analysis?

My first book, *The JFK Horsemen*, is the result of six years of meticulous work. I used digital computer technology to analyze the Altgens 6 photo, the one of the man in the doorway of the Texas School Book Depository. Using forensic digital overlays, I was able to positively identify the man as Lee Harvey Oswald, which means he wasn't on the sixth floor shooting Kennedy. I also analyzed the backyard photographs with Oswald supposedly holding a rifle, and I discovered these photos were manufactured to frame him. All of this proves Oswald should be exonerated.

On the Altgens 6 photo, the first thing you notice is it's been highly altered. It has a lot of airbrushing. There are researchers who say that because it's such a tiny area in the photo, the enlargement changes the features of the people. I don't agree with that because I did the overlays for the man in the doorway, and when I overlaid images of Oswald onto blowups of that man, the features lined up perfectly. When I did that with Billy Lovelady, the man the Warren Commission concluded was in the photo, they didn't. I focused mostly on the face and the features, but there's an anomaly over the left shoulder where it seems like the man behind him is both in front and behind because the shoulder has been retouched.

I published this on a website called academia.edu, where a lot of academics and researchers publish papers. I published the study as a scientific paper, with an abstract, introduction, methodology, results, and conclusion. I give people step-by-step instructions on how to replicate the work. Since then, the paper has been cited over 2,500 times in other papers and books. In the methodology, you start with a probe image, an unknown or control, and then you bring in your known images, superimpose them and digitally work with the images, adjusting the opacity and the scaling. And you pay close attention to the inner pupillary distance and setting those because they can't change. Then you can work with the rest of the features and determine if it's the same person or not.

With Oswald I did a superimposition, where I start with the lower values and increase the opacity, and gradually you see the transformation and the features line up perfectly with the man in the doorway. When I used this methodology with a photo of Lovelady, it wasn't even close. Since 2016, I've challenged anybody who's willing and able to refute the findings to follow the methodology and prove it's Billy Lovelady, and to this day nobody has been able to do it. I've had people from Hollywood contact me and say, "Hey, you're right on the money with this."

Did you use the same methodology with the backyard photos?

The backyard photos are purported to show Oswald holding the rifle. I applied the same techniques to those photos and was able to prove the man who stood in for the photos was Roscoe White of the Dallas Police Department. When you superimpose a picture of White onto the backyard man, everything comes out perfectly. The only thing they did was put the face of Oswald onto White, and White did the altering himself because he was highly trained in photography. When you superimpose a picture of Oswald from that time frame onto the backyard man, it's

One of the controversial backyard photos that appears to show Lee Harvey Oswald holding a Mannlicher-Carcano rifle and a newspaper. (Photo by © CORBIS/Corbis via Getty Images)

absurdly scrawny. The shoulders are much higher because the neck isn't as long. The shape of the shoulders and the torso aren't even close, and the inner pupillary distance proves it's White.

If you look at the doorway and backyard photos, you see the amount of sophistication employed in trying to make Oswald a patsy. They even had *Life* magazine publish this on its cover. You start to realize the magnitude of this whole operation and the effort to keep it under wraps, hidden from public opinion. You also realize the mainstream media were obviously complicit in not revealing this information. Instead, they continue with the lie that Oswald did this. Even though the best riflemen in the world said the shot was impossible—two hits on a moving target through foliage with that rifle and a defective scope. The best tried, but nobody could do it.

You also produced a 3D model of Dealey Plaza to determine where the shots came from. What have you learned from that analysis?
When you go to Dealey Plaza, you realize the headshot came from the storm drain. Jim Garrison[5] said this many years ago. Researcher Penn Jones Jr. used to climb into it through the manhole cover, but all of that has since been altered because too many people were starting to realize the headshot came from below. If you look at the Zapruder film,[6] at the trajectories, it's obvious it came from below. Kennedy's head was at a 60-degree angle and the road sloped down. To get that headshot, it had to come from below. When I created the 3D model of Dealey Plaza, I was able to look at the trajectories, and I'm 99.99 percent certain the headshot we see so graphically displayed in frame 313 came from the storm drain.

If you go there and look from the picket fence, the trajectory is wrong. Any bullet from there would've gone through and hit Jackie. Roy Kellerman of the Secret Service was riding shotgun in the limo, and in his testimony before the Warren Commission he said it was a shot coming from below. I don't profess to have all the answers, but I'm confident in the work I've done using computers to analyze images and create the 3D model. I was supposed to testify at the mock trial in Houston in 2017, but I was excluded at the eleventh hour. My doorway and backyard photos would have exculpated Oswald right away.

What did you learn from analyzing the Fred Newcomb tapes?
Fred Newcomb wrote the book *Murder from Within* with Perry Adams in 1971. Newcomb interviewed several witnesses for the book, and these interview tapes have given us a whole new perspective on what happened on Elm Street. I think there were seven different police officers interviewed for the book. Newcomb sent the Zapruder film to these police officers, then followed up and interviewed them over the phone. And all of them said what's on the film isn't what happened.

These tapes are real because we have videos of Bobby Hargis on YouTube talking about the same thing, and the voice is the same. All these guys have died, some of them prematurely. James Chaney died in 1975, and I don't think he was even fifty. I was in touch with Douglas Jackson's son, who wanted copies of the tapes, and he verified it was his father talking. That information changed everything that happened on Elm Street, and it confirmed what we see in the Zapruder film is false.

What kinds of challenges did you encounter while doing your research?
Sifting through all the misinformation and false leads. People are actually paid to run disinformation. "Limited hangouts" is what we call it. They indicate they're proconspiracy, but they're really creating a lot of confusion and arguments, and they give out bad information that has already been hashed out before. That's why I don't participate in online forums because it's a waste of my time. You can spend hours there when you could be doing other things. We've always had shills coming in and stirring the pot, creating false leads, misinformation, and disinformation. That's why I like to go straight to the documents, form my own opinions, and combine that with other things we need to do, like interviewing witnesses.

Were there any low points along your journey?
Realizing how the mainstream media are in concert with the government to perpetuate the cover-up. That's when you realize what you're up against. They control what goes into the minds of young people in schools. Our history books all have Oswald shooting from the southeast window of the sixth floor of the Texas School Book Depository and then have him jumping on a bus. That's ridiculous, and Jim Garrison made this point. He

said Oswald would be the only assassin he'd ever heard of that used public transportation to leave the scene of the crime.

What was your biggest "eureka" moment as a JFK assassination researcher?
The first was when I was analyzing the Newcomb tapes in the summer of 2014, and I heard James Chaney clearly say both the JFK limo and the Queen Mary limo behind them stopped. He said, "Bobby Hargis got off of his bike, ran in between the two limos in front of me." You don't see this at all in the Zapruder film.

Also, Douglas Jackson said five Secret Service agents dismounted and surrounded the JFK limo with guns drawn. Jackson was the so-called "knoll rider." He rode his bike up the embankment, then dismounted and drew his gun. He hid behind the little wall there, where Zapruder was. He was trying to find out where the shots came from. Again, you don't see any of this in the Zapruder film. When Newcomb sent him the film, Jackson said it had been altered; he couldn't see any of the things that actually happened.

In the Newcomb tapes, there's an anecdote about a piece of Kennedy's skull landing at the feet of a kid on the curb of the south side of Elm Street. The only kid there was Joe Brehm, Charles Brehm's son. You see them in the Zapruder film from frames 279 to 290. That's another thing that proves the film has been altered. He's behind his father, and suddenly he's in front, and that type of movement is impossible.

Stavis Ellis, the supervisor of the motorcycle cops, is interviewed for almost an hour on the tapes, and he says a big chunk of skull landed on the south curb and a kid picked it up. And then a Secret Service agent took it and tossed it into the limo. That was compelling because it changed everything. Newcomb didn't realize the importance of what he had on those tapes because he only heard a small portion of them and didn't transcribe them the way I did. It took me eight months, and I've only shared them with select members of the research community because the owner of the tapes doesn't want them to fall into the hands of people who would misuse them.

The other eureka moment was when I superimposed the man in the doorway with Oswald and all the features lined up perfectly. I said, "Man, I'm in trouble here now."

What have been the ripple effects of the assassination, good and bad?
In my mind, the assassination is one of the seminal events in the history of the United States. It changed the course of history as we know it. But as far as ripples are concerned, I can't see any positive ones.

As a result of this coup d'état, you had individuals who became presidents who should never have been presidents, starting with LBJ, who was about to be thrown in jail for all the murders and the influence peddling he was involved in.

You have all these enemies of JFK who benefited from the assassination—J. Edgar Hoover (whom Kennedy was about to retire), the oil millionaires, the Cubans, and even the Israelis because JFK didn't want Israel to have the atomic bomb. Then you have the military-industrial complex, which desperately wanted to expand the war in Vietnam. And let's not forget the Federal Reserve . . . JFK wanted to stop this privately-owned bank from loaning money to the US government at interest. He wanted to replace the Federal Reserve with the US Treasury and create a currency backed by silver and gold. All these people and organizations benefited because of Kennedy's death.

What would you want younger generations to understand about the JFK assassination?
In 2013, my nephew was a senior in high school in Puerto Rico. His history teacher invited me to give a short presentation on JFK. They weren't too interested until I showed the Zapruder film. I ran it a few times, and that's when they had their eureka moment because they could see he was shot from the front. But in their history books, it still says Oswald was the lone gunman.

I want these kids to realize the United States, as hard as this is for most people to accept, is a fascist government controlled by the military. Everything here is controlled by the military contracts that go out to every state to keep the vast middle class going, but you have a small upper echelon that controls everything.

What is your biggest motivation, at this point, to continue your work?
Now I'm focused on the new declassified documents related to Mexico City. Some of it relates to the supposed affair between Oswald and Sylvia

Duran, but the witnesses giving evidence of this all have highly suspect reasons for doing so and really can't be trusted. None of their testimony holds up.

Then there's Orestes Peña, who owned the Havana Bar in the French Quarter of New Orleans. He saw Oswald many times hanging out with federal agents, including FBI, ATF [Alcohol, Tobacco, and Firearms], and Customs Agents. It was obvious they were working together. Warren de Brueys was an FBI agent in New Orleans and had Peña informing on the anti-Castro and pro-Castro Cuban exiles. Peña testified before the House Select Committee and said de Brueys and Oswald knew each other and went to Dallas before the assassination.

This tells us Oswald wasn't some lone nut, but instead he was working closely with federal agents. That's the dangerous game Oswald was play-ing. After the assassination, de Brueys went into Peña's bar and threat-ened to kill him if he talked. The documents on that were classified until 2018, but Peña had started to work with researcher Harold Weisberg, and some goons beat the heck out of him. He called Weisberg from the hospital and said he wanted to go after those guys. He testified before the Warren Commission and asked why they weren't talking to de Brueys, but of course they didn't follow up on that.

This is a perfect example of how the old information from the Commission and the newly declassified documents are coming together to fill in more pieces of the puzzle. There are a lot more, too, that implicate many people in government, the military, and the intelligence community.

The documents also tell us Oswald was a patsy and was being manipu-lated. He was a foot soldier, just like Jim Garrison said. Oswald would get his assignment for the day. "Go pass out leaflets on Canal Street." Okay, done. Then it's, "Lee, we have an investigation in Dallas. The owners of the Texas School Book Depository are involved in running guns, probably to Cuba. We need you to investigate." That's how they got him into the building.

There have been papers written on the history of the Texas School Book Depository building and the companies that occupied it at the time of the assassination. Some of those people were major right-wingers, like the Byrd family. They owned a lot of land in Dallas and were good friends with LBJ. You can see pictures of them at football games together. Bill Shelley, Oswald's supervisor at the Depository, was CIA and had connections to the John Birch Society and other right-wing, anticommunist groups. It's a complex rabbit hole.

Do these declassified documents suggest there may have been "backup" patsies?
They do. The first announcement regarding the rifle used for the assassination mentioned a British Enfield .303. Who owned an Enfield? Wesley Buell Frazier, who worked at the Book Depository and gave Oswald rides to work every day. I did a Freedom of Information Act[7] request for his army records, and they tell quite a story. He disappeared for six hours on the day of the assassination. The gun was then reported as being a Mauser, and then, hours later, it was a Carcano. These threads tell me Frazier was the first patsy in line. That's why he's been removed from the Altgens 6 photograph. After the assassination they drafted him into the army.

The next patsy in line was Joe Molina, a Mexican American who worked at the Texas School Book Depository for sixteen years. At 1:30 a.m. in the early morning hours the day after the assassination, authorities raided his house and woke up his wife and children. They sent an assistant district attorney, a captain, and two lieutenants to serve the search warrant. They told him they were looking for bombs, explosives, guns, or whatever could link him to Oswald. He was surveilled, harassed, and eventually lost his job at the Book Depository.

Another possible patsy was Billy Lovelady. Before he worked at the Book Depository, he was court-martialed out of the Air Force for stealing guns from the armory and trying to fence them at a bar. He worked with a couple of other guys on this. I know this from a FOIA request I filed. In one of the files, it reads "court-martial not in file," which tells me there was indeed a court-martial, but those documents disappeared. Lovelady got a fine, which he started paying, but then he bolted from Maryland and wound up working at the Depository building. The FBI tracked him down and arrested him, but the vice president of the Depository paid his $1,000 bond.

So, what kind of relationship did Billy Lovelady have with these right-wingers at the Book Depository? With the type of record he had, he's another possible patsy, because what if Oswald steps out of the building? You must go to plan B or C or D, and it just so happens all four of them were in the Altgens 6 photograph in the entrance of the Texas School Book Depository. Oswald, Lovelady, Molina, and Frasier . . . all four of them.

And they're standing there with Bill Shelley, who was Oswald's handler. There's a document that details the Sheriff's Office interview with Shelley, and in it he said he had been working very closely with Oswald since he started working there. There are very few pictures of Shelley, but there are documents that show he was ex-military, had worked for the CIA, and was working as a foreman at the Depository at the time of the assassination.

Is there anything else you wish to add?
A colleague of mine always says, "Just keep writing, researching, and publishing because future generations *are* going to revise this case. They're going to set things straight." We might not see it in our lifetime, but that's the motivation for me. The revision of history is No. 1, and the exoneration of Oswald is No. 2.

I'm pretty sure it's like the Lincoln assassination. At the time it was John Wilkes Booth doing it by himself, but eventually the conspiracy revealed itself, and that's what's accepted today. We've already been through the fiftieth anniversary of the assassination, but hopefully by the 100th the truth will be known.

CHAPTER 3

PHIL NELSON

Phillip F. Nelson has worked in the property-casualty insurance industry and as an independent business owner. He retired at the age of 58 and began his extensive research into the murder of our 35th president. His books, *LBJ: The Mastermind of the JFK Assassination* and *LBJ: From Mastermind to Colossus*, provide strong evidence that shows Kennedy's successor, Lyndon B. Johnson, played an active role in plotting the young president's death and the takeover of the White House. Nelson's careful and meticulous research has led him to uncover long-buried secrets about Johnson and his participation in several scandals and murders. He is also the author of *Who Really Killed Martin Luther King Jr.?* and *Remember the Liberty!: Almost Sunk by Treason on the High Seas*.

What triggered your involvement in this work?
When JFK was assassinated in 1963, I was eighteen years old. I was shocked, as was most of the country. And yet I tried desperately to believe the government was on top of it, they got their man, and that was the end of it. I wanted to believe it was a simple case of some screwball lone nut because like most people, the alternatives were so daunting, so frightening, I just didn't want to go there. I think many people were in the same boat, and many of them still are. They just don't want to go there.

But over time, through reading books by the earliest researchers, I became convinced the whole thing was a scam. These books were revealing little factoids that all added up to a very believable story. And yet the official story was sort of hammered together and brought forth in such huge volumes. There were 26 volumes in the Warren Report, and when you got into it, you realized it was a bunch of nonsense. I could go on for an hour talking about that, but just to illustrate the point, they talk at great length about Jack Ruby's mother's false teeth. I realized they were trying to pad the files and make it impossible for people to ever get to the truth through those files, because so much of it was just extraneous nonsense.

Can you provide some examples of why the Warren Commission Report isn't credible?

They interviewed somewhere between sixty and eighty witnesses in Dallas, and then they took the information back to Washington and didn't allow the witnesses to read them before publication. Even the Dallas officials weren't allowed to read most of them. It became obvious later they changed much of the testimonies, including those of the Dallas doctors, as well as everything they said about the bullets and the trajectories.

The FBI and Secret Service sent their agents down to Dallas and forcefully told these witnesses that what they thought they saw they really didn't see. Two of JFK's closest aides, Dave Powers and Kenneth O'Donnell, reported everything they witnessed, including that they heard two shots come from behind the fence on the Grassy Noll.

Decades later, former Speaker of the House Tip O'Neill asked them about that, and O'Donnell told him: "I told the FBI what I had heard, but they said it couldn't have happened that way and I must have been imagining things. So, I testified the way they wanted me to. I just didn't want to stir up any more pain and trouble for the family." This information had never been reported until O'Neill put it in his memoirs. And this misinformation came from two of Kennedy's closest friends, so you can imagine how testimony from other witnesses was twisted to conform to the FBI narrative.

Both were just a few cars back in the motorcade. They also reported smelling gunpowder in the kill zone. The wind was blowing the other direction that day, so they couldn't have smelled gunpowder from the sixth floor of the Book Depository. They also said they heard multiple shots, more than three. Other witnesses talk about seeing the limousine slowing or even stopping briefly, but that isn't in the Zapruder film. This led some researchers to investigate whether the Zapruder film has been tampered with. Those kinds of things have been cropping up one at a time for more than fifty-six years now.

When did you first become suspicious of Lyndon Johnson as both a person and a politician?
Back in 1961 or 1962, I was still in high school, and one of the first things that caught my attention about Lyndon Johnson was news that came over the PA system. It was a Monday afternoon in February, and there was an airplane crash at LBJ's ranch. The actual airplane crash was three days earlier because it was on Friday, but it was only just hitting the news. That seemed strange, but the focus of the announcement at the time was "Don't worry. LBJ is fine. He wasn't even on the airplane." And that was the end of it.

It turned out taxpayers had paid for a runway on his ranch. So even before he was vice president, he somehow got the government to build an airstrip on his ranch. All of this started making me wonder what he was all about. We learned the flight shouldn't have been attempted due to bad weather, and there was a mystery over the ownership of the plane. They had to rush around and file changes of title for the airplane after the crash. All of it was steeped in mystery, like everything else about him.

The point of this is there were these incidents that happened in 1961. Then in the spring, summer, and fall of 1962, every paper you could find featured articles on a businessman and financier named Billie Sol Estes, and the interest stemmed from his association with LBJ. They were partners in fraud. This was being revealed on the pages of every newspaper; it was on the evening news shows, television shows, and so forth. At Sol Estes's trial, there were news outlets from around the world covering it, but if you look for his name in the history books and biographies written about Johnson, you aren't going to find it.

Robert Dallek has a brief mention of him in his book *Flawed Giant: Lyndon B. Johnson and His Times, 1961–1973,* but he dismissed all the assertions of Estes as "not credible." That single point reveals how Dallek went to great lengths to reach a perfunctory, ridiculous conclusion. He ignored the finding by a 1984 grand jury that the 1961 "suicide" finding of a Department of Agriculture agent named Henry Marshall by a corrupt sheriff and coroner should've been "homicide," and that the men named as the perpetrators were Lyndon Johnson, Cliff Carter, and Malcolm "Mac" Wallace.

Marshall had extensive evidence of the frauds committed by Estes on behalf of Johnson, and it should be noted the "suicide" finding was issued on Johnson's orders and was patently absurd given that Marshall was beaten so severely that one eyeball was hanging from its socket, he had a high concentration of carbon monoxide in his lungs from a failed attempt to kill him with a tube attached to his truck's exhaust, and he was shot five times from a long rifle when he had a lame arm—three of those shots would have been fatal.

Even though Estes and Johnson were raking in tens of millions of dollars for at least five years and defrauding US taxpayers, this is often removed from Johnson's history. And as much as I've uncovered on Johnson so far, I've only scratched the surface.

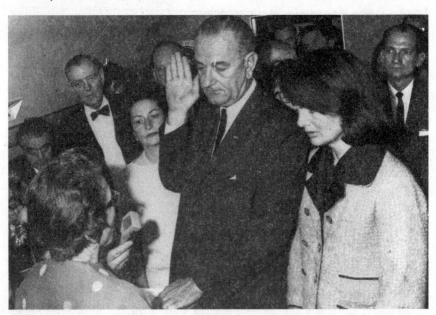

Vice President Lyndon B. Johnson is sworn in as president aboard Air Force One in Dallas, Texas, hours after the assassination of President Kennedy. At farthest left in the background is Jack Valenti. (Source: Bettmann via Getty Images)

What conclusion have you come to regarding Lyndon Johnson's role in the JFK assassination?
Everything I've learned in my research tells me he was the mastermind of the JFK assassination. People want to pin it on the CIA and leave it at that, partly because they know it'll be buried there, and you'll never be able to figure out what really happened. And they don't want to acknowledge the military was heavily involved, more so than the CIA in my humble opinion. Just look at what happened to the corpse. That was military all the way. They effectively stole the body from Parkland Hospital. They took it right out of the hands of Dr. Earl Rose, the medical examiner for Dallas County. He was required by Texas law to do the autopsy, but the Secret Service just stole the body—at gunpoint, by the way—then turned it over to the military, loaded it up on Air Force One, and hightailed it back to Washington, where all kinds of nefarious things were done to the corpse.

How would you describe Johnson's psychological profile?
To talk about the psychology of Lyndon Johnson, we must start from childhood, when he developed what I would call a maniacal lust for power. I believe he learned this at the heels of his father, Samuel Ealy Johnson Jr., who was a Democratic member of the Texas House of Representatives. He got voted in and out of office over the course of twenty years or so. His father lost the family farm in 1922 due to a fall in the price of farm commodities. I believe LBJ felt his father wasn't ruthless and conniving enough.

Robert Caro did a lot of work on these aspects of LBJ, but Caro and a lot of biographers stopped short of following the darker aspects of Johnson's life and some of the characters he was connected with, including Mac Wallace, reputed to be his hitman, and Harold Barefoot Sanders, a federal judge whose name you won't find in the history books, either. He was involved in the case of the death of Henry Marshall, the Texas agricultural agent who was investigating the graft and corruption involving Sol Estes and Johnson.

It was Sanders, as a US attorney in 1962, who handled the first grand jury called by Texas Ranger Clint Peoples to review the "suicide" finding and made certain it wasn't changed to homicide. He did that by refusing to let the grand jury see almost the entire file Marshall had kept on Estes and Johnson to ensure they saw nothing with Johnson's name on it (which was on 153 of the 175 pages). He released only the twenty-two pages that had no reference to Johnson.

LBJ was also manic-depressive. When he had depressive episodes, he would stay in bed for days. He would describe feeling like he was in a Louisiana swamp, drowning with the alligators and snakes and everything. And he would lash out at anybody who came in, the nurses and so forth. It was awful. Caro talks about it, as does Richard Goodwin in his book *Remembering America*. He devoted forty-five pages to Johnson's psychological problems.

He was also morally corrupt. It was part of his narcissism. A narcissist and a sociopath are very similar. If you're a sociopath, you're generally a narcissist, and vice versa, though I don't believe they're technically synonymous. They can do anything they want to people and not be burdened by guilt. That's why most cutthroat criminals are sociopaths and narcissists. Hitmen like Charles Harrelson,[1] actor Woody Harrelson's father, were absolutely that way. One of Johnson's strongest traits was the ability to identify fellow sociopaths, and he could manipulate people by exploiting their needs, as he did with biographer Doris Kearns and White House Press Secretary Bill Moyers.

This doesn't paint a pretty picture of Lyndon Johnson at all. Based on your research, you found he wasn't opposed to "eliminating" people who were in his way, correct?
Johnson was involved in murders from back in 1951. The first we know of involved John Douglas Kinser, who was the golf pro at a little pitch-and-putt golf course near Austin. Kinser was a lady's man and took a liking to Lyndon's sister, Josepha, as well as Mac Wallace's wife, Mary DuBose Barton. Wallace was working at the Department of Agriculture in Washington as an economist. He had a degree from the University of Texas and was studying for a master's. The job at the department was arranged by Lyndon.

So, there was a ménage à trois involving Kinser, Josepha, and Mary. Mac's wife was promiscuous and said to be bisexual. This became publicly known, and Lyndon was vexed. He didn't want to be embarrassed so decided to put an end to it. He put this in the hands of Mac, who drove into the parking lot of the golf course and went inside. This is when people heard a series of shots, so careless was he about how he handled the murder. Everyone around the clubhouse and parking lot saw him get back into his car, which was very identifiable because of the Virginia license plates, and he was subsequently arrested.

He was tried and found guilty of murder with malice, but the judge gave him a suspended five-year sentence. He was essentially put on probation, and at the end of five years, the whole thing was erased from the record. Basically, he killed someone in cold blood and didn't spend a day in prison for it.

We understand there was blatant jury tampering, including a visit to a juror by a thug with a shotgun to make the point. And it's likely the judge was blackmailed, as well as the prosecutor, who, after a very perfunctory presentation, seemed to admit as much when he left the courtroom even before the foreman was finished reading the verdict. This established Mac Wallace's credentials as a hitman, and from then on, he was at Johnson's beck and call. He murdered several people who were connected to Billie Sol Estes.

What happened to Josepha, Lyndon's sister?
Josepha Johnson died mysteriously on Christmas Eve in 1961. [2] She was supposed to be getting her life together and not embarrassing Lyndon, but from time to time she would go off the rails. They had a party that night, and Mac Wallace was there. She was found dead the next day, and without even looking at the body, the coroner pronounced it "death by natural causes" over the telephone. She was buried the day after that. No one will ever know exactly what happened, but the fact that Mac Wallace was there suggests he was given another assignment.

What was your biggest "eureka" moment as a JFK assassination researcher?
One of them relates to the Altgens 6 photo. When I was writing *Mastermind*, I noticed Johnson wasn't in the car with Lady Bird and Senator Yarborough, his bitter enemy. They were right there and clearly

smiling, and they hadn't reacted at all to the first shot, but that same photo shows JFK clutching his throat, and you couldn't get Johnson's reaction because he was nowhere to be found. He had already ducked. I believe he knew the shots were coming, and so he ducked before the limo even made the turn.

One of the policemen, B. J. Martin, said Johnson ducked even before they turned the corner.[3] He was already hunkered down, pretending to listen to a radio the Secret Service used. He didn't need to duck for that, but that was his excuse.

It's important to understand what I mean by the word "mastermind." It doesn't mean LBJ had anything to do with the details, such as the planning and the people who were selected. He put it out there and delegated to certain people, such as Allen Dulles[4] and James Angleton[5] in the CIA, Hoover in the FBI, and James Rowley at the Secret Service. They all knew one another, and Johnson knew he could get people to do things for him. And he left them to develop the internal planning and the selection of who else could be trusted to get it done. But it was always under his auspices and with the promise that "Don't worry. You'll never be caught. They'll never solve this. You'll never face prison time." He had the power to control all of that.

John F. Kennedy campaigning with Lyndon B. Johnson. (Source: Bettmann via Getty Images)

Jack and Robert Kennedy probably never realized just how vicious he was and how he'd be willing to do anything, because it was his lifetime goal to become president since he was a child. He would tell his friends he would one day be president, and it was as certain as the day is long. Again, Robert Caro documented this in detail. All the other biographers—Doris Kearns, Robert Dallek, Michael Beschloss—agree on that. That was always his goal, and he would let no one stand in his way.

In your opinion, was Lee Harvey Oswald a patsy?
For the first few years, I wanted to believe the government's story, but I can't remember being convinced the case was ever really made. Once I understood enough about it, I could never believe he was guilty. It would be impossible, I believe, because he wasn't even on the sixth floor. He was standing in the doorway. Through the photography skills people had back then, it wasn't just the Zapruder film that got modified to show what they wanted it to show; it was some of the other photographs, including the Altgens photo. There has been a lot of research on that by others who convinced me it was Oswald standing in the doorway and not Billy Lovelady.

Oswald certainly wasn't capable of the shooting performance the Warren Commission established, which was three shots in less than six seconds. The very best sharpshooters tried to replicate it and couldn't. But interestingly, Mac Wallace's fingerprints were said to be found in the Book Depository. Wallace was a good shot, and he practiced. Oswald, by contrast, was said to be a poor shot, according to his Marine records. You only get to be a good shot by knowing your rifle and practicing.

Why does the JFK assassination still matter all these years later?
This coup d'état changed the course of history and the whole nature of the United States. JFK was trying to foster a benevolent society, which not only protected its own but wasn't a threat to others, and he was guided by the best of intentions. Instead, we turned into a sort of a paranoid society, a national security police state. It really comes down to that, doesn't it? It's difficult for a lot of people to come to terms with this.

Lyndon did enact important civil rights legislation, but in my view that was more subterfuge. It was something that had to be done. It effectively created a contrived legacy for him, but the coup has left us in a perpetual state of war. For the last twenty years, all you hear about and see is more war. And I think this came out of the growth of this military-industrial complex, which was also congressional and now incorporates the media and the entertainment industry.

It seems we've reverted to a mind-set of threatening the rest of the world, trying to manipulate economic advantage through the threat of force. The whole deep-state mentality is basically replicating Lyndon Johnson's whole persona, in my estimation. I believe all the darkest elements of it are the direct result of what he set in motion. And all their lies were converted to myths that must be sustained. To this day, almost sixty years later, they still haven't released all the classified documents related to the case.

What would you want younger generations to understand about the JFK assassination?
A lot of the stories they hear about the infallibility of the United States, the exceptionalism, are simply false. If you want to feel a sense of patriotism, the real patriotism is getting the country back on the right track, and I think it's incumbent on all of us to somehow work toward that end. It's going to be a long journey because our politicians focus far more on reelection than on serving the country.

I've been accused by some people of dwelling in negativity. But I regard what I'm doing as shining a light in all the dark places and trying to expose it so we, as a country, can learn something from real history and not perpetuate these myths. I apply to my work the axiom that if you don't know your history, you're bound to repeat it, and this is especially true for young people. All I've tried to do is correct history. We need to understand where we went wrong so we can figure out how to correct it. We must make a lot of mid-course adjustments if we're ever going to get back on the right track. Sometimes I think it's doable and achievable, yet I still have difficulty in getting the word out there that I think represents the truth.

What have been some of the challenges in doing this work?
My first book was successful, especially for an unknown author who had never written anything other than insurance reports back in my corporate

career. I wrote this 700-plus page book about what I felt were real truths, and I've convinced a fair number of people I'm on the right track. Some very influential people have endorsed my work, and the book sold enough to get me on some lists. I got some very fair reviews from *Publisher's Weekly*, *Booklist Review,* and others.

After those reviews came out, a very prominent fellow in New York, an art collector and dealer, liked it so much he bought fifty copies and gave them as gifts to his closest friends. We were talking by phone for a while, and he told me that at a dinner party he sat with someone from the Book Review section of the *New York Times* and attempted to interest them in doing a review. This guy told him they didn't review assassination books unless they supported the Warren Commission.

On another occasion he met Bill Moyers, the former White House press secretary, who owed a lot to Johnson. This guy told Bill about the book, and he responded by turning on his heel and walking away, saying, "That case was solved forty-seven years ago." What really made him angry, I'm sure, was that the book somehow made it through the maze he thought had been constructed to keep this kind of book out of the public eye, but it got reviewed by two of these significant literary journals, so bookstore owners and librarians around the country would see it being written up in a very fair way.

The next three books I wrote didn't get reviewed by any of those journals, and you have to wonder if Moyers had some role in that.

Suppression of material that goes against approved government narratives is something you would imagine happens in communist countries, but not in the United States.
Exactly. In 2003, when the series *The Men Who Killed Kennedy* came out—and this is on public record—Moyers and Jack Valenti, another Johnson crony, got together, and they brought in Jimmy Carter, Gerald Ford, and Lady Bird, and they went to The History Channel and read them the riot act. They told them they couldn't make these kinds of assertions about our beloved President Johnson, and they threatened them in all kinds of ways.

No one will ever know for sure exactly what they threatened them with, but we do know they demanded to know the names, addresses, and phone numbers of everyone who participated in the documentary series. Nigel Turner, the man who produced the series, apparently refused to cooperate, but he also went back to England and became a recluse. He had previously been very outgoing, gregarious, and excited about doing this series. This was his passion, and then suddenly it was all over. I have no reason to think he's not still alive, but no one knows because he disappeared.

I would point to that as evidence in my assertion that Moyers did much the same thing with my book, but he never consulted with me. It just happened. How else would you explain it? The two journals reviewed my first book when I was a complete unknown author. On the back of that success, I did three more books and none of them got reviewed, none are in bookstores or libraries.

You mentioned Jack Valenti. His name keeps coming up since I've started writing this book.
Valenti was in the same league of corruption. He was very close to Johnson, and it was no accident that one of Johnson's Hollywood buddies, Lew Wasserman, got Valenti appointed in 1966 to be the president of the Motion Picture Association of America. If you want to know all about him, it's in my book on Martin Luther King Jr. He had connections to Carlos Marcello[6] and Jack Ruby and got his original film experience through the genre of pornography, including the kind involving children.

Why is it critical to keep searching for a higher truth, especially in this matter?
In the alternate universe where Lyndon B. Johnson and J. Edgar Hoover resided, both believed they could do anything either wanted to do and get away with it, one way or the other. Johnson proved that repeatedly throughout his life, in a series of nearly unbelievable but ultimately successful feats that numerous people witnessed, but about which all were forced to remain silent. That was done through every device available to those who have access to the deadliest tools of covert operations and their cover-ups: murder; personal threats; bribery; changed, destroyed, or fabricated testimony; and—for those in the military or in possession of

high security clearances—merely standard government secrecy protocols accompanied by threats of prison, or worse.

Explaining my interest in finding real truths to people more inclined to accept the officially sanctioned propaganda has always been difficult for me, or anyone else for that matter. We approach that task with the presumption most people have read George Orwell's books, particularly *1984*, and have at least a smidgen of critical thinking skills, but then we're invariably disabused by that before long.

But one need only consider that this dilemma has been around for many writers for a very long time. Start with Hunter S. Thompson, and before him, Aldous Huxley and George Orwell, H. L. Mencken and Bertrand Russell. And further back to Mark Twain. There were countless others through the ages of Voltaire and Shakespeare, and on back to Plato, Socrates . . . and finally to Homer, whence it all began (which brings us full circle to a point where even the term "mythology" meant essential truths).

Finally, as I've long believed, when the seeds of officially disseminated disinformation have finally been exposed and disposed, the real truths of the 1960s assassinations will be revealed just as Shakespeare predicted when he wrote, "the truth will out." And those revelations will connect the tens or hundreds of thousands of dots that will explain the truth of LBJ's reign of tyranny, which is to say that Lyndon B. Johnson, helped along by J. Edgar Hoover and Allen Dulles/Richard Helms (and, subsequently, their successors or assignees), were the primary founders of the modern "deep state" that has now been well established and made ever more insidious. And that it exists on the same foundation and uses the same tools they originally perfected, though its reach has now grown to a global, even a celestial, scale.

Whether it's ever defeated is the great unknown.

CHAPTER 4

WILLIAM MATSON LAW

William Matson Law's interest in the assassination of John F. Kennedy began in 1975, when he first saw the Zapruder film on television and later when he picked up the book *Best Evidence*, by David Lifton, in a local bookstore. He is the author of *In the Eye of History: Disclosures in the JFK Assassination Medical Evidence*, with Allan Eaglesham. The book is essential to any reader seeking to gain insight into the events surrounding the handling of the slain president's body on and after November 22, 1963. Law spent years collecting interviews from many firsthand witnesses who had contact with the president's body. His work has appeared in well over thirty books on the assassination. For more information, go to williammatsonlaw.wordpress.com.

What triggered your involvement in this work?
I've wondered most of my life about what happened to Kennedy, and I remember thinking as a teenager, "Somewhere out there, somebody knows the answers to this, and someday we're going to have the answers." I didn't give it a whole lot of thought. I'd watch the occasional documentary, but I hadn't read much about it. I remember arguing with my father when I was a teenager. He said, "You can bet that son of a bitch Johnson had something to do with it." To which I replied, "Dad, you're talking about the president of the United States." I really had a problem with that.

Then toward the end of the 1980s, I was browsing in a bookstore and saw this book titled *Best Evidence* by David Lifton. I started looking through it, and what caught my attention immediately were Kennedy's autopsy photos, which I'd never seen before. I remember standing there transfixed, looking at these photos, so I decided to buy it. The premise of the book is that at some point after the president was assassinated, his body was intercepted, and a preautopsy autopsy was performed before the body arrived at Bethesda Naval Hospital. I thought this was absolutely insane.

I read the book, and I'm thinking this is nuts, but I became obsessed. I started reading every book I could get my hands on . . . all the old classics, but what held my intention was this theory that President Kennedy's body was intercepted. I thought, "Had we been duped all these years?" At the time I was about thirty-eight years old, so I also thought, "I've got to stop this. Grown men with children don't obsess about things like this."

I stumbled across a magazine article that talked about this upcoming JFK symposium in Dallas. I didn't even know they held things like this. I thought, "I'm going to go to this thing, get it out of my system, and put it to bed." I went and had a wonderful time. They had panels on different topics, and I listened to all of them. One morning I was sitting at a table having breakfast with George Michael Evica, the author of *And We Are All Mortal: New Evidence and Analysis in the Assassination of John F. Kennedy.* He was the chairperson of the conference.

I didn't know how important he was when I was talking to him, so I said, "If you want to find out what really happened, you need to study the medical evidence. That's where the answers are."

He looked up from his food and asked, "Would you like to go onstage and talk about that?"

I replied, "No, I don't want to do that. I'm just saying this is where you need to go."

At the end of the conference, he asked me, "Would you like to put together a medical panel for next year's conference?" So, I found myself trying to put this panel together, and the people I really wanted to talk to were the guys who were involved with Kennedy's autopsy and the movement of his body.

The first person I contacted was Jerrol Custer, the radiology technician at Bethesda Naval Hospital who was asked to take X-rays of Kennedy's body. I was brazen enough to ask if he'd sit with me for an interview, and he agreed. About three months after I told myself I was going to put this whole thing behind me, I'm sitting in Jerrol Custer's living room talking with him about the autopsy X-rays he took of Kennedy. That's how it all started; one thing just led to another, and it took me off in directions I never thought I would go.

Can you describe for readers what happened to Kennedy's body from Parkland Hospital to Bethesda Naval Hospital?
After the president was shot, they took him to Parkland Memorial Hospital. The body was taken out of the limousine, put on a gurney, and taken to Trauma Room One, where the medical staff started performing lifesaving procedures. They cut down on one of his arms and one of his legs to give him Ringer's Lactate. They performed closed heart massage on him at one point, but it didn't take them long to realize he wasn't going to make it.

There was a wound about the size of the end of your little finger in the front of his throat. It was ragged, not perfectly round. There was also a wound to his head that was somewhat in the back but also to the side about the size of an orange or a large egg. They *did* see brain in the president's skull cavity. At one point one of the doctors said the cerebrum, which is the brain, and cerebellum, which is in the very back of your head that's a different color and texture than the brain itself, were all oozing out onto the cart. One doctor said the cerebellum was "literally swinging in the breeze." Dr Robert McClelland said he had a good chance to stand at the head because he was asked to hold open the throat wound and was able to look at it.

Dr. Malcolm Perry came in and made a small slit across this wound in the throat at the necktie knot. He did this to put in a trach tube to allow the president to breathe. After the president was pronounced dead, they washed the body, meaning they dabbed up the blood. They wrapped him in sheets with extra sheets around his head. They brought in a 400-pound Britannia casket from the O'Neill Funeral Home and laid some plastic across the inside of the casket to keep body fluids from seeping onto the lining. They put the body into the casket and closed the lid.

At this point, the doctors had a scuffle with the Secret Service, who said they didn't want an autopsy done in Dallas. Dr. Earl Rose,[1] who was the medical examiner for Dallas County, should have been able to do the autopsy, but the Secret Service wouldn't allow him to do it. They told him if he didn't get out of the way, they were going to roll over him, or words to that effect. Dr. Rose was finally talked into letting them leave with the body.

Where did the Secret Service take the body?
They hurriedly whisked the body out and put it in an ambulance. They drove it to Love Field and put it aboard Air Force One at 2:14 p.m. Jacqueline Kennedy came aboard the plane at 2:18 p.m., and they had the swearing in of Johnson at 2:47 p.m. The theory has been posited that while Jacqueline Kennedy and everyone else were watching Johnson being sworn in, the body of President Kennedy was taken from the casket, put into a body bag, taken off the other side of the plane, and put into a luggage compartment that was on that side of the plane.

Now, this seems ludicrous, but if these guys were willing to kill the president of the United States in public, they were definitely willing to take his body and put it in a luggage rack. You must realize Kennedy meant nothing to them while he was alive, so he sure as hell didn't mean anything to them now that he was dead. So, they put him in the cargo hold, and I've seen pictures of the inside of that. There's plenty of room for the body to have been in the cavity of the plane. The Britannia casket, unbeknownst to Jackie, was now empty.

A few hours later when the plane landed at Andrews Air Force Base, while Johnson gave his "I need your help" speech, sounds of a helicopter were heard, and researchers believe this is when they loaded the body onto a helicopter and whatever was done to the body was done. When Johnson finished his speech, the Honor Guard, or Joint Service Casket Team, unloaded the ceremonial casket from Air Force One and put it in a light-gray Navy ambulance, at which point the official motorcade to Bethesda Naval Hospital started.

Jackie Kennedy and Attorney General Robert Kennedy watch as the casket of the late President Kennedy is lowered from the plane after its return to Andrews Air Force Base, Maryland. (Source: Bettmann via Getty Images)

What happened next?

It took about forty-five minutes for the motorcade to get to Bethesda Naval Hospital from Andrews Air Force Base. The Honor Guard, which shadowed the motorcade by helicopter, got to the hospital about ten to fifteen minutes before the motorcade. And here's where it gets weird . . . when the motorcade got there, the Honor Guard was expecting to follow the ambulance to the hospital morgue loading dock, where it would take the casket out of the ambulance and into the morgue. According to Hugh Clark, one of the Honor Guard, at some point after the motorcade arrived, when it came time to follow the ambulance to the morgue loading dock, the ambulance took off quickly, prompting the head of the Honor Guard command to order his men to get in a truck and follow it.

They chased the ambulance into the dark, following its taillights. Bethesda Naval Hospital is a huge complex, so they were going around this enormous circle, and at one point the lights on the ambulance disappeared, and they got lost. They finally found it, at which point they performed their ceremonial function of following the ambulance to the back of the hospital and carrying the casket to the morgue cold room. The Honor Guard claims to have delivered the casket to the morgue at 8:00 p.m.

Dennis David, a First Class Navy Corpsman serving as Chief of the Day that night at Bethesda, claimed a Secret Service detail, which had literally taken over Bethesda that afternoon, gave him orders to gather a working party of six or seven enlisted men from the dental school to unload the president's casket when it arrived that evening. When David encountered what he described as a black Cadillac hearse on the hospital loading dock later that evening, he asked the driver, "How did you come up?" And the driver said, "We came up the back way through Jones Bridge Road." David noticed these guys weren't dressed in scrubs; they were dressed in suits. He said later, "I've always remembered these guys had shiny shoes."

David gathered the enlisted men, who were all dressed in their Navy uniforms, and had them take a cheap metal shipping casket out of the black Cadillac hearse, up the steps and into the morgue itself (not the cold room), where they put it on the floor and left. Now keep in mind the official people, the Honor Guard, took in the ceremonial Britannia casket from the motorcade at 8:00 p.m. Dennis David said he and the enlisted men took a cheap metal shipping casket out of the black Cadillac hearse and into the morgue at about 6:35 p.m.

That's a big-time difference, but we know this is accurate because USMC Sergeant Roger Boyajian, whose Marine Barracks security detail provided physical security during the autopsy, logged 6:35 p.m. into his after-action report. I got a third party to confirm the time.

To clarify, you're saying there were two coffins being unloaded into the hospital.

Yes. Two or three days after the autopsy was concluded, in response to a question from Dennis David, Dr. Thornton Boswell, one of the three pathologists who conducted the autopsy, confirmed that JFK had been in the shipping casket David's working party unloaded from the black Cadillac hearse at the morgue loading dock hours earlier. In fact, David told author David Lifton in 1979 that both Dr. Humes and Dr. Boswell (the two Navy pathologists who participated in the autopsy) were present on the loading dock, along with their commanding officer, Captain Stover, and two others who he believed to be the Surgeons General of the Army and Air Force.

To complicate things even further, Secret Service agents James Sibert and Francis O'Neill said they unloaded the casket at 7:17 p.m. When I was in Sibert's home and read him this piece out of *Death of a President* by William Manchester, which basically talks about all these men in their respective dress uniforms unloading the casket, he said, "I've heard about that, but I didn't see anything like that. Nobody in dress uniform helped us. There may have been a few people who came in from the medical building because it was a heavy casket and the four of us couldn't have handled it alone, but I don't remember anything like that."

His partner, Frank O'Neill, told me he took the casket in with the Honor Guard at 8:00 p.m., but that's not what he said in 1978 to Andrew Purdy, who took his testimony for the House Select Committee on Assassinations. He basically said the same thing Sibert said, that it was he, Sibert and two other Secret Service agents, Kellerman and Greer, who picked up the casket, put it on a gurney, and took it in.

O'Neill only changed his story after he read *Best Evidence* and realized he had been had. So rather than admit that, he decided to toe the official line that the Honor Guard took the casket in because to say anything else would point to conspiracy. And he didn't want to involve himself in that, didn't want to risk his pension or his official standing. The thing about it is, if you're not exactly telling the truth, you can't always keep all that stuff from coming out from under the door because it's not based on a framework of truth.

Did you have a eureka moment doing your research?
In a memo the FBI put out, what they call a FD302, it states two FBI agents—James Sibert and Frank O'Neill—were sent to the morgue to keep an eye on the body of the president. They were told to stay with the body and take whatever evidence was taken from the body to the FBI laboratory. While they were in the morgue, they wrote five-and-a-half pages of notes. And in those notes was a quote they had written down, which

read, "There has been a tracheotomy performed, as well as surgery of the head area, namely in the top of the skull."

David Lifton told me this "surgery of the head area" statement personally changed his life because there was no surgery done in Dallas other than the cutdowns on Kennedy's arm and leg for the Ringer's Lactate.

I made all these phone calls to O'Neill to get him to talk to me. He finally sent me a chapter from the book he was writing on Kennedy, and it concerns the autopsy. In it he describes "some cutting of hair or slight removal of tissue from the president's head had been performed," and he told me they made the "surgery of the head area" statement in their notes because one of the doctors doing the autopsy noticed this and said something. In essence, I had, from O'Neill's own book manuscript and typed notes, what I considered to be proof there was surgery performed before Kennedy's body got to Bethesda.

Another big moment was when I spoke to Jim Sibert. He agreed to have me come to his house in Florida and allowed me to set up a camera on him, the first time it had ever been done. I have a big blowup of what they call the "stare of death" photograph, which is basically Kennedy stretched out on the morgue table. His eyes are slightly open, and his mouth is also open. You can see the throat wound. I held this up in front of him so he could look at it, and I could see him staring at it because it's thin paper and the light was shining through it.

And he said, "I've often wondered, whoever that marksman was, if he used an exploding bullet." We know if it was Oswald, he didn't use an exploding bullet. So now I have another FBI agent, on record, and he's wondering if "whoever that marksman was used an exploding bullet," which told me, of course, he didn't believe Oswald killed Kennedy.

Was it a challenge getting these people to talk to you about what they witnessed?

I feel like people are always afraid to reveal everything they know about the JFK assassination because they're terrified. I tell people this, and they ask me, "You're saying these guys are still afraid to talk all these decades later?" and I say, "Some of them are most definitely terrified, some are just a little bit scared, and some don't want to deal with it simply because it's a hassle in their lives."

What convinced you these men were telling the truth?
I talked to Jim Sibert in his house, sat with the man, watched his body language, watched how he responded. When you sit across a table from somebody, you can watch their face, watch how they hold themselves, watch the movement of their eyes. That all plays into everything. Every little thing is a part of the whole, and those things give you an insight into other things you might not get otherwise.

I interviewed Jerrol Custer, the radiology technician at Bethesda Naval Hospital who was asked to take X-rays of Kennedy's body. I got to his house, and he came out dressed in a sweater and a pair of slacks, and he said he and his wife were just having some dessert. I came in and sat at the table with them. After dessert, we started talking about the autopsy, and the moment that stunned me was when he held up an AP X-ray, which is a frontal X-ray he took of President Kennedy's head, and he said, "They wanted this man dead, and they did a good job of it."

Now, it's one thing to read this in a book, but it's quite another thing to sit across from a guy who you know, because it's in the record, had his hands on the body of the president. I was three feet away from him when he said this, and it blew my mind.

There were others who were at Bethesda that night who you spoke to as well, correct?
Paul O'Connor was a medical corpsman and student at Medical Technology School at Bethesda and one of the men in the morgue who helped the doctors with the autopsy. He had a gregarious personality, loved people, loved life, and would freely talk to you about anything. I had several conversations with him, and he agreed to come to Oregon because he'd never been there before.

What makes this thing come together is that O'Connor was the man who first brought attention to the fact President Kennedy's body was brought into the morgue in a cheap metal shipping casket. He told me they put it on the floor, and it was his job that night to remove the brain.

He explained, "We opened the lid of the metal casket and saw this body bag. We unzipped the body bag quickly, and there was the president. He was totally nude except for wrappings around his head. We took the body and put it up on the table. When we unwrapped the head, there was a large gasp that went through the room because his head was a mess. There was brain matter everywhere, his hair was bloodied, and the wound in his throat was a big open gaping gash."

Let's go back to Dallas and Trauma Room One. Remember when I said the only thing that was done to President Kennedy to sustain his life was to make some cutdowns on an arm and a leg to put in Ringer's Lactate. At the time, there was a small round wound they considered to be a wound of entry in his throat. Dr. Perry made a small incision across that wound to put in a trach tube to allow the president to breathe. Other than that, there was nothing done to Kennedy's body, but by the time the body was taken out of this cheap metal shipping casket at the morgue in Bethesda, the wounds had changed. The wound in his throat that started out the size of the end of your little finger had morphed into a "big open ugly gash." And the wound to his head was now four times larger than it was in Dallas.

What caused the wounds to change so drastically between Trauma Room One at Parkland Hospital in Dallas and the morgue at Bethesda Naval Hospital in Washington, DC? What happened to the body? That's the crux of the whole thing. You can argue all day about whether Oswald could shoot Kennedy from the sixth-floor window of the Texas School Book Depository. You can argue until hell freezes over about what each individual witness saw. You can play with that all you want, but it's not going to get you answers.

The only answer I was looking for was whether there was a conspiracy in the death of the 35th president of the United States. That's as far as I wanted to take it. If I could get more, I'd take more, but that was my goal.

These individuals spent more than a few minutes looking at the president's body. They had their hands on him and moved him around. They had close-up views of what was in his cranium and the wounds on his neck. These are trained medical personnel, but they're also the people on the edge of the stage of history. They're the little guys who are low on the totem pole, and they see these things, but they don't say anything because they're the very last rung of the ladder.

Doctors Humes, Boswell, and Finck, the autopsy doctors, had their careers. They gave the orders, and they were right in the middle of it, but you could never get a straight answer out of any of them. But talk to the men who stood beside these doctors. They'll tell you what the hell went on. That's why I was interested in what they had to say, and I got more than I bargained for.

What else did you learn about President Kennedy's brain?

Jim Jenkins was a fellow student of Paul O'Connor's and his partner in the morgue on the night of the autopsy. Jenkins is reclusive and doesn't talk about it. He went on with his life, and when I found out he hadn't been interviewed much, I wanted to talk to him. I remember he spoke with a soft Southern drawl and said, "The autopsy was nothing but show. That body had been gotten to before we saw it."

I eventually met him in New Orleans. I didn't sleep well the night before the interview because my adrenaline was flowing, and the next morning I met him in the lobby of my hotel, and we went to a little restaurant around the corner. We sat down and he started telling me about his experiences, "I don't trust people; I don't trust the government. And this [autopsy] thing was the start of it."

I realized at this point I wanted to get him on camera, and he agreed to come to my room. Once we settled in, I asked him about Kennedy's brain, and he said, "I was given a brain to infuse that night . . . Dr. Humes uttered something . . . he said the damn thing fell out in his hands."

I asked, "What does that mean to you?"

He looked at me and said, "I think that means the brain was removed and then replaced."

At this point I was trying to remain professional, but when he told me that I swear it took everything I had not to fall off my chair. We went down to the lobby after the interview, and my head was spinning from what I just learned from this guy.

I said, "Jim, if you'd like, I could arrange for you to go to a conference this year in Dallas where you can talk about this."

He introduced me to his wife, Jackie, who was waiting in the lobby, and said, "I don't want to go to Dallas." He then turned around and was gone.

Did you keep in touch with these witnesses?
I kept my relationship up with them over the years, and we became friends. I needed to test their veracity. Not only that, but if I was in your life and we talked about things, it wouldn't only be about JFK. I'd learn about your kids, your likes and dislikes. I'd meet your wife if you were married. That's what happened with these guys. I got so close I considered them extended family.

Do I believe Paul O'Connor? I do. Do I believe Jim Jenkins? I do. I've never met more honest human beings in my life. I would bet my life on anything they said.

I worked hard to earn the FBI guys' trust. The chapter on the FBI agents is the part of my book I'm most proud of because these guys didn't talk to anybody. Jim Sibert invited me to his house on more than one occasion, and I spent twelve hours once in his office talking to him. To get this stuff on film, it's there for all time. There's no denying it.

What have you concluded about the assassination based on your research?
President Kennedy's body, at some point between Dallas and Bethesda, was intercepted. I believe, as do all the witnesses I talked to who were in the autopsy room, that Kennedy's body had been gone over before it reached the autopsy room at Bethesda Naval Hospital. The fact the wounds on his body differed so much from what doctors at Parkland Hospital saw and what people at Bethesda Naval Hospital saw point decisively to conspiracy in the death of President Kennedy.

I wish I didn't know what I know because it breaks my heart. For all my wanting to know, that little teenager in me is there saying, "Dad, you're talking about the president of the United States."

To have your idealism crushed like that is hard.

What have been the ripple effects of the JFK assassination?
Some of them have been tsunami-like, and some of them have been tiny little ripples. I believe we wouldn't have had a Vietnam War, at least to

the extent we did. So, whoever pulled that trigger not only killed John
Kennedy, but they also killed 58,000 other Americans. I believe Robert
Kennedy would've eventually run for the presidency, but he wouldn't have
been killed.

The real cost of this conspiracy is the world we live in today. I believe
Kennedy tried to keep the so-called "extreme right" clamped down, and
when we lost him, they gained a foothold and knew they could get away
with anything. And they did. Think about Richard Nixon and all his shenanigans in the White House. We have the most corrupt political system
in the history of this country, and I believe that manifested because there
was a vacuum.

There was a death of innocence in the 1960s. They killed all our
heroes, the leaders who the flower children believed were going to make
this a better world. That vacuum has been left to the point where we
just had the worst president, Donald Trump, in history. Someone asked
Benjamin Franklin after the Constitutional Convention in 1787 what
we had, and he responded, "A Republic, if you can keep it." I think
we're at the point where we may not keep the Republic created by our
Founding Fathers.

People ask me, "Why don't you leave John F. Kennedy alone? He's
dead. What difference does it make?" The difference it makes is that idealism in the United States for younger generations died. In the early 1960s,
both older and younger generations believed we were the best and the
brightest nation. There was nothing we couldn't do, nothing we wouldn't
do for the betterment of mankind. That kind of idealism was destroyed
with the deaths of John Kennedy, Martin Luther King Jr., and Bobby
Kennedy.

**You got the opportunity to speak with Marina Oswald. Please share
that experience.**
I called Marina Oswald Porter about twenty-five years ago because I
wanted to meet this woman, reach out and touch history. I got her number and called her, and she picked up the phone and said hello. When I
recognized her voice, I said hello and told her I was a JFK researcher. And
she said in a Russian accent, "Oh, wonderful. Just wonderful."

That's how we started off the conversation. You could hear in her voice she regretted picking up the phone, but I managed to ask her some questions. I didn't record anything, but I remember asking her about the backyard photographs and if she took them. She said, "I took them, but in the photographs I took, Lee was holding something else, not a gun."

We talked for about twenty minutes, and years later I called her again, and we had this wonderful conversation. The reason I called her was that Judyth Vary Baker's story had just broken, and Baker claims to have had an affair with Lee in New Orleans in the summer of 1963 (see Chapter 7). So, I called and introduced myself again, and I told her there was a story that recently broke about a woman who says she had an affair with her husband. I asked, "What do you think about that?

I was expecting this loud explosion of Russian anger, but she said, in a very calm voice, "Well, this sounds plausible to me."

I almost fell off my chair, and I said, "You were married to him, surely you would know this."

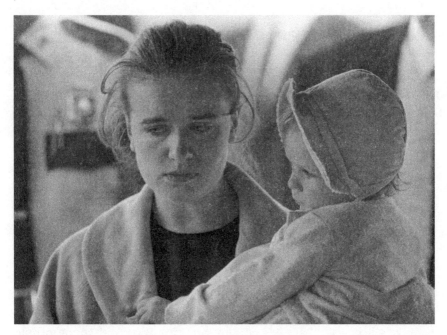

Marina Oswald weeps as she views the body of her husband Lee Harvey Oswald shortly before his burial in Ft. Worth, Texas. She is holding her twenty-two-month-old daughter, June. (Source: Bettmann via Getty Images)

And she responded, "How do I know what he does when he leaves the house?"

It blew my mind to hear that. We talked about all kinds of stuff, but I didn't want to push her too hard because this was only my second call to her. I did ask her about her feelings toward the government, and she said, "The government is the government. It doesn't matter whether it's Russia or whether it's America."

I felt we had really connected; she was warm and open and wonderful. I asked if there was some time when we could meet? And she said, "Oh no. I cannot do that. I am busy. I have to cook dinners and things like that."

At one point I told her that whether she liked it or not, she was part of the history of this country.

And then, in a sad voice, she said, "I am wife of assassin. I do not like it."

This was heartbreaking. It's one thing to hear me tell you about it, but it's another to hear the emotion in her voice. I'll never forget that.

What do you want younger generations to understand about the JFK assassination?

Young people today are growing up in a cynical world, and they see the latest former president of the United States, Donald Trump, who comes out and literally lies straight into the camera without any sense of decency or remorse. I want them to understand that once, a long time ago, there were politicians who really did have the best interest of this country and its people at heart, and unfortunately, they paid a big price for that. All of us paid a price for that.

We've gone from a time when we wanted to do the best we could for all Americans and for the world because that's what we're supposed to do, to a time of cynicism, outright lying, and untruth. John Kennedy was once asked what his definition of happiness was. He referred to the Greeks, who said happiness is full use of your powers along the lines of excellence. I believe that's who John Kennedy was. I believe that's who Martin Luther King was. I believe that's who Bobby Kennedy was. And young people need to understand where we find ourselves today is a direct result of the JFK assassination.

What is your biggest motivation at this point to continue this research?
My sense of longing for what could have been. Kennedy had enough brains during the Cuban Missile Crisis and knew what he was dealing with. He knew how dangerous it was, but he had a Joint Chiefs of Staff that was going to fight him every step of the way. He knew enough to bring in the very best people, and instead of reacting like, "I'm going to bomb the shit out of them," he knew that eighty million people could be dead in an hour. So, instead of sticking his chest out, he gathered all the people he knew were the best and the brightest, and he worked this thing out. Instead of sticking it in Nikita Khrushchev's face, he let him have some space and breathing room so both countries could back off and let tensions ease.

I'm motivated because a man like Kennedy, who can do that and literally gave his life for the pursuit of peace, deserves to have the truth be known about what happened to him . . . for our history, for his family, and for his memory.

What has this journey meant to you?
In life, we think things are going to turn out a certain way, but that very rarely happens. How did I go from standing in a bookstore to interviewing all these people? This pursuit allowed me to sit with a man, Jim Jenkins, who participated in Kennedy's autopsy, to be in a car with him as we drove through Gaithersburg and Washington, DC, down the road he used to drive every morning going to work at Bethesda Naval Hospital. I'm looking at this man, who has now become my friend, and I'm thinking, "How did this happen?"

Next, we visited Kennedy's grave at Arlington National Cemetery, which was the first time for both of us. And I'm standing beside this man who worked on his body, which is now in front of him, six feet under the ground. I'm thinking, "God, this is amazing. How the hell did I get here?"

Going to a bookstore one day changed the whole course and meaning of my life . . . and that must have been how it was for the people in Dallas who saw Kennedy assassinated, thinking they were going to go see the president pass by, and the people in Bethesda Naval Hospital, who suddenly found themselves standing over the president's body. Obviously for them the event was more visceral, but it boggles my mind that going to a bookstore led me down this pathway to where I am now. I don't understand it. I just embrace it for what it is, and I thank God for it.

CHAPTER 5

VINCE PALAMARA

Vincent Palamara was born in Pittsburgh, Pennsylvania, and graduated from Duquesne University with a degree in sociology. He has studied the largely overlooked actions—and inactions—of the United States Secret Service regarding the Kennedy assassination in unprecedented detail, having interviewed and corresponded with more than eighty former agents. He has also interviewed many surviving family members, White House aides, and Parkland Hospital and Bethesda Medical Center witnesses. He is the author of five books on the Kennedy assassination: *Survivor's Guilt: The Secret Service & The Failure to Protect President Kennedy* (2013), *JFK: From Parkland to Bethesda* (2015), *The Not-So-Secret Service* (2017), *Who's Who in the Secret Service (2018).* and *Honest Answers About the Murder of President John F. Kennedy: A New Look at the JFK Assassination* (2021). He has appeared in several documentaries, as well as on radio, in newspapers, print journals, and national conferences. Palamara's original research materials, or copies of them, are stored in the National Archives, the John F. Kennedy Presidential Library, Harvard University, the Assassination Archives and Research Center, and the Dallas Public Library.

What triggered your involvement in this work?
When I was twelve, my parents lit a fire in me about both JFK and his untimely death. This was in 1978, during the House Select Committee on Assassinations investigation. At the same time, I was very much into

reruns of the classic television show *The Wild Wild West* (still my favorite show), which was a fictional take on the Secret Service of the 19th century. The two interests merged, and, more than forty years later, I'm interested in President Kennedy and his assassination, especially through the "lens" of the agents assigned to him.

What kinds of challenges have you encountered while doing your research?

I was threatened once by the executive secretary of the Association of Former Agents of the United States Secret Service (AFAUSSS)[1] to "cease and desist" from contacting any more of his associates. This scared me for a day or so, then it dawned on me. I wasn't doing anything illegal. There's no crime in calling someone. Former Secret Service agents Rufus Youngblood, Sam Kinney, and Bob Lilley sided with me, stating that the executive secretary, Hamilton Brown (formerly on Joseph Kennedy Senior's detail), was not the boss of anyone.

I was also harassed at my former place of employment. There was a gentleman who is friends with former agent Gerald Blaine (of *The Kennedy Detail* fame) who started bothering me online, trolling my YouTube videos, leaving nasty comments on my Amazon page, getting my reviews on Amazon deleted and deleting my blogs. He basically admitted as much. He's a retired Military Intelligence officer and apparently has a lot of time on his hands.

I believe what sent him over the edge was my contacting the proposed director of Blaine's movie-in-progress with a summary of why his book couldn't be trusted. I did this in a scholarly, nonpersonal way. Coincidence or not, the film was suddenly scrapped, and the amazing litany of Oscar-winning technical people connected to the film, including the *Life of Pi* technical advisor, disappeared from the movie's website.

I received a call from the human resources department while at work saying they needed to speak to me, but I was to go to a private conference room. It was there they told me this man wrote a lengthy letter to the company CEO requesting I be terminated because my writings were "unpatriotic" and "grossly unfair" to his former Secret Service agent friend.

If that weren't enough, he sent another letter a week later, and I got another call from the HR lady explaining all of this once again. Luckily, they screened the CEO's calls and letters, and he never received them. Also, the HR lady laughed and said what I was doing was perfectly fine and nothing remotely criminal, immoral, or job-jeopardizing in nature. In fact, she said if he wrote again, I could press charges against him. He then disappeared . . . for good.

I have repeated this story a few times on radio shows and at conferences to demonstrate this is still a current event that can ruffle the feathers of (former) government-connected folks wishing to whitewash history to their benefit.

What was your biggest "eureka" moment as a JFK assassination researcher?
It was on September 27, 1992. I spoke to the head of the White House Detail, Gerald Behn, who told me President Kennedy did NOT order the agents off the back of his limousine. He said, "I don't remember Kennedy ever saying he didn't want anybody on the back of his car." Soon, many of his colleagues corroborated his shocking statement, stating that President Kennedy was a very nice man, never interfered with their actions at all, did not order the agents off his limousine, did not order the motorcycles away from the limousine, and did not order the bubble top off his car. Several of these men believed there was a conspiracy in the death of JFK.

Were there any low points along your journey?
In 2007, I briefly and begrudgingly became a "semi-lone-nut" believer due to being burned out on the case. I was still trying to get published, my personal life was sort of "blah" at the time, and it seemed like the case could go no further. I was briefly "smitten" by Vincent Bugliosi's lone-nut book, *Reclaiming History*, before others would go on to debunk and dismantle it and provide me with the proverbial slap in the face I needed to get me back on track. I always believed there were multiple conspiracies to kill Kennedy, but after reading Bugliosi's book, I thought Oswald beat them to the punch, but this erroneous belief only lasted a few months. One

might say my latest book, *Honest Answers About the Murder of President John F. Kennedy: A New Look at the JFK Assassination*, is more of my "penance" for my sin of once drifting over into the "dark side."

Have you ever feared for your life because of your research?
Not my life, although I did entertain some paranoid thoughts briefly when I was younger. In addition to my mail being opened several times in the early millennium (former agent letters slit perfectly down the sides, as if someone read the contents and carefully put the letters back), the above-mentioned harassment at work was both humorous and troubling, all at the same time. It wasn't so much physical harm as it was mental harm—fear of losing my job, primarily. I was relieved by the HR lady's comforting words both times, but it still unnerved me, as it did my family when I told them what happened. My dad summed it up best when he said, "Son of a bitch. Well, Vince, if there's nothing to your work, they wouldn't be doing all this, would they? You're really onto something. Keep going!"

Secret Service agents standing on the rail of the car trailing President Kennedy as the motorcade passes by the Texas School Book Depository. (Photo by © CORBIS/Corbis via Getty Images)

What have you concluded about the case based on your research?
I believe if the Secret Service had done its normal, thorough, and professional job, JFK would have survived that day. Also, the medical evidence demonstrates the official story of one lone shooter from the rear (Oswald or anyone else) is false, and doing research for my latest book has convinced me beyond a shadow of a doubt there was a conspiracy in the death of JFK.

What have been the ripple effects of the assassination, good and bad?
Mistrust in government. The Vietnam War became a full-blown ground war with boots on the ground and tens of thousands of American boys dead. And then there's the succession of presidents—LBJ, Nixon, Ford, Carter, Reagan, Bush 41, Clinton, and Bush 43. If Kennedy doesn't die, LBJ, Nixon, Ford, and Carter are never president; and Reagan and Bush 41 are doubtful to possible only. LBJ became president via the death of Kennedy, and Vietnam sealed his fate. Nixon came "back from the dead" politically, but Watergate brought about his vice president, Ford, taking over. Carter, a good man, was the nation's protest vote over the Nixon/Ford years of corruption. Kennedy's murder was a coup d'état that demonstrated that a small, shadowy part of the government used bullets instead of ballots to change things.

In your opinion, was Lee Harvey Oswald a patsy?
Yes. Definitely. My new book provides further details (the nuts and bolts), but simply put, Oswald wasn't on the sixth floor when the assassination happened. Someone else fired his rifle, but he didn't. I guess you could say Oswald's rifle was guilty . . . but he wasn't. In addition, there was also another assassin from the front. Oswald may indeed have been a part of the conspiracy, but he wasn't a shooter. His rifle led straight to him, which was the intent of the plotters.

Why does the JFK assassination still matter all these years later?
Besides the millions of people still living who remember him well and still are touched by his tragic death, JFK has almost become a two-part metaphor: for "Camelot," an almost innocent time in America, before the

1950s truly gave way to the 1960s with its drug culture, antiwar demonstrations, and loss of faith in government. Kennedy's death is mentioned by many researchers and authors as merely the start of other government shenanigans—Watergate, Iran-Contra, Iraq War/WMDs, etc.—that continue almost unabated to this day. Most Americans, as well as people across the globe, believe Kennedy's death was the result of a conspiracy, and he's viewed quite fondly to this day and is still one of the most popular presidents ever. As JFK assassination researcher Robert Groden said, "It may be too late for justice in this case, but it's never too late for the truth."

What would you want younger generations to understand about the JFK assassination?
That President Kennedy—"alive and well" thanks to countless YouTube videos, newsreels, television programs, books, images, etc.—was our last assassinated president and *only* ten presidents ago. Before 9/11, 11/22/63 was *the* touchstone date in American history, and, to an older generation, despite the loss of 3,000 people, the death of JFK was more shocking and personal. People liked Kennedy and felt as if they knew him. Like my mom said, "9/11 was shocking, but I didn't know those people. I felt like I knew President Kennedy, and I loved him."

Also, his assassination is an unsolved murder, and there are two government verdicts: the Warren Commission's lone-nut conclusion and the House Select Committee on Assassination's "probable conspiracy" verdict. Then there's the Assassination Records Review Board (ARRB), a relatively recent government body that looked at the assassination from 1994 to 1998, which held an unofficial medical evidence investigation and released millions of documents that have spawned some of the best books ever on the case just in the last few years.

In addition, millions more documents were released to great fanfare in 2017 and 2018, and more are scheduled for release soon. And, just as Abraham Lincoln is one of the very few presidents still well known, liked, and admired all these years later and to whom Hollywood spawned a blockbuster movie, *Lincoln,* in 2012 that attracted many young people to theaters all over the world, President Kennedy is also among that very rare pantheon of presidents who's still well known, liked, and admired all these years later and to whom Hollywood also spawned a blockbuster Hollywood movie, *JFK*, in 1991 that's still extremely popular.

All other assassinations and attempts are known about, so there's no mystery there. However, the death of JFK isn't only the greatest murder mystery of the 20th century, it still resonates into the millennium because, once again, he was the last assassinated president, and we don't know the full story. JFK is the great American mystery, and he represented the closest thing we ever had to a royal family. Last, image can be and often is everything; perception is reality. Kennedy was our most attractive president, and his lovely wife and children added to the triumph and tragedy of his story, the ultimate soap opera and reality program. To use the vernacular of today, "JFK was dope."

If you could get the answer to one question in the case, what would it be?
Where is President Kennedy's brain today? Dr. Cyril Wecht, the forensic pathologist who was given permission to examine the assassination evidence in 1972, was the one who discovered that Kennedy's brain had gone missing, and to this day nobody knows where it is. Also, can we ever get a responsible, discreet exhumation to answer, once and for all, the medical anomalies in this case?

What is your biggest motivation, at this point, to continue your work?
My admiration for President Kennedy and my sadness at his tragic death . . . and a fire still burns in me to discover more of the truth, even at this late date.

Is there anything else you wish to add?
Although many of the main players have passed away, Marina Oswald and her daughters, Ruth Paine, Clint Hill, Paul Landis, Abraham Bolden, Buell Wesley Frazier, Mary Ann Moorman, Beverly Oliver (whatever one thinks of her claim to being the "Babushka Lady,"[2] she definitely was a dancer at the Colony Club and knew some of the players in this case), Tina Towner, the Newman family, James Jenkins, Hubert Clark, and others are still with us. And, central to my area of the case, Clint Hill, Gerald

Blaine, and roughly fifteen or more former Secret Service agents are still with us, some of whom are falsely propagating a "JFK-is-to-blame" mantra that infuriates me to no end.

This is another reason I carry on—to debunk the false notion that Kennedy was somehow responsible for his own death by ordering the agents off his car, ordering the top off the limo, ordering the motorcycles away from the limo, etc. Hill and Blaine wrote a bestselling book, *The Kennedy Detail*, with a documentary/DVD *and* media blitz (from Simon & Schuster) that not only demonstrates the tremendous interest there still is in JFK, his death, and, to a certain extent, the agents who protected him, but also demonstrates why I must carry on to debunk their nonsense.

PART 2

NEW ORLEANS: THE SUMMER OF '63

The CIA could not face up to the American people and admit that its former employees had conspired to assassinate the President; so, from the moment Kennedy's heart stopped beating, the Agency attempted to sweep the whole conspiracy under the rug.

—Jim Garrison, New Orleans district attorney (1961–1973)

CHAPTER 6

ED HASLAM JR.

Edward T. Haslam was born in Kansas in 1951. Soon afterward, his father was appointed to a teaching position at Tulane Medical School in New Orleans. As a child, he got to know one of his father's colleagues, Dr. Mary Sherman, who was later found murdered in her apartment in 1964. In 1990, he began to investigate her death and her relationship with David Ferrie, one of Jim Garrison's JFK assassination suspects. In 1995, Haslam published *Mary, Ferrie & the Monkey Virus*. He continued his research and, after compiling more compelling evidence, published *Dr. Mary's Monkey* in 2007. In this book, he examines the nefarious connections between Sherman, Ferrie, Dr. Alton Ochsner, Lee Harvey Oswald, covert cancer/bioweapon research, and the assassination of John F. Kennedy.

What triggered your involvement in this work?
It all starts with Dr. Mary Sherman. She and my father worked together at Tulane Medical School back in the late 1950s and early 1960s. I remember they took a British doctor out to dinner one night, and the three of them came back to our house to talk about subjects they weren't comfortable talking about in the restaurant. I was eight or nine years old at the time, and I sat on Mary's lap as they talked. She and my father taught orthopedic surgery and occasionally did surgeries together, mostly at Charity Hospital. They were friends and would travel to orthopedic conferences together, and they hung out with each other because they both liked to

drink scotch, smoke cigarettes, and do shop talk. Mary told dad a lot about her life at the University of Chicago, where she worked with Enrico Fermi and Harold Urey, both of whom were Nobel Prize winners and the top scientists behind the Manhattan Project.[1]

Also in the 1960s, when I was ten years old, my father told me they were researching monkey viruses from Africa at Tulane Medical School. That was a memorable experience for me, and I wrote about it in my book *Dr. Mary's Monkey*, which is first and foremost an inquiry into the death of Mary Sherman in New Orleans in July 1964.

Later, after Mary's death and when I was in high school, I heard that Mary and David Ferrie[2] were involved in secret cancer experiments. New Orleans District Attorney Jim Garrison mentioned this in an interview in *Playboy* magazine in 1967. A few years later I heard Mary and David were in fact mutating monkey viruses to develop a biological weapon to kill Fidel Castro, who was then president of Cuba. I remember feeling this was a dangerous activity, particularly if the virus escaped into the human population.

Around 1992, I finally fell down the rabbit hole. The fact that the AIDS epidemic was caused by a mutated monkey virus was certainly a trigger for me, and I also found out that in 1960, scientists discovered a cancer-causing monkey virus in the polio vaccine that was administered to tens of millions of Americans from 1955 to 1963. Then I got the CDC [Centers for Disease Control] statistics and discovered the magnitude of the current soft tissue cancer epidemic in this country.

In 2000, *60 Minutes*, the CBS News show, introduced me to a woman they were vetting named Judyth Vary Baker [see Chapter 7]. Judyth was saying she worked with Mary in the summer of 1963 on a project involving David Ferrie and that she worked as the technician in the laboratory in Ferrie's apartment. It was Judyth who led me to Lee Harvey Oswald's involvement, and you simply can't talk about Oswald without getting into the JFK assassination.

So, Mary Sherman's murder was the starting point for me and the glue that held the story together. Eventually, I wound up staring at the JFK assassination and a cancerous biological weapon made from irradiated monkey viruses the CIA then tested on prisoners from Angola Penitentiary

The CIA attempted to eliminate Cuban dictator Fidel Castro many times, and by any means necessary, as soon as he came into power in 1959. (Source: Bettmann via Getty Images)

in southeast Louisiana. This story came to me rather than me going to it. Call it fate if you like, but it was a scary journey.

What do you remember about Mary Sherman?

I thought she was severe because when she came to the house, she was wearing a dark-blue silk dress and pearls, and her hair was swept up on top of her head, like a French twist or something. And she had a scotch in one hand and a cigarette in the other. She kind of debated me when I talked to her, and my father was unhappy I was there during their conversation. I could tell he was looking forward to getting me out of the room. I knew my father had enormous professional respect for Mary because she was the Chair of the Pathology Committee of the American Academy of Orthopedic Surgeons, which made her one of the highest-ranking women in medicine.

How did you react when you heard she was murdered?
In the summer of 1964, we had just moved into a new house that had some louvered doors in it. My father was sitting in the living room, and I was hiding in the hallway eavesdropping, and I heard him crying. My father was an old Navy doctor from World War II, and he just didn't show much emotion. In fact, I'd never seen him cry before. When I walked out into the living room, my mother was sitting with him, and I asked, "What's wrong with daddy?" And she said, "A woman he knew from the office has died. He'll be alright. He's just sad right now." Later, when I found out about David Ferrie's laboratory and working with the monkey viruses, I talked to my mother about it, and she said, "Oh yeah, he was doing that with Mary."

Then she told me about the murder and how Mary was found naked and stabbed. "Dismembered" was the word my mother used because her right arm was missing. That's how I found out about it. What I learned later was the public had not been made aware of what my mother told me, so I had two different versions of the story. I later learned my mom's version was the right one, but I didn't know this until I got my hands on the documents, such as the autopsy protocol and the crime scene and morgue photos, which show very clearly what happened to her, and which was not revealed to the public.

The press reported she was set on fire in her apartment, but the fire didn't burn anything. Nobody reported seeing flames. It was just a smoldering mattress fire, yet her entire right arm and rib cage had been disintegrated by heat. But the hair on her head and pelvis wasn't burned at all, and hair is the easiest thing to burn. So, there was a fundamental problem with the forensics of the murder in the first place, and it wasn't until I got my hands on the core documents that I was able to articulate it.

There comes that moment when you make the commitment, right?
I was looking into it mostly for my own reasons. I was pulling thorns out of my paw, if you will, and I didn't know if I was going to talk about it publicly. I'd never written a book, and I really didn't want to write one, but I wanted to know what happened to Mary. The big point of commitment was when I realized there was a cancer epidemic that erupted after the polio vaccine. In my opinion, that was because there was a cancer-causing monkey virus in millions of doses of the polio vaccines released between 1955 and 1963. And nobody disputes this fact because it's public record. They grew the polio vaccine on the kidney cells of the rhesus monkey, but they also got all the viruses in the monkey, which is where simian virus 40 (SV40) comes from.

The only people who won't admit SV40 causes cancer in humans is the National Cancer Institute because of the politics of it. Nobody who wants to get funding from them can say it, but I had guys who were FDA virologists tell me to my face it's the most carcinogenic entity they've ever studied. There's absolutely no question it's what's causing the cancer, and it's almost certainly from the polio vaccines, though I'll add it's also sexually transmitted, so if you had sex with anybody who got those polio vaccines, you may have gotten that cancer.

So, you begin looking into the death of Mary Sherman, and suddenly, you're connecting dots, and the scope becomes far-reaching. What was this like for you?
The process was like putting a puzzle together. I had the general idea of what happened way back in the '60s. I was told by my physics professor, a Jesuit priest, that there was a linear particle accelerator in uptown New Orleans close to Tulane campus, and he couldn't give us any more information because they were doing things there that they didn't want to talk about. Linear particle accelerators create beams of gamma ray radiation. Gamma is the stuff that's stronger than x-rays. It burns out tumors in people, so I knew it was there, and I knew it was dangerous and secret.

And I knew Mary and David were mutating monkey viruses, and radiation is a good way to mutate monkey viruses.

I didn't know where the linear particle accelerator was when I started this, but the important evidence came to me in pieces. I got a friend to do some research in New Orleans for me, and he tracked down a building engineer who confirmed there was a building in uptown New Orleans with strange wiring in it, and I was told by other engineers that this wiring was enough to run a small city. If you have a 5-million-volt machine, you need a lot of electricity. We finally found the facility that matched the descriptions I'd been given—on the campus of the US Public Health Service Hospital.

Did you eventually get to speak with Judyth Vary Baker?
Yes. She originally was from Bradenton, Florida, and I happened to live there. Her mother was still alive, so she came to visit, and we went out to lunch and sat there for about three hours while she went through all these three-ring binders of the evidence she collected over the years— newspaper articles about her winning science competitions in high school and research about cancer-causing viruses. She trained up in Buffalo, New York, at the Roswell Park Cancer Institute. She worked in the lab of one of the guys who founded the American Association of Radiologists and was close friends with Dr. Alton Ochsner,[3] who had been president of the American Cancer Society and is a major player in this story.

I finally asked her, "You're telling me you personally stood in David Ferrie's apartment with Lee Harvey Oswald at your elbow, day after day, and did experiments on cancer so you could develop a biological weapon to kill Fidel Castro? Do I have this right?" And she said rather matter-of-factly, "Yes."

So, when you have this kind of information coming in as you're doing your research, it's not a clean, linear kind of model. It's like working on a moving mosaic, putting pieces in and seeing how they fit. I think the book captures some of that, but I tried to keep it as simple as I could so readers could follow it, but it was a challenging and complex issue. I had to go to medical school libraries and do my own research. When people found out what I was working on, they started calling me, sending me stuff and feeding me information they didn't want to say in public, so it was a complex process with lots of moving parts.

What have you concluded as a result of your research?
I researched a murder and discovered an epidemic.

And talking about the murder is a good place to start because the public was never told about Mary's missing arm. At about 4:00 a.m. on July 21, 1964, someone smelled smoke at the Patio Apartments and called the police, who came and found one of the doors open and Mary's apartment full of smoke. The police called the fire department, which came and pulled the mattress out of the apartment, and on the floor, they found a naked body of a woman who was badly burned and stabbed.

They did the whole crime scene thing, but things didn't add up. The curtains next to the bed didn't burn, the rug didn't burn, the books on the bookcase didn't burn, and the top of the headboard didn't burn. The paper label on the sherry bottle on the nightstand didn't burn, but her arm was disintegrated. So, what burned off her arm? There was nothing in her apartment that could possibly explain the damage to her body, which is why they didn't tell the public about it. They didn't want anyone going to uptown New Orleans looking for a powerful electric machine capable of burning off her arm.

And because she was working on the medical equivalent of the Manhattan Project, this linear particle accelerator was well hidden. There were about thirteen buildings on the campus of the US Public Health Service Hospital, and it was hidden in a building named the Infectious Disease Laboratory Building, which kept out the casual traffic. This was the building that had all the weird, heavy-gauge wiring in it and a steel wall that was grounded with a big heavy cable to protect the equipment operators from the radiation they were exposed to. A beam was shot down at the ground, and there was a platinum pyramid on the ground floor that divided the radioactive beam into equal doses and reflected it back into these asbestos-lined chambers where they kept their test tubes and stuff for the experiments.

A lot of this detail came to me because there was a doctor who was madder than hell about this. He worked at a cancer hospital on the East

Coast that had a linear particle accelerator, and he knew the guy who installed it. He took the guy out for a drink after he and I became friends and started asking him about this place, and the guy said, "Well, there are things I can't tell you because I had to sign all these non-disclosure agreements with the government, but I can tell you a couple of things about it."

He proceeded to tell my doctor friend that most of the linear particle accelerators, which are very expensive pieces (about $10 million in those days), were usually financed like the mortgage of a house. You pay off little pieces of it over time. On this particular project, he was given six different checks within a week that paid off the entire thing, all drawn in different amounts from different banks. If you're not in the drug business, I'll point out this is money laundering, so who would launder that kind of money and why?

Let's get back to Mary Sherman's apartment. I finally meet this woman, Victoria Sulzer [see Chapter 8], who was Mary Sherman's neighbor and lived next door to Juan Valdez, the guy who called the police because he smelled the smoke. Victoria also went to middle school with Lee Harvey Oswald, so she recognized him when he came to the Patio Apartments in August 1963. And where was Oswald going? To see Juan Valdez. And what were they doing there? Victoria and her ex-husband both told me the same story, which is when Lee would go into Valdez's apartment, they would flush the toilet twenty-five to thirty times in a row. Victoria told me the headboard of their bedroom was up against the wall, and on the other side of the wall was Valdez's bathroom, so the pipes from the bathroom ran down that wall. Every time he flushed the toilet, they heard the water running down the pipes. This happened night after night for almost a month.

Now, once you get Judyth's story out on the table, you realize this was right at the end of her research, when they were killing up to 500 mice a day and had to get rid of these cancerous tumors they were cutting out of the mice at David Ferrie's apartment. It was there where they made slides, put them under microscopes, put them in test tubes, and took all the samples over to Mary's apartment for her to analyze. Mary, who was in charge, wasn't going to stand over the toilet and flush biomedical waste down it. They had somebody else doing that—Oswald. Oswald was picking up this biohazard waste from Mary's apartment and bringing it to Valdez's apartment so they could flush it down the toilet.

Who sanctioned this research?

Who wrote the six checks for the $10 million? To me, that's CIA. Let's also consider the time frame. The Eisenhower administration started mass inoculations of the government-approved Jonas Salk polio vaccine in 1955. One year earlier, however, Dr. Bernice Eddy, PhD, a veteran scientist with the National Institutes of Health, found that a sample of the vaccine contained live, infectious virus that gave polio to a test monkey. She knew something was wrong and told a friend "there was going to be a disaster." Four years later, Dr. Eddy and Dr. Sarah Stewart, MD, PhD, discovered the vaccine contained SV40, and their fear was that the continued inoculation of polio into humans would result in a human cancer epidemic.

Despite Dr. Eddy's presentation of evidence at the New York Cancer Society in 1960, millions of additional people were needlessly exposed to the cancer virus in the polio vaccine. Between 1955 and 1963, something

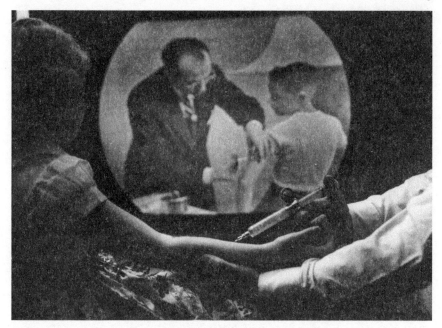

An eight-year-old girl receives a polio vaccine while she watches a closed-circuit television broadcast showing Dr. Jonas Salk inoculating a boy. (Photo by PhotoQuest/Getty Images)

like ninety-eight million Americans were exposed. When Dr. Eddy tried to get the word out to colleagues, she was muzzled and stripped of her vaccine regulatory duties and her laboratory.

So, what do you when you're the responsible party that authorized the release of this? The first thing you do is stamp it as a national security secret so nobody can talk about it, and then you get busy trying to find a solution before the public finds out because they're going to lynch you. So, they set up the medical project in New Orleans with the linear particle accelerator to mutate monkey viruses and develop a vaccine that would stop SV40 from causing a cancer epidemic.

The big question here is, do we have a cancer epidemic? And the answer is yes, we have an enormous cancer epidemic, particularly an elevated rise in soft-tissue cancers—breast, prostate, melanoma, and lymphoma—in the last fifty years. I left out brain cancer for technical reasons, but brain cancer, particularly childhood brain cancer, would be the fifth one in that cluster.

Just to clarify: The cancer-causing virus is discovered, which prompts efforts to stop the SV40 from causing a cancer epidemic. But the US Government also commissions covert projects through the CIA with the purpose of weaponizing cancer to eliminate political enemies such as Fidel Castro, which was what Alton Ochsner, Mary Sherman, Judyth Vary Baker, David Ferrie, and Lee Harvey Oswald were working on— in various capacities—during the summer of 1963. Is this accurate?
Yes, and I believe Mary was working on both projects, but it would be a whole lot easier to tell you what the CIA did if the CIA was willing to tell us what they did. The reason they don't tell us is they don't want us to have the document trail connecting the development of a biological weapon and testing it on human prisoners, which is what happened that summer.

In 2006, the CIA got a new director, Michael Hayden, and he decided he wanted to establish a new atmosphere of openness at the agency. His director of security told him, "Boss, you're new here, and there were a lot of things we did you don't want to tell people about." So, Hayden com- missioned his director of security to draft a document with everything the CIA did between about 1956 and 1964 that was either flat-out illegal or embarrassing to the agency. This document, named the Family Jewels, had eight items in it. When Hayden called a press conference in 1977, he said, "Here are the family jewels; we're opening up the kimono!"

Family jewels two through eight were things like using the mafia to kill Fidel Castro and Operation Mockingbird, in which they went about gaining control of the American press, but jewel No. 1 is 100 percent redacted . . . all three pages, every single word of it. It's not redacted; it's obscured and obliterated.

So, what's family jewel No. 1? Is it that the CIA used its money-laundering operations to pay for a linear particle accelerator on the grounds of the US Public Health Service Hospital so they could mutate monkey viruses to find a vaccine to stop a cancer epidemic, which was caused by a cancer virus in the polio vaccine the government released? But then the Russian missiles came into Cuba, so did they change this noble-but-dangerous mission into weaponizing these same monkey viruses to create a biological weapon to kill Fidel Castro . . . and anyone else they wanted to get rid of? Example: Jack Ruby.

That would explain Mary Sherman's death being covered up.
My mother told me the investigation was shut down from above. It was all very hush-hush. In 1970, six years after Mary's death, I tried to get a copy of the police report. I had a girlfriend whose father was an investigator for the DA's office. He did murders and capital crimes, so I asked him if he could get me a copy of the file, and he said, "Sure, no problem. I do it all the time. Call me back in forty-eight hours." I called him back in forty-eight hours, and he screamed at me, "What did you get me into? I almost got fired for asking to see this file!"

You look at the front page of the newspaper the day after Mary's death, and it reads, "Orleans Woman Surgeon Slain by Intruder; Body Set Afire." And then underneath that, a smaller headline reads, "Clues Lacking in Killing of Dr. Sherman." What clues lacking? It's not clues lacking; they're just not going to tell you.

What do you think really happened to her?
She was electrocuted at the laboratory, and I believe it was sabotage. Somebody messed with the wiring so whoever turned on the machine

would get all five million volts back up through their arm. And the reason her feet didn't blow off, which is normal in such high-voltage electrocutions, is that she was standing in front of the steel wall I mentioned that had the grounded cable. The electricity came up her hand and went back into the wall, which is why her rib cage was disintegrated. You could see the internal organs of her body through where her rib cage was supposed to be. Her right arm and rib cage are missing, and all around her body, the hair is still there.

And because the electricity went up her right arm and out of her rib cage, it didn't cross her heart. Often in these high-voltage electrocutions, if it crosses the heart, the person dies instantly. But if it doesn't, the heart can keep beating, so the person is technically alive. So, whoever was there with her, colleagues with medical knowledge, stabbed her carefully with a slim surgical-style instrument between the fifth and sixth ribs, directly into the center of her heart, in what was a mercy killing. Whether sabotage or not, the linear particle accelerator and the project at the US Public Health Service Hospital could *not* be exposed, so that's when it was decided to bring her body back to her apartment and make it look like an intruder killed her there.

One of the interesting things I found was a newspaper article from July 22, 1964. It tells what happened on the previous day, July 21, in Washington, DC, when President Johnson received some startling information and jumped into his limousine without telling his staff where he was going. He told his driver, "We're going to the Pentagon right now!" After his sudden Pentagon visit, he came out and told his driver to go to Arlington National Cemetery, where he exited the car and stood at John F. Kennedy's grave.

Does this strike you as unusual behavior? My guess is he finally realized what Kennedy was dealing with and the potential of what could happen if this type of information got out to the public.

So, during the summer of 1963, you have a covert, CIA-sponsored biological weapon project, a covert linear particle accelerator project, and the Kennedy assassination chicanery with David Ferrie, Clay Shaw, Guy Banister, and Lee Harvey Oswald ALL happening in New Orleans. Is it fair to say the Crescent City was a busy place?

Absolutely. I knew a cop who was investigating the Kennedy assassination for the House Select Committee on Assassinations in the 1970s, and he said New Orleans in the 1950s and 1960s was like Casablanca, with all these intelligence operations going on because of its proximity and trade with South America, Central America, and Cuba.

But why people do things is often a mystery. Ferrie was involved with a lot of people . . . with the mafia, with Carlos Marcello, so was he doing this for him? He was already looking for a cure for cancer on his own, and that's the texture of this story; there aren't a lot of clean answers to these

The New Orleans house in which David Ferrie was found dead on February 22, 1967, and where he allegedly worked on secret cancer-related experiments (under the supervision of Dr. Mary Sherman) in the summer of 1963 with Judyth Vary Baker and Lee Harvey Oswald. (Source: Bettmann via Getty Images)

things, but reality is a lot stranger than fiction. I did a presentation at a conference where I talked about Oswald's summer in New Orleans. He comes into town, and on his first day there, he intercepts Judyth Baker at the post office. On the second day, he introduces her to David Ferrie. On the third day, he introduces her to Mary Sherman at a party at David Ferrie's apartment. On the fourth day, he introduces her to Guy Banister.[4] This is the first week in New Orleans for a guy who hasn't been there for ten years.

How is this possible? I mean, someone is writing his script, giving him his marching orders, and it's quite openly, at this point, Guy Banister. But you're talking about stuff people didn't want known, so it's buried. You have to piece the thing together—a little oral history there, a document here, an inference around the corner. Then later, many times those inferences get filled in by harder documentation. It's a messy process, but I had to accept that, or I wouldn't have been able to write the book.

Were you able to determine if Mary Sherman was directing Judyth, Lee Harvey Oswald, and David Ferrie, and probably a few others, in this medical project?
Yes, but it was all under the direction of Dr. Alton Ochsner. I've got his FBI file. He was approved by J. Edgar Hoover for a sensitive position in the US government in October 1959. He had decades of secret assignments for the US military and other intelligence agencies, including the FBI and presumably the CIA. And he did secret work for the US Public Health Service, where he would go and pick up his paychecks from the government. So, saying these people were innocent little doctors is simply not in line with reality.

I read that Dr. Ochsner was a staunch anticommunist who believed Fidel Castro was Public Enemy No. 1, so it's not a stretch to consider he was working with the CIA to create a cancer-causing biological weapon with which to eliminate him.
Correct, and if you go to the front of the Ochsner Medical Center today, there are nineteen flagpoles flying the flags of the countries of Latin America. One CIA director testified before Congress and said the CIA was

responsible for financing 159 hospitals in the United States using a combination of seed money—which they either got from one of their buddies like Texas oil millionaire Clint Murchison or from the Hill-Burton Act[5]—to build.

Ochsner's hospital was originally nicknamed Splinter Village because it was a bunch of one-story military barracks and offices he had somehow secured from the military. Then they moved into what looks like the Emerald City. You're talking about hundreds of millions of dollars, and you have the CIA director saying they did this so they could do experiments. What do these medical experiments have to do with gathering foreign intelligence, which is supposed to be the sole purpose of the CIA?

What kinds of challenges did you encounter while doing your research?
First, I was looking into a murder no one wanted to talk about, particularly not the police. And second, I was investigating some of the wealthiest and most important people in New Orleans, so many individuals were reluctant to talk to me. I was dealing with issues like contaminated vaccines the pharma industry and the federal government didn't want discussed, and particularly their involvement in releasing millions of doses of the contaminated polio vaccine, which consequently caused our current cancer epidemic. So, I had to proceed very carefully.

My biggest challenge was when I finally got my witness, Judyth Vary Baker. Her credibility was being rudely criticized, unfairly, by both sides of the JFK aisle, so I became her champion and even became the editor of her book, *Me and Lee*, which was way more difficult and challenging than I anticipated, but it's what I needed to do in order to preserve her credibility.

Was there a specific low point for you during this long journey?
It was when I realized my worst fears were in fact founded in facts, particularly the dimensions of the cancer epidemic that resulted from the contamination of the polio vaccines in the 1950s. That was a genie I couldn't put back in the bottle; I had to deal with it. Whatever the price to me, I was now headed into a dark, lonely tunnel looking for a

public health disaster of unimaginable proportions. And I remembered my father's warning about crossing swords with these people. I felt very alone, and I wondered what I'd gotten my family into. It was a very difficult time.

Did you ever fear for your life because of your research?
Yes. It comes with the territory, but I was never threatened. You must realize assassins don't threaten you; they simply kill you when they're told to do so. I learned to be very careful and cautious. I worked with a loaded gun next to my keyboard. I had children at home, and I had to tell them, "Daddy's guns are loaded, so don't touch them."

The most stressful time for me was right before I published because if they shut me up then, nobody would know what I had to say, and my family would be left without a breadwinner. It was a scary situation. I did the original draft of the book and sent it to half a dozen friends to read because you can't proofread your own stuff. They all marked it up and send it back to me, and five out of six of them told me I was going to get myself killed. And they were serious; they weren't joking. It was very stressful, but I wasn't going to stop.

One of the reasons I self-published the book was I needed to control the content, but I also needed to keep a low profile until I published because I knew once I got sunlight on me, I would be safe. I had to get the story out quickly and quietly. As the sunlight shone on me, my safety and security improved. My stress levels went down. I'd worked through the hard part.

Is there a burden associated with knowing the things you know?
Yes. I was a kid who grew up believing all these things about the Founding Fathers, the truth, the democratic system of government, and it's just not that way. We're an oligarchy,[6] and I'm disappointed in a lot of stuff. It's like Jackson Browne said, and I'm paraphrasing a little bit, "When you see through life's illusions, there lies the danger."

Now, I worry about my plants. I'm sitting here looking out into my backyard. We've got bird feeders, and we have water features. It looks like a Disney film with the animals playing. This is what I do nowadays . . . because I've already done the dark stuff.

What was your biggest eureka moment in your research?
The best moment was when Jim Marrs agreed to write the foreword to *Dr. Mary's Monkey*. I was very insecure about my knowledge of the JFK assassination because it's very complex, and I was late to the party, and Jim was a world-class expert on it. He had written *Crossfire*, which was a *New York Times* bestseller and a book used by Oliver Stone as a source for *JFK*. I knew having Jim on my side as an ally would mean smoother sailing in the JFK waters. He also came on board for Judyth; he wrote the afterword to *Me and Lee,* and I wrote the forward to it. When I was editing, I'd edit a chapter and send it to Jim. I wanted him looking over my shoulder on all the JFK content, so I wound up with this wonderful ally. We became very good friends.

What have been the ripple effects of the JFK assassination?
The first ripple effect of the JFK assassination was the Vietnam War, and that was a bad one. JFK inherited a small war from Eisenhower with less than 1,000 troops involved. He did increase that number to about 60,000, but then he realized it wasn't our war and was going to pull them all out. LBJ became president as a direct result of the assassination, and he increased the military presence in Vietnam to more than 500,000 soldiers at one time. Their average age was twenty-one, and a total of 2,700,000 Americans served in that theater over the years, and 58,000 of them died, as did millions of Asians.

The next ripples were the Martin Luther King and Robert Kennedy assassinations. And then there was the election of Richard Nixon, which led to Watergate and more secretive corrupt activities they attempted to cover up.

Why does the JFK assassination still matter all these years later?
If JFK had died a natural death, the country would've just moved on. But because there was an assassination, it inspired a whole generation to ask hard questions and ultimately inspired today's culture of criticism,

which replaced the culture of obedience from the Cold War. It's obvious the government's JFK narrative doesn't hold water at all, and Lee Harvey Oswald is the keystone in that whole thing, and when you realize who he was, what he did and didn't do, and why he was murdered while in the custody of the police, everything starts to come into focus.

They sacrificed one of their own to get away with it, and what younger generations need to know is that Lee Harvey Oswald DID NOT kill JFK. He was framed. He was set up to take the fall to protect the real conspirators. He learned about the JFK plot in July of 1963 and tried to stop it, but he was in too deep. JFK was killed by powerful people who wanted to control the US government. It was a coup d'état, and they framed a twenty-four-year-old father of two as the murderer so they'd have somebody to blame . . . somebody who was disposable, who could be sacrificed, and this was to protect the real criminals who planned and carried out the assassination. This was a trick they pulled off because they controlled law enforcement and the media.

Abraham Bolden was a secret service agent who was in Chicago preparing for Kennedy's visit there, and he said they got a message from an undercover agent named Lee telling them there was going to be an assassination attempt there. They subsequently found some hard evidence of that, so they canceled his visit. Then on November 17, five days before the assassination, Oswald marched into the FBI office in Dallas and handed them a note that said a right-wing group was planning to kill Kennedy. This is why Judyth's book is so important, and I hope people read it because it provides a much better picture of Oswald and the day-to-day that led up to the assassination.

If you could get the answer to one question in your case, what would it be?
I'd like to know what the CIA's family jewel No. 1 is.

Is your work finished?
I wrote *Dr. Mary's Monkey*, which wasn't an easy task. I brought Judyth Vary Baker into the spotlight. I've spoken publicly for twenty-six years about this. The only thing left for me to do is make a documentary series,

which would bring the story to a wider audience. Other than that, I've done what I can do.

Is there anything else you wish to add?
The problem is we have the best government money can buy, but it's not a very good one. The United States has become an oligarchy that runs a war machine known as the military-industrial complex. It's all a rich man's trick, and we need to learn to turn off the television set and think for ourselves. If we don't, we'll be led wherever they want to lead us.

CHAPTER 7

JUDYTH VARY BAKER

Judyth Vary Baker developed a keen interest in science while attending Manatee High School in Bradenton, Florida, where she received national attention for her cancer research and guidance from two Nobel Prize winners in biochemistry. In 1963, she was offered a summer medical internship in New Orleans through Dr. Alton Ochsner and Tulane Medical School. That summer she met Lee Harvey Oswald, David Ferrie, Guy Banister, and Jack Ruby—all of whom would be implicated in the assassination of JFK. Judyth has provided compelling evidence (which has been confirmed by eyewitnesses) that she and Oswald became lovers that summer and that she worked with him and others to develop an aggressive strain of cancer as part of a CIA plan to assassinate Fidel Castro. Despite having endured major character assassination attempts from those who wish to discredit her, she courageously stands by her story and has written three books on the topic: *Lee Harvey Oswald and Me*, *David Ferrie: Mafia Pilot*, and *Kennedy & Oswald: The Big Picture*. She also runs the annual JFK Assassination Conference in Dallas and continues to speak out to vindicate Oswald.

When reading your book, I felt like it was the first time I was reading something about Lee Harvey Oswald the human being, not the lone-nut assassin or patsy. Who was the real Lee Harvey Oswald . . . the person *you* knew?

Judyth Vary Baker aged seventeen doing a cancer nicotinic acid study. (Source: Judyth Vary Baker)

Well, he wasn't perfect. I mean, as much as I adored and loved him, when you're young, things must be ironed out. He had manly pride, and it burned him to a crisp in the end.

What was he like to spend time with?
His first impulse was to try and help people. I loved that about him. And he was very thoughtful. He wasn't a person who talked a lot, but boy, once you got him started, he loved to get into deep conversations. I would get him going on a topic, and then we would talk for hours. He was very knowledgeable about a lot of things.

It seems like we get such completely different versions of his patriotism. What was your sense of his patriotism? Where did his heart lie in that sense?

Freedom. Freedom for everybody. Even though it wasn't against the law, the signs that read "Colored" were still up in the back half of buses in New Orleans, but we'd sit in the back with all the colored people anyway, and they loved us. When Lee had to go to court and pay a $10 fee for disturbing the peace and handing out those leaflets,[1] the courtroom was divided with whites and blacks, and he sat with the blacks. And I loved that because I was the same way. He just wanted people to get along . . . he was all for peace. As far as his patriotism was concerned, he saw flaws in both the United States and the Soviet Union. Today, I think you'd call him a liberal. It's hard to say. You couldn't put a label on him.

In the time you knew each other, did you get to know him well enough to see into his past and what it was in his childhood that created that love of freedom?

When Lee was a little boy, his mother read him a book titled *This Is the Christmas*. The author was from Serbia, and this is important, because this is what formed him. I asked him, "What's the first book that really impacted you?" We were both readers. Lee read voraciously even though he had dyslexia and had a lot of difficulty with writing. He saw a "9" as a "6," for example, and it made things hard for him. Nevertheless, he conquered all of that and loved to read.

So, he's a little boy reading this Serbian story about a blind two-year-old baby who is lost in a horrible storm, and people in this Serbian village adopt him, but nobody likes him because he is from a group of people who have darker skin than they do. So, here's this little boy and he's blind, and they won't even let him go to church. He's sent out to take care of the sheep, and every Christmas, he hears them all going to church. He hears mothers call their sons to go to midnight mass, but he never hears his name called.

The way the story ends is amazing. The little boy is all by himself out in the fields with this little lamb who has a broken leg, and everyone in the village has gone down to church and left him alone again. He's hungry and he's freezing, but then somebody comes and visits him and says, "Touch my face so you'll know who I am," and "I'm a boy like you," and it was Jesus Christ. Christ comes and visits him, and people are coming out from midnight mass and there's this light in the valley, and it's just filling the valley, and they go to see what it is, and they see Christ with the boy and the little lamb with the broken leg. And they finally realize they treated the boy horribly. The boy did nothing wrong, but they neglected him because his skin was dark.

That's the way the story ends, and it really affected Lee because he was sensitive. He cared that much. Lee was known to have said, "I would lay down my life for my black brothers." That was the kind of person he was.

I went and found that book at the library. I went to the front desk and asked, "If I give you a donation of $25, will you let me have this book?" and they said yes. It hadn't been taken out for years. So, I have the book, and it's very precious to me.

Was Lee an intelligent person?
Lee was a highly intelligent man, but sometimes he had to act stupid. He told me once, "All you have to do is keep your mouth shut and act dumb, and they'll say anything in front of you." In New Orleans we got together with some very suspicious people, including Jack Ruby and others who were going to visit Clay Shaw,[2] and Lee told me, "I want you to act dumb, Juduffki." Juduffki was his nickname for me. My family called me Juduffski because I loved Russian literature and music, and I learned some Russian, but Lee said the s shouldn't be in there. So, these guys drove up in a beat-up green-and-brown Chevy, and we got in the car, and I said, "Oh, I get to put my little bottom on the Godfather's car upholstery!" But there wasn't room for me, so I had to sit on Lee's lap, and one of them said, "Well, it looks like you had to put your little bottom on him, and he doesn't mind at all!" That was the status I had with this group . . . the only girl, just acting like a bimbo.

Do you remember the best and worst days you spent with Lee? Do you have strong memories of those sort of shared experiences?
The best day of my life was when Lee and I were at the Roosevelt Hotel in New Orleans, which was after we had a big showdown. He was struggling with being married to Marina and being in love with me. He said, "I love my little girls too much, my baby and my baby to come. I'll never

see them again, so we can't be together." And he went to the bathroom because he was really upset, and I left. I wrote a letter on a napkin saying I would love him forever but that he had to do what was right. I was crying and distraught because I loved him very much, but I knew he also loved his family, so it was tearing him apart. He didn't love Marina, necessarily, but even if he got a divorce, we couldn't stay in the country. It would be too dangerous, even for her.

So, I went back to the house where I was renting an apartment, and I was sad, but a couple of days later, Lee came tapping on my bedroom window. I hid under the bed because I was too upset to see him, but I knew he could get in because we had left a key outside. He was about to get the key when the house dog, Collie, chased a cat up a tree, so Lee pulled a ladder from under the building, propped it up against the tree, and brought this rather ornery tomcat down. The cat scratched him pretty good, but Lee told the cat, "Mr. Cat, you know you've got to stay away from this neighborhood because Collie is always going to try and get you." After he let the cat loose, he got the key and came inside. So, I said, "Please, just go away and go back to your family," and he got down on his knees and looked under the bed, and he said, "I planned to get down on my knees to you today, but I didn't think it'd be like this. Will you marry me? I know your husband never asked you to marry him, so I will ask you one hundred times."

I said, "Ask me again," and I got out from under the bed. He asked me while standing on his head, with his ears plugged, and by the time we got back to the room at the Roosevelt Hotel, he was still asking me. While he was taking my clothes off, while I was taking his clothes off, he kept asking me, repeatedly, and by the 100th time, I said, "Yes," and we consummated our love, and it was so beautiful. It was just beautiful.

When did this happen, exactly?
This was sometime in July of that summer, the summer of '63.

How did he treat Marina?
People say, "Look how mean he was to Marina. He kept her isolated, wouldn't let her have any friends and wouldn't let her learn English," but

he did that to protect her because if she learned English and had lots of friends, she could be accused of being a Russian spy. Lee literally saved her life. She knew a lot more English than she pretended, but the point is, she had no friends, no connections. And how could you be a spy if you never went anywhere? So, that's what they did, and I think it's wonderful he did that, but people think he was abusive because of that.

He told me he hit her more than once, which horrified me. But he also said that happened after she kicked him a bunch of times and said, "If you don't hit me back, you're not a man!" I was mad at Lee when he told me, and I told him I couldn't be with a man who would hit a woman, but I could also tell he truly regretted doing it. It wasn't in his nature to do that.

There seems to have been a depth of connection and understanding between the two of you. Have you ever felt his presence over the years?
I wanted to kill myself when I saw him get shot on live TV, but Lee was smart, and he made me promise him something before he left New Orleans. He said, "Promise me you'll have babies for me." So, I had to stay alive and keep my promise, and I ended up having babies with my husband, but I had to wait until they were grown up before I ever said anything to anyone about Lee. Finally, when my youngest child left the house after getting married, I called a reporter from Baton Rouge and told him I'd written some stuff down and wanted to get it on record in case it got stolen or something happened to me.

I began to speak out, but here's the point: I had nightmares during which I would see Lee on a Ferris wheel, going up, and people were shooting at him, and finally they shot him, and he came crashing down to the ground, and his skull broke open and this red light came out of his eyes. It was the most horrible nightmare you could imagine, but I never had it again after breaking my silence about him.

Was Lee a religious man?
When I met Lee, I was an atheist, and he was an agnostic. He said he was a reluctant agnostic because as much as he'd like to believe there was somebody running things, everything was such a mess. I remember him

saying, "Here's the problem I have. We have all these different religions, and the founders of these religions all say they've talked to God, and God talked to them, or they got inspired by the Holy Spirit. Yet they all believe different things and fight with each other, which means God's not a very good communicator. Therefore, I am not responsible."

What was David Ferrie like?

Dave was a nervous and very conflicted man. It turned out he had been abused by a priest when he was a kid, yet this other priest rescued him and believed him when nobody else did. He had a nervous breakdown over that first priest, and his hair started falling out. It was his first bout with alopecia. That's why he had no hair on his body. Dave was one of the most brilliant men I've ever met, and multitalented. He decided to become a priest thanks to the second priest who befriended him, but in the seminary, he again found himself sexually assaulted, and when he reported it, he was kicked out. Dave believed God didn't want him and that maybe he was supposed to be a homosexual. It's very strange how he came to that conclusion.

He told me, "Nobody wants to be around me. I mean look at me." His thick eyebrows were pasted on . . . they were little pieces of pubic hair. He had a board with samples of pubic hair on it from all his conquests. I actually said to him, "Dave, you know it makes you look really strange," and he said, "Well, it saved my life. I'm a pilot." He had no eyelashes, so when he put his goggles on, stuff would get in his eyes. The pubic hairs glued to his eyebrows sealed the goggles so stuff wouldn't get in his eyes.

People don't realize this, but he just got into the habit of it and didn't care what he looked like because he was really demoralized that way. I saw him take off his toupees. He had several of them, and they were all in terrible condition. I mean this guy didn't care at all. One was made of monkey fur. I'm not joking.

Another one of Dave's talents was his ability to hypnotize people. I don't know where he learned to do it, but I saw him hypnotize the two Cuban kids who would bring the boxes of mice to his apartment. Lee and I couldn't be hypnotized, for whatever reason, but a lot of people could be, and Dave knew how to do it.

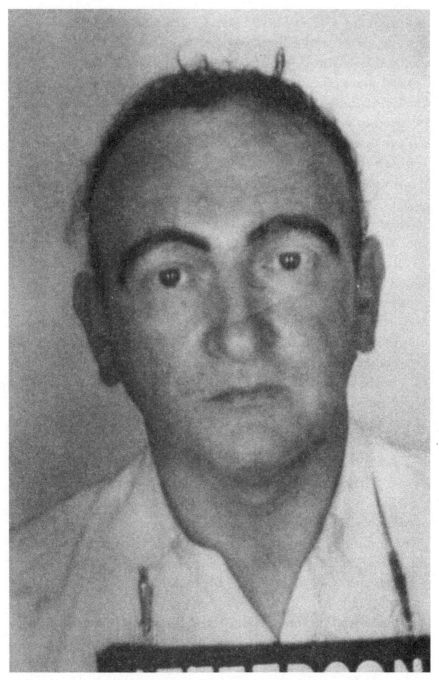

David Ferrie was introduced to Judyth Vary Baker through Lee Harvey Oswald. (Source: Bettmann via Getty Images)

What kind of relationship did David Ferrie have with Lee?
Lee told me the story of how they met. When Lee was about thirteen or so, he was part of the Civil Air Patrol Cadet Program in New Orleans, and Lee and all the other cadets looked up to Dave, who was the commander of all the patrols and was also a pilot. One day, Dave took Lee and a bunch of the other cadets to his house, where a rowdy party ensued. Lee, always curious, went upstairs to look at this big mannequin Dave had created . . . it was a medical skeleton with blue and red veins running through it, and it had lights where all the nerves were. Dave came upstairs and was surprised to find Lee there, so he slammed the door and locked it, which scared the heck out of Lee. Dave said, "What are you doing up here?" Lee apologized, but Dave started walking toward him. Lee was afraid he was going to do something to him, so he backed up and broke a window with his elbow, took a piece of the glass, and said, "Don't you come near me."

Dave was infuriated that Lee threatened him with glass, so he beat the heck out of him. But then he realized what he did, because he bloodied him all up, and Lee's mother happened to be dating Carlos Marcello's driver at the time. Plus, Lee's uncle was one of Marcello's best friends, so Dave realized they would cut him up into little pieces for what he did. So, Dave cleaned Lee up as best he could and took him home, but Lee had no key, so he sat on the porch while Dave went to get ice cream because his mouth was bleeding so bad. When he got back, Lee was inside. But Dave had said, "Please don't tell on me," and Lee said, "I'm not going to tell on you. I'm no snitch, but I don't ever want to see your ugly face again." Later, Dave said, "I owe you for not telling on me," and recommended Lee as a possible recruit in espionage training.

At the time, Lee thought he was a total creep, but as time went on and they found themselves working together on different "operations," they came to respect each other and became friendly.

Are there any other stories about David Ferrie you could share?
I'll tell you a little story about "Ferrie's Berries." We had these morning glory seeds, which we called berries, and it was rumored that these seeds, which were legal to have, could give you a serious high. Well, Lee wasn't so sure about that, but Dave said it was true and cooked the berries so we

could try them. They tasted terrible and nothing happened, so Lee, who was always curious about everything, went to the New Orleans Juvenile Division to see if morning glory seeds were on the list of hallucinogenic substances.

He needed an excuse to walk in there and ask them about this, so he pretended he was reading Aldous Huxley's *Brave New World* and wanted to know if soma was a government-produced drug. It's on the record that he went there, but researchers don't know why. He also went to a chemist in New Orleans and the New Orleans Police Department, but he went because he wanted to know if morning glory seeds produced hallucinogenic effects, and if "Ferrie's Berries" were mentioned as a legal or illegal drug.

It's the little things the public has no idea about. For example, he got mad at Marina for smoking when she was pregnant; it just made him furious. He was a health nut who always ate healthy food, except he loved Dr. Pepper.

Was Lee the kind of person who had a lot of friends?
Well, the issue was he couldn't be too friendly and open with people. When you're a spy and trying to infiltrate, you can't make outside friends and say, "Hey, let's go out and have a beer together." He couldn't make new friends because that could interrupt the trajectory of what he was doing. He had to act distant, but after the assassination, all this stuff came out about how unfriendly he was. He was a spy and had to be a bit standoffish to most people, but the reality was he was kind, friendly, and funny. I remember once we got on a bus and went to the back, but people wouldn't move over for us to sit, so he pretended to sneeze hard, and people got out of the way fast. It was hilarious, and he wrote a poem about it afterward. I memorized it. "I sneezed a sneeze into the air; the droplets fell, I knew not where; but everyone inside the bus moved over and made room for us." He had an incredible sense of humor.

Let's fast-forward to the fall of 1963 . . . Lee is sent to Dallas, you're in Gainesville, Florida, and David Ferrie is still in New Orleans, but you're able to communicate with one another?

Lee Harvey Oswald distributes Hands Off Cuba flyers on the streets of New Orleans, Louisiana. (Photo by © CORBIS/Corbis via Getty Images)

Lee knew what was going down at this point. He pieced together enough information, and he knew he was in trouble, but he was also able to contact the FBI with information to save Kennedy's life in Chicago. He told me this, and researchers have confirmed someone named "Lee" was able to help thwart the assassination plot in Chicago.[3] It was during our last phone call, as a matter of fact, when Lee told me about it. He said, "I believe I saved Kennedy's life three weeks ago."

The other thing Lee told me was that the name of the operation to assassinate Kennedy was called "The Big Event." It wasn't until many years later that Saint John Hunt's father, CIA operative E. Howard Hunt, came forward and said on tape that the name of the op was The Big Event. I had actually been filmed by The History Channel and said Lee called it that just a few months before E. Howard Hunt said the same thing into his tape recorder, which was the recording he gave to his son. So, you can see how close Lee got to the center of the plot, and he knew it would probably end with his death.

So, once he gets to Dallas, he follows his orders, meets with some of the Cuban operatives, and realizes what's happening?
Yes. He told me he was probably going to die.

So, he realizes they're trying to set him up?
He first suspected something bad was going to happen back in July, when he met with some of his CIA handlers. He always had problems with James Angleton, whom he called "Jesus" because that was his middle name. He told me, "Jesus has made it clear they're not going to let me advance. I'm not going to go to college like they promised, and that means only one thing."

He added, "If I've come back from Russia, but they're not going to use me and advance me, I'm somebody who is compromised and in the way. They could use me as a patsy."

For a long time, he believed he was trying to save Kennedy's life. But in July, and especially after he got to Dallas, it became clear to him. I remember he told me, "I can see it now, how they're setting me up as a possible patsy." He knew he was expendable because they weren't going to invest in him. He said, "They don't trust me."

Why didn't they trust him?
Lee explained it to me. He came back from the Soviet Union, but James Angleton would've been happier if he came back dead because it would've proved he was loyal. There was a big political problem because when Lee went over, it was during the Eisenhower administration, and during that administration, they had a good network of spies set up. This was with the OSS, but when the OSS turned into the CIA, things changed. So, now he comes back having been embedded in a life there, complete with friends and a new bride. And he becomes a liability because he wouldn't have been the first spy to become a double agent. You know, go over there and really become a communist. Lee was expecting, because of the good work he did, that he would be rewarded, have his college education paid for and moved up the ranks. And when that didn't happen, he knew he was doomed. If they don't invest in you, and you have knowledge that could leak out somehow, you're a liability. Toward the end, he honestly felt like he was a walking dead man.

What was that last phone call with Lee like?
I hate talking about this. This is like if you had to talk about the last days of your grandmother as she lay dying or something. It's not easy. That last phone call was an hour and a half long, and it was very emotional. Lee told me he didn't think he was going to make it out of the situation alive, and I begged him to leave Dallas and fly to Mexico. I told him I'd meet him there, but he was convinced there was no way out at that point because they would kill his entire family, including his children, if he aborted. Besides, he told me if he stayed in Dallas, there would be one less gun pointed at President Kennedy. He still believed he could help stop the "Big Event" from happening, but in retrospect, that was wishful thinking on his part.

I mean, he did go to the local FBI office and leave a note. I think it was warning them about the assassination and may have said something like, "Please meet me. I have something important to tell you." But they pretty much ignored it. And after Lee was shot, they destroyed the note and said he had threatened to blow up the building. But if that was true, they would've used the note to prove he was violent.

His main concern, and we both knew this, was that I had to stay alive somehow, and he wanted to make sure he did everything he could to erase every record that we ever knew each other . . . everything you could think of. And people attack my story and say, "Where is she? She's not on the record." Well, Lee was always very careful about making sure we weren't in any photos or videos together. In the beginning, I think it was a combination of his spy craft and the fact he was married, but at the end, it was all about keeping me alive.

And David Ferrie helped you to stay safe, correct?
Yes, he did. He called after Lee was killed and said, "You have to be a vanilla girl. You can't get your name in the papers." I wasn't to say a word about anything that happened that summer, including the cancer research. Dave's message was very clear: Stay invisible. I also stayed away from my family because I was concerned for their safety. I couldn't go to my own sister's wedding. My four grandparents died, and I couldn't go to their funerals. It wasn't until 1977 I dared to go to my father's funeral.

I got on with my life as a wife and mother, and I eventually moved to Europe.

It feels like so much of what you've been sharing has been about the costs to you.
Well, there are many other costs, of course. One of the worst of them, in my opinion, is defaming John F. Kennedy and making him seem non-consequential. The Smithsonian Institution wrote an article about him on what would've been his 100th birthday, and it said Kennedy didn't contribute anything except charm to the presidency. It was like the Cuban Missile Crisis never happened . . . and his incredible heroism during WWII in the Solomon Islands never happened.

The media always emphasize the womanizing, doing everything to minimize the greatness of this man, and he *was* a great man. Lee was convinced of his greatness. Kennedy gave us hope. He wanted to have peace between us and Russia. He's assassinated, and we've been at war with one country or another ever since.

If Lee was in fact a patsy, then that must be the biggest injustice in all of this?
He has been the ultimate pariah in the American public's mind since the assassination. He's been portrayed as a malcontent . . . a confused and violent malcontent who was also a communist sympathizer. But the truth is he was a kind, intelligent, and thoughtful man who loved Kennedy and what he was trying to do. People forget he had two young daughters who have had to grow up and live their lives with this stigma surrounding their family. Imagine living with the thought that your father was the assassin of John F. Kennedy? Whether they believe that or not, it's a horrible burden to carry through life.

You had to not only keep quiet about your relationship with Lee, but also about the research you were doing for Dr. Sherman and Dr. Ochsner, correct?
That's right, and I have serious objections when people say my story has nothing to do with what happened and that it's only peripheral. My

experiences that summer show there were sinister things afoot, and there were other reasons to cover those things up, not just because of the assassination, which is bad enough, but the fact we were working on a virus to use as a weapon. We were weaponizing cancer so the CIA could use it for their own nefarious purposes against enemies of the state.

And we know where that has taken us. We have an industry in big pharma that makes a heck of a lot of money by treating cancer, not curing cancer. I truly believe we could've cured it in the '70s, but we still haven't done it because it doesn't make money. And that could be a bigger story than the Kennedy assassination.

Do you think Lee's name can ever be exonerated?
I do. When I first started speaking out and said Lee tried to save Kennedy's life, people called me a liar and a fraud, but over time, a number of witnesses have stepped forward who have provided evidence verifying my association with him. The latest witness saw Lee at my apartment so often, she thought he lived there. And I think more and more people realize Lee was a patsy, and what happened in New Orleans the summer before the assassination was very telling and important.

My whole life I've just wanted to help people, which is why I got into medicine, and the other thing I wanted to do is have a life with Lee. We talked about having babies and living a simple life. We imagined having our things paid for because we really believed we could be informants for the CIA in Mexico and live a peaceful life. And Lee would be able to see his kids in the States. You know . . . I guess it was an ideal fantasy.

To be honest, it's only because of people like you, who aren't afraid to tell the human side of these stories, that the essence of truth gets out. I've been vilified for telling my story. People hate me for daring to put a wrench in their perfect theories. They accuse me of wanting to make money off this, but my entire life was turned upside down the second Lee was arrested in Dallas that day. I had to be the "vanilla girl" Dave told me to be in order not to be taken out. One minute I was working for prestigious doctors on cancer research, and then I had to disappear. I was approached by a movie company, and they said, "We can make you a millionaire, and all you have to do is say Lee lied to you, and we'll portray you as a tragic figure in the movie." I couldn't believe it, and of course I didn't do it.

Would you give up those months you had with Lee to have lived the kind of life you thought you were going to live before you met him?
I'll put it this way, and I mean this with all sincerity. I was loved and cherished enough to last a lifetime, and I'd never exchange one minute of it for anything else. If I think about it too much, I'm going to cry. People say, "Oh, look at how emotional she is." You must know I wouldn't react this way if Lee was an ordinary man, but he wasn't. He was extraordinary. We loved each other completely. I know that true love does exist.

Do you miss him?
I think about the little dog who, when his master dies, sits near his master's grave until he dies. Well . . . that's me. I just want to be buried next to Lee. This guy named Abedin bought the burial plot next to Lee's as a joke. If only he would let me, I would buy that plot from him. I would ask people to help me buy it so I can be buried next to Lee in Rose Hill Cemetery. I love the name of it . . . Rose Hill. That's my dream.

Judyth, thank you for taking the time to speak with me and for being so open and honest with your emotions. And thank you for letting the world know a little bit more about the man you knew.
I had to do this because he would've done it for me. And I don't care if I die now. I'm seventy-seven, so if they do something to me for telling my story, then so be it. I mean, the truth must get out, and I'm part of that truth.

CHAPTER 8

VICTORIA SULZER

Victoria Sulzer is a retired educator, self-taught artist, mother of six, and grandmother and great-grandmother of twenty-one. She received her Bachelor of Arts and teacher certification and did her postgraduate work at Tulane University in New Orleans. Her studies centered in criminal justice, the social sciences, education, and business applications. She also served in multiple capacities at the university, including as a faculty and student grievance advocate, academic advertiser, campus Senate representative, and national adviser for adult continuing education. She has contributed to the books *Who Really Killed Martin Luther King, Jr.?* by Phil Nelson, *Dr. Mary's Monkey* by Ed Haslam, and *Farewell to Justice* by Joan Mellen, as well as the documentary *A Séance for Mary Sherman* by Stephen C. Tyler. She has been a featured speaker at David Denton's JFK Historical Group, the annual Lee Harvey Oswald Conference, and the annual New Orleans and Dallas JFK assassination conferences.

What are your earliest recollections of Lee Harvey Oswald?
In the late 1950s, I was a seventh-grade student at P.G.T. Beauregard Jr. High School in New Orleans, Louisiana. I assumed Lee was older because I specifically remember he was in a ninth-grade civics class right before my class. His teacher, Mrs. Marcotte, ran late all the time, so we would wait in the hallway outside the classroom and could hear what was going on inside. She would call his name a lot, and I can only assume it was because

he was raising his hand and either knew the answers or was inquiring further. There was a group of boys who teased him, but there was also another group that stuck up for him. I'm not quite sure why he was teased, but I remember him as being a well-mannered, polite person, and a nice boy.

After my husband and I married, we moved to Dallas for about a year and then moved back to New Orleans. In December 1962 we moved into the Patio Apartments, located at 3101 St. Charles Ave., the street the

A young Lee Harvey Oswald at the zoo. (Photo by © CORBIS/Corbis via Getty Images)

trolley car ran on. We lived there until the spring of 1964. I was in my early twenties at this point, married with a small child and pregnant with my second. The Patio Apartments were very nice, and there was a long waiting list of people who wanted to live there.

We had some interesting neighbors, including Juan Valdez, a rather mysterious man I nevertheless became friends with. He would sometimes visit Mary Sherman, a respected doctor, who lived in one of the back apartments. Each apartment had a cubicle patio and lots of privacy based on the way they were laid out. There were sixteen apartments total on two levels.

I would see Mary coming and going, and we would often say hello to each other. She wasn't really a conversationalist, but she was always polite and asked me about my daughter and pregnancy now and again. I knew she was a doctor, so that was a little intimidating. She appeared to be nice and kind, and she definitely had an aura about her that was professional.

When did you see Lee Harvey Oswald at the apartments?
One day, I heard a knock at my patio door, and there was a young man standing there who asked me if this was Juan Valdez's apartment. He had a box in his hand about the size of a child's shoe box. Suddenly I realized I knew him. I said, "I know you. We went to Beauregard Jr. High School together." We had a polite exchange, and he asked me if I could take the package if Juan wasn't there. He went over to Juan's, and when he wasn't there, he came back and asked if I could keep the box in my refrigerator until Juan returned. He asked me to do this at least a few times over the course of several weeks, and at the time I didn't think anything of it.

You must understand that at the time, these were just moments in time, nothing more. I didn't know these people would play a role in some of the biggest stories of the twentieth century. So, I took the package, which was wrapped in plain brown paper, and put it into my refrigerator. When Juan got home, I would knock on my wall, which was adjacent to his apartment, and tell him he had a package, and he would come over and pick it up.

What was Juan like?

Juan was an interesting man, to say the least. He grew orchids, and they were all over his patio. He was also into antiques, and I heard a few years later he worked at the New Orleans International Trade Mart. The truth is nobody ever knew what he did. To my knowledge, he disappeared after Mary's murder. While in my apartment, I could often hear conversations in Spanish coming from his apartment, and from time to time I could hear his toilet flushing repeatedly. It seemed very odd to us, and this always occurred late at night, from like 10:00 p.m. to the early morning hours.

Where were you when JFK was assassinated, and Oswald was arrested?

My husband and I went to the Saenger Theatre in downtown New Orleans to watch a movie. It was our first time out together since the birth of our second child. Halfway through the movie, the screen went blank, and the lights came on. I thought the projector had eaten the film or something, but then the manager's voice came over the loudspeaker, and he said, "We are discontinuing the movie. The president of the United States has been shot." Then he said something about offering refunds.

We left the theater and walked down Canal Street toward Maison Blanche, a department store that had an electronics department with TVs on. We watched the news coverage for a while and then caught a trolley car back home. I remember feeling a little afraid and worried, but it never occurred to me that the president would die.

Shortly after we got home, we were watching the news and heard Lee's name. They had arrested him in connection with the shooting, and I remember thinking to myself, "This doesn't make sense." As I started thinking about it days after he was shot and killed, I was angry and upset, and again I thought, "This can't be right." I can't explain why I felt that way, especially when everyone else thought he got what he deserved. I talked to anyone who would listen because something just didn't smell right to me. Lee getting shot the way he did seemed like a stage play, and to this day it still replays itself in my head. He certainly wasn't a bully in school, and I always remembered him being polite and soft-spoken, so it didn't sit well. It was the first time in my life I saw something that made me realize bad things can happen to good people.

Let's fast-forward again to July 1964 and Mary Sherman's murder.
We moved out of the Patio Apartments and to Metairie about a month before Mary's death. A few days later, I got a phone call and am convinced to this day it was Juan Valdez. He never said his name, but I recognized his voice. He asked, "Have you heard about Mary Sherman?" to which I replied, "No." Then he told me, "She was murdered. I just want you to be careful about what you say and who you say it to." Then he hung up. The phone call frightened me because we had an unlisted number, yet this person, who I recognized as Juan, found the number and called, I believe, to warn me.

Juan was always a very kind person to me and my family, and we had established a friendly relationship during our time at the apartments, so I think he was trying to protect me. There were a lot of rumors going around at the time about many people who knew Dr. Sherman either disappearing or dying mysteriously. It wasn't a good situation at all, and you could tell there was some kind of cover-up going on.

Do you ever look back and think to yourself how synchronistic these events were?
Looking back now, it's unnerving to me when I think about how important all of it was, but as a casual observer I didn't grasp the significance of the moments. Mary was my neighbor, Juan was my neighbor, Lee was in middle school with me. Of course, now I realize I was most certainly in danger simply by association. Maybe, as human beings, we need to be more aware of our surroundings. For example, I remember Juan asked on several occasions to use our phone for long-distance calls, for which he would reimburse us right away. It wasn't until after we moved when I realized it was suspicious because he had his own phone, and I could hear him talking on his phone, but my brain didn't connect it at the time.

After the assassination, I suggested to my husband we turn over our phone records to the New Orleans Police Department. It's my understanding the police then forwarded them to the FBI. We were told they would be returned to us, but we never got them back. At one point we were told they were never delivered. I assume now either my husband

A young Lee Harvey Oswald in Marine uniform. (Photo by © CORBIS/Corbis via Getty Images)

never took them to the police department, or there were points of interest in those records, and that's why they never returned them to us.

And for some reason I didn't think anything of Lee asking me to put those packages in my refrigerator until Juan got home. Now, of course, after reading *Dr. Mary's Monkey*, I have a better understanding of what could've been in those packages . . . you know . . . biomedical waste, but at the time I was just doing a favor for a polite young man. I now understand, based on more current research, these packages might have contained cancerous mice tumors that were being developed as a bioweapon to be used against Fidel Castro.

What do you think now when you look back on those events?
Years later, I started asking myself why I was there for all of this. In the early 1960s, my husband was a draftsman, and we moved to Dallas for almost a year. In December 1962, we traveled to his family home in Baton Rouge for Christmas, and when we returned to Dallas, he announced we would be moving back to New Orleans immediately. He had already secured an apartment without my knowledge. He had a connection to NASA and did some work out at the Michoud Assembly Facility.

My questions now are: How did we get into Patio Apartments so quickly when there was such a long waiting list? Why did we live next door to Juan Valdez? Why did we live in the same complex as Mary Sherman? And why did we have an unlisted phone number that the person I identified as Juan was able to find? I've asked all these questions as I continually try to piece it all together.

At the time I thought these were random, insignificant events—Lee knocking on my door with a box and asking me to keep it in my refrigerator for Juan, Juan asking to use our phone for long-distance calls, hearing his toilet flushing repeatedly in the middle of the night—but looking back they become historic in nature. I just think if we can sometimes get out of our own personal space and be more "in the moment," we may recognize these moments are more significant than we realize.

Why does the JFK assassination still matter all these years later?
Of course, like many people, I felt and still feel history was altered and detoured onto a negative path far beyond one that President Kennedy

could ever have envisioned. To me, putting aside the horror of it, it confirms how discouraging it is there are factions in place that can change our daily lives, and we have no control over it. It upsets me to no end we're raised to respect authority because they have our best interests in mind, but sadly, in my opinion, it's not true. We're mice running through a maze, and this is terrifying to me. History needs to be rewritten. I talk about this with my children and grandchildren, but people today don't seem to understand the significance of the assassination's effect on the course of history.

What would you want younger generations to know about the JFK assassination?

I would encourage them to read as much as possible about the assassination, and to do so with an open mind. Follow the chain of research while trying to relate that information to other political assassinations of that decade. And think about all the people, many of them nameless, who were "rubbed out" by these perpetrators who were doing wrong. You don't have to change the world, but you should be proactive and aware of the realities of the world we live in today. If we don't want this to keep happening, ask yourself how, as an individual, you can make your little corner of the world a better place.

Open your eyes, look and ask yourself what you can do to make sure something like the JFK assassination never happens again.

Any final thoughts on Lee Harvey Oswald?

Today we know a lot more about him, not just as a lone nut or a patsy, but as a father, a husband, a patriot, and a person who served his country. To me, he was a regular young man who seemed sweet and gentle. He certainly didn't appear to be the type of person to knock off a president.

In fact, I feel strongly, knowing what I know now, he was part of an abort plan to try and *save* the president that day. I believe he tried to warn the Dallas FBI office that there would be an attempt on Kennedy's life. Research strongly suggested he was an asset for the CIA and the FBI, and he was involved in all kinds of spy craft, including delivering secret packages to Juan Valdez, a man many researchers believe was also a CIA asset.

I think Lee was set up to be the patsy, and by the time he knew what was happening, it was too late. And had he been able to stop the assassination, I believe he would have.

PART 3

MY FATHER WAS IN THE CIA

My whole outlook on life has changed just by hearing that there's evidence that completely exonerates this man of the crime of killing the president. Now, I'm not saying that he is not involved. I believe he's involved or else why would he be there? But I don't know. I really believe, though, that he didn't kill the president. And my whole life has been plagued by this idea that my father is the murderer of one of the most loved persons in the world. And if he's not responsible for that, then it means a great part of the burden I have to carry is gone.

—Rachel Oswald Porter
Daughter of Lee Harvey Oswald

CHAPTER 9

SAINT JOHN HUNT

Saint John Hunt was born in 1954 in Washington, DC, and subsequently lived with his family in Japan, Uruguay, Spain, Mexico, and the United States. In 1970, his father, E. Howard Hunt, told him he had worked for the Office of Strategic Services and Central Intelligence Agency since WWII. In 1972, his father was arrested as a Watergate conspirator, and his mother was killed in a suspicious plane crash. In his father's final confession to his son, E. Howard Hunt told Saint John that key figures in the CIA were involved in the plot to assassinate JFK in Dallas, and that he himself was approached by the plotters, who included the CIA's David Atlee Phillips,[1] Cord Meyer Jr.,[2] William Harvey, and David Morales,[3] as well as Watergate burglar Frank Sturgis.[4]

When you were young, were you aware of what your parents did for a living?
I had no knowledge of what my parents did. The ongoing story was my father worked in the State Department and my mother worked for various embassies. I knew their jobs had something to do with why we traveled so much because we traveled from the time I was six months old, first to Japan, and it never stopped after that. It was totally normal for me to be a gypsy. I didn't realize at the time what kind of impact it would have on me, but it turned out to be quite devastating on many levels because we would stay in countries for two to sometimes up to five years, and I was

never able to make close friends because we were kept in this little protective box, going to certain schools that were designated as being "approved" by the CIA.

I also didn't understand the language in the countries we lived in. I spoke rudimentary Japanese at the age of three, then we moved to Uruguay, and everybody spoke Spanish, but I went to a French school. Those are the kinds of crazy things you start to realize as you get older. When I was sixteen, both my parents sat me down one day. I thought I was in trouble, but they told me Papa worked for the Central Intelligence Agency (I had no idea what that was), and Mom also did contract work for the agency. They told me, "You must never speak about this to anybody, including your friends." This really wasn't a problem because I didn't have too many friends.

It wasn't until a few years later the gravity of the situation started becoming clear. Since then, it's just been a process of digging deeper and deeper, at least as much as I wanted to and as much as I could. I eventually got a handle on most of what was going on with my parents, why we moved around so much and why my childhood was the way it was.

I've come to the realization that my sisters and I . . . not so much my brother because he was much younger . . . were part of this false image of two normal people, a married couple with children who traveled around for the State Department or the foreign service or what have you. We basically lived a life of continual lies. We would always have dinner with my folks, but they didn't spend a whole lot of time with us because they were so wrapped up in what they were doing. They had governesses and nannies take care of our day-to-day rearing. I feel like we were baggage they needed to carry around as part of their cover, but I think that's probably how it goes for CIA kids.

Yet, you had a good relationship with your parents, correct?
I did. I had a very good relationship with my mother, especially. When my father was around, he was kind of a person to be feared, but he also had a gentle side that came through. I don't remember a lot of interaction with him in my grade-school years, but later when I started writing music, singing, and teaching myself guitar, he was extremely helpful. He

E. Howard Hunt, who pleaded guilty to all charges against him in the Watergate bugging trial, talks to newsmen upon leaving court after posting $100,000 bond on January 11, 1973. (Source: Bettmann via Getty Images)

was quite the musician himself. He had a perfect pitch, a great ear, and he could formulate a note or chord just by listening. He was good at piano and trumpet. He helped with copywriting about eighteen of my songs back in 1969–1970. He would take me down to Blues Alley, a jazz club in Georgetown, and he would hobnob with the headliners, people like Gene Krupa, Willie the Lion Smith, and Jimmy Rushing.

I learned a lot about jazz music thanks to him; he had a huge record collection, and he shared his music with me. So, we had a good bond. I had no problems with him other than the fact I felt it was generous of him to spend some of his time with me because I knew I was a failure in his eyes. He did his best to hide that. It wasn't such an obvious thing where he would look at me and make a disgusted face or anything like that. It wasn't like that, but I was very underweight (ninety pounds), wasn't good at any sports, had double vision, and I stuttered to the point where I could barely speak.

We all had a great relationship with my mother, and then later during the Watergate years, even though it was brief, we spent a lot of time riding horses and talking, and I was really coming to understand her as a human being rather than as just a mom, and that's why it was such a terrible time for her to be taken away from us. She never saw me blossom, and I was never able to fully explore the relationship we could've had and were on our way to having as equals.

It's sad because she was such a wonderful human being and such a strong person. She was also a deeply spiritual person. She put up with a lot from my dad. She was going to divorce him when she got back from Europe, but then Watergate happened, and she stuck by him, which was amazing to me.

What was it like the night your father came into your room and asked for your help?
It was sometime after midnight on June 17, 1972. I was seventeen, and I was scared because I could tell something was severely wrong. I didn't know what it was, but I just leapt at the chance to help my father. It seemed like he needed me to do something, and for Christ's sake, for the first time in my life, I felt like I could do whatever he wanted me to do.

I'm thinking, "Yes, I'll get dressed. I'll run upstairs. I'll be quiet. I'll do whatever you want me to do." It was an epiphany in a way, a realization that I had value to him.

So, you wanted to help?
Oh, yeah. I would've done anything. I did everything he wanted me to do, and I felt really good about it, even though the whole situation was getting worse and worse, and there was more and more tension and stress.

I didn't understand a lot about what was going on, but in the year prior to the Watergate break-in, there were a lot of rumblings in our house about things. Some of my father's Cuban friends would come over, have dinner with us, and retire with my dad downstairs in his office. Also, my parents started to argue, and I never heard them argue, ever, not once in my entire life. My room was just below theirs, and I could hear the raised voices and the disagreements, although I didn't know what it was about.

When my mother started opening up to me about what was going on, it became very clear my dad had promised her he wasn't going to work in the intelligence community ever again. He was going to become a full-time writer, stay-at-home dad, and make up for lost time. But he went back on his word, and this was the final nail in the coffin for her. She put up with his infidelities throughout their entire marriage. Unfortunately, this happened to lot of women back then. It was simply the way things were; men did what they wanted to do, and women had to suck it up. But my mom was over it.

In a very short period, you lose your mother in a plane crash (December 8, 1972) and your father is sentenced to a maximum of thirty-five years in prison (March 21, 1973), and all as a direct result of Watergate. What was this like for you and your siblings?
Everything was happening so fast I didn't have time to assess how I felt about all of it. It was like being on a roller coaster. You're just in the moment, and the next minute or hour or day comes at you, and you just have to pray you can get through it. Mom died, and Papa was having all these legal problems and eventually went to jail. Suddenly it was me, my sister Lisa, and my brother David left to pick up the pieces.

Before my mom died, when the Watergate situation was heating up, she came back from Europe and wanted to remove me from the situation. She handed me a little pile of cash and said, "Go buy a car or van and take your girlfriend around the country or do whatever you want. Just go. I don't want you around here. You need a break from this."

With Mom and Dad gone, and with my older sister, Kevan, back at school, the responsibility of taking care of David fell to me and Lisa. I don't know how we got through it because Lisa was literally falling apart, crying all the time, and needing me to hold her and tell her things would work out. We were trying to raise my little brother, but then they took him away from us.

We were also told we had to leave the house under the premise it was being sold, and I discovered many years later when Papa died this was a complete lie just to get us out of the house. The governess didn't trust us and told our dad we were doing drugs. The truth is we were drinking a little wine and smoking a little reefer, but Jesus Christ, with all that was going on, was that so bad? A survival instinct must've kicked in for me,

Watergate burglar Frank Sturgis (right) after his arrest on charges of threatening a woman who reportedly told authorities that he shot at President Kennedy in Dallas on November 22, 1963. (Source: Bettmann via Getty Images)

and I did what I had to do to stay afloat. If you're drowning, you paddle; you keep your head above the water somehow.

William F. Buckley Jr. was one of the individuals who came to the house to take your brother and tell you the house was being sold, correct?
Yes. He was our godfather. We called him Uncle Bill. Buckley's sister Patricia married Brent Bozell, the conservative activist, and they had a big country farm in rural Virginia. We would go down there for a few weeks every summer. The Bozells had ten children, so it was fun. I remember when Uncle Bill would come over and have dinner, and he'd retire into the living room to have a cocktail with my parents. I would sit there and listen to this guy talk because he was so eloquent, and I didn't know who he was at the time . . . that he was the CEO of *National Review* or this major Republican figurehead. To listen to him and my dad converse was amazing. I was very, very taken with that.

But one afternoon some men came by the house with instructions from Uncle Bill, telling us we had to vacate our house. They told us that because of our dad's financial troubles, he was selling the house and everything in it. Then they told us David was going to be removed from our care and sent to live with his godfather in Miami. It was really upsetting and completely changed my opinion of Uncle Bill. My sister and I reacted with rage and anger because we couldn't understand it. It was the ultimate betrayal.

When did you realize your father might be involved in the JFK assassination?
My father served thirty-three months in prison for Watergate, and it was after his incarceration the first accusations came up linking him to the Kennedy assassination. I was living in Oakland, California, at the time, and I remember seeing this poster on a telephone pole announcing a lecture at San Francisco University with activist Dick Gregory. And on top it read, "CIA killed President Kennedy." I knew very little about the JFK assassination up until this moment.

On the poster, I also noticed photos of the three tramps[5] who were in Dealey Plaza that day, and my dad's photo was on either side of the older tramp, comparing his face to that of the older tramp's face, and this just blew my mind. I tore the poster off the pole, folded it up, and brought it home.

Later, I just kept looking at it, repeating to myself, "What in the hell?" I could barely wrap my head around it. And Papa, of course, when I asked him about it, said, "It's all lies. Don't believe a word of it. It's not true. They're just trying to get me. These guys are left-wing radical kooks and there's no truth to it at all." And he kept up his story for years, in all his testimony in the Senate Congressional Hearings and the trial with Liberty Lobby and Mark Lane . . . he denied any involvement time after time after time. But what else was he going to say?

Your father eventually moved to Miami. Did you continue to have a good relationship with him?
I did. I mean, we never had a bad relationship, especially after what I did for him during Watergate. I was able to go down there and visit, which was about once a year. We went fishing, spent time listening to music, cooking meals, and talking. I helped with chores around the house and fixing stuff. We had a very good relationship.

How did your dad finally tell you what he knew about the Kennedy assassination?
I started putting two and two together. Before he actually revealed anything to me, I would question him on a few things, such as, "Do you think Oswald was part of an assassination team?" And he just kept up the whole denial thing, saying things like Oswald was a communist, etc. I guess that's what he was supposed to say. This went on for years, and then when I was living in Eureka, California, he called me about his leg having to be amputated. He said he didn't know if he could go through with it and that he might not be around very much longer. He wanted me to come visit him because there were things he wanted to talk to me about.

I went to Florida and convinced him to go through with the amputation. I said, "Look what you've gone through in your life already . . . The Bay of Pigs, the whole Guatemala coup,[6] Nixon, Watergate, and the loss of Mom . . . so you're not going to give up now. Your family needs you. You can do this."

Around this time, I learned he was serving as an adviser on the Oliver Stone movie *Nixon,* and there were conversations happening with Hollywood people regarding my dad being paid to tell what he knew about the JFK assassination. So, he asked me to come down to Florida and talk to him about some things. He was recovering from his amputation, and I think he felt like he still wasn't going to be around for much longer. I pushed hard for him to reveal what he knew.

I told him, "Think about all the people who made money off your name, writing books, accusing you of being involved, alleging you were one of the tramps . . . they've all dirtied your name and made money off it. You're like one of the last guys standing, Papa. Doesn't it make you mad this is the legacy you're leaving your family? All these accusations without any attempt on your end to clear them up, without you coming forth and telling what you know."

I think I got him riled up enough to where he was invigorated, but between pressure from his second family, as well as from Bill Snyder, the attorney William Buckley picked, nothing ever happened.

When did he send you the recording?
About a month after I got back to Eureka, he sent me a cassette tape in the mail, and this is what has come to be known as his deathbed testimony or deathbed confession, but I never called it that. They called it that on Coast to Coast,[7] and it just stuck.

When you listened to the recording, did you feel like your father was being totally honest or still holding back?
I felt he was holding back, but the reason for this was because some project negotiations were still going on with the Hollywood people. He didn't want to give out too much information, to them or anybody else but me, about his prior knowledge of the assassination. He also realized he could still be prosecuted if he implicated himself too directly, even if he was old and sickly. They could still make life difficult for him, so I felt he was holding back and choosing his words very carefully.

He referred to himself as a "benchwarmer" in the assassination, but this doesn't mean you're not involved in the game. It means you're there at the game, and you're a participant in terms of your understanding of game strategy. My dad was the guy who knew where the safe houses and escape routes were. He knew what to do, where to go, and how to handle things. He was a good manager in that respect, and I think he knew the overall plan. He says he was offered a more active role in the assassination, which he turned down, but it's still somewhat of a mystery.

I think in time things will come out substantiating further what his role may have been, but there have certainly been a lot of allegations, and he's been on the hot seat for a long time.

Did your father "handle" the Cuban exiles as part of his role with the CIA?
Yes. He was well known and well loved in the Cuban exile community. When I went down to his memorial service, I wrote and read the eulogy, and members of the Bay of Pigs Brigade 2506 came up and gave me hugs as a measure of great love and respect for Papa, which floored me.

Do you resent your father for who he was, or have you forgiven him?
I don't harbor any resentment toward my dad at all. The only thing I'm sorry for is the fact his own ego was so big he went back on his word to my mom about not working for Nixon. She didn't want him to, and he promised he wasn't going to get involved in anything like that ever again. So, I feel really ashamed of him for doing that.

Second, and maybe more importantly, is the fact he let these guys play him. My dad was a very intelligent, highly educated spy craftsman, and he devoted his life to what he believed were patriotic things. They took advantage of him, and he allowed it to happen because of his swelled head. He was thinking, "I'm working for Nixon, so we'll be able to get the Cuban exiles back in Cuba so they can overthrow Castro."

I'm still finding out about stuff. We went to Spain in 1965, and I didn't know why at the time, but we went because Papa was on a deep cover mission, and he was meeting assassins in Madrid and Barcelona to continue the assassination plots to kill Fidel Castro, Raul Castro, and Che Guevara.

It never stopped for him, and when Charles Colson[8] offered him the job at the White House, my dad took it in a heartbeat. Truth is, my dad had been working Colson for almost a year so he would hire him, and he was reporting back to the CIA about what was going on in the White House. So, he was acting as a double agent.

Did you ever blame him for your mother's death?
I never really felt that blaming him . . . it just never occurred to me to blame him. My sisters did, but I never thought it was his fault she died. In some ways, of course, it's all interrelated, but how could he know the plane was going to be brought down? Maybe he should've known, maybe he shouldn't have sent her to Chicago with a bunch of money to pay people off with, but it happened the way it happened, and it was a great loss to both him and his children.

Do you think your father justified the things he did as an intelligence operative because he was doing them for love of country, or do you think there was a part of him that knew he had blurred the lines between right and wrong?
I think deep down inside he must've known and felt the line was being blurred, but his overriding mentality and strongest feeling was sometimes you need to get dirty to clean up a dirty mess. That's the mind-set of a lot of these intelligence people, that the end justifies the means.

I asked him one time, "Papa, how do you justify all the deaths that occurred after your successful coup in Guatemala?"

"What deaths?" he responded. "What are you talking about?"

"The 40,000 to 60,000 to as many as 100,000 people who were rounded up, imprisoned, tortured, and killed," I replied.

And he said, "That's just the price. You know, freedom doesn't come cheaply."

I was like, "Freedom for whom? The whole Guatemala thing was about money. Maybe the coup was against communists, but it was really about the United Fruit Company. John Foster Dulles[9] and Allen Dulles were board members of United Fruit, and the Guatemalan government was nationalizing all the plantations. It seems to me, Papa, that the United

States was involved in that coup to secure the financial holdings of the Dulles brothers and keep the peasants at bay."

And he said, "No. That's not it. It was about Communism."

He just didn't want to open up about anything.

What have you personally concluded about the JFK assassination based on your research and what your father told you?

I think the JFK assassination was meticulously planned, sometime way before Kennedy's campaign for a second term in office. I believe it was an inside job. The mafia was *not* involved, and neither were the KGB and Cuban intelligence, for that matter. It was strictly an in-home cleaning job.

There were many things JFK was doing that frightened the intelligence community. We know what those things were, but there was also his erratic use of methamphetamines. It got to the point where he was getting injections two to three times a day. This exacerbated his sex drive, which was already in overdrive, and he was risking a great deal by bedding women who were dual-edged. Some were associated with gangsters and others were foreign intelligence agents. Hoover knew all this, as did Bobby Kennedy. Additionally, JFK's proposed withdrawal from Vietnam spelled disaster for the intelligence community and military-industrial complex, so they weren't going to let that happen.

Oswald was groomed to be a patsy. He was sheep-dipped. He wasn't a communist. He was part of the CIA's false defector program in 1959, which was run by William Harvey, who was sending Marines over to Russia. All of this was being built little by little to come to this grand conclusion in Dallas. It's amazing, and it wasn't only Dallas. It was Tampa, Chicago . . . three or four other cities where they had people in place to kill JFK. It just happened to mature in Dallas.

What do you think your father's role was in the assassination?

My dad obviously knew about one or more plots, and I think he stayed on the fringes of things, as he said, a benchwarmer, but that doesn't mean he wasn't involved. It certainly gave him prior knowledge, and I think he would've been a person in Dallas that morning, immediately available to create confusion or direct the assassins to safe quarters. I think he was there to do those things. My mom actually told us that Dad was away in Dallas that weekend.

You grew up in a world of half-truths, and the road you've traveled on was paved by conspirators and corrupt, powerful people. As someone who has lived this, what is the true cost of conspiracy?
It's horrible. I think I've learned to handle it well, but for a lot of people it's much harder. In terms of the nation, it's devasting. Conspiracy of our

David Atlee Phillips had a 25-year career in the CIA (1950–1975) and rose to the Agency's chief of operations for the Western Hemisphere. (Source: Bettmann via Getty Images)

own government continues to go on randomly today . . . in terms of the government withholding information from its citizens and all the dirty tricks the CIA has played over the years. We continue to push this false image of freedom and democracy. And, yes, we're better off than most other countries in the world, but still, we're being told a lie.

And the people in these intelligence agencies who are controlling things continue with this sick mind-set, this warped mentality that in order to maintain a "safe" society, we have to lie and kill and plot and backstab, and they don't care about the collateral damage. They have these black budgets, and where do you think that money comes from? The sale of drugs and weapons on a worldwide scale.

Why does the JFK assassination still matter all these years later?
Because it's an injustice that needs to be rectified. It's a murder, and you always want to find the killers, right? You can't just let this murder go and say it doesn't matter anymore. Yeah, it matters. This was the president of the United States, and his assassination brought the whole military-industrial complex into focus. There may be no one left alive to prosecute, but the people must know this was what our country was up to. And maybe if they knew that, they might conclude there are things we need to pay attention to, instead of staring at our freaking cell phones all the time. There needs to be justice. Justice must happen.

What would you want younger generations to understand about the JFK assassination?
Younger generations need to understand that the truth may never come out. I don't think any government in the United States, any president, whether it's the next one or the one after that, is ever going to announce, "We did it. It was an inside job. Sorry." This will never happen, but we're getting pretty close to the truth because of the work citizens are doing, and I think it's important for younger people to understand they shouldn't always believe everything the government tells them. Question authority. Do your own research. Find the truth behind the headlines on the front page.

If you could get the answer to one question regarding the assassination, what would it be?

I don't know if it's a question, but I want Lee Harvey Oswald to be exonerated for what he was accused of and murdered for. I think his murder is just as relevant and important as JFK's murder. It's a terrible injustice to his family, to his children. Jesus Christ, if you think I've had a tough time with all this, what about Oswald's two daughters? He's known as the worst human being in the world, and that's just wrong. JFK is still the hero; he has the eternal flame. We forgive his many infidelities and all the election stuff with the mob. But Oswald . . . come on. We need to get this guy off the hook.

Any final words about your father?

I think he was as much a victim as he was a perpetrator. My father was an intelligent, articulate, accomplished man. He loved his family. He wrote and published eighty-eight novels. He was very creative. And as far as the CIA is concerned, if you ever saw the movie *The Good Shepherd*, that's my dad. He was a dedicated, old-school, Cold War spy who was, for better or worse, a product of his time.

Letter from Saint John Hunt to Caroline Kennedy
Sent in November 2017

11/2017
TO CAROLINE KENNEDY

It is with the deepest respect and honesty that I reach out to you. I feel a great deal of sorrow for actions involving my father which may have led to the death of your father.

In 1963 my father, E. Howard Hunt, as a CIA officer, had knowledge of plans to eliminate your father, President John F. Kennedy. I know this because my father confessed this to me shortly before he died. It is a burden I will always carry.

I cannot imagine the loss you experienced at such a young age. In the ensuing years you have carried yourself with great dignity and grace in the face of public speculation about your father's death. No one has ever, to my knowledge, offered any kind of apology for this horrible and unforgivable crime. It seems an insignificant gesture to apologize, but that is all I am able to do. I can empathize with your loss because my mother Dorothy was killed (in 1972) under very curious circumstances after threatening to "blow the White House out of the water."

So, for what it's worth, I am **deeply** regretful for my father's role, whatever it may have been, in the death of your father. I am so sorry that history has been cruel to your family in ways most of us won't even understand. Despite it all, you have chosen not to be hateful and for that alone, I respect and admire you. From the bottom of my heart, I offer this sincere apology and hope that you find it comforting that someone cares enough about you and what you've lost to come forward and say, "I'm sorry."

Sincerely,
Saint John Hunt

CHAPTER 10

PETER JANNEY

Peter Janney is an American writer, psychologist, and lecturer who grew up in Washington, DC, during the Cold War era of the 1950s and 1960s. His father, Wistar Janney, was a senior career CIA official who began work at the Central Intelligence Agency shortly after its inception in 1947. The Janney family was intimately involved with many of Washington's social and political elite that included the family of Mary and Cord Meyer, as well as other high-ranking CIA officials, such as Richard Helms, Jim Angleton, Tracy Barnes, Desmond FitzGerald, and William Colby. In his book, *Mary's Mosaic: The CIA Conspiracy to Murder John F. Kennedy, Mary Pinchot Meyer, and Their Vision for World Peace*, Janney makes a detailed case that ex-CIA wife and John F. Kennedy mistress Mary Pinchot Meyer was murdered by the CIA to cover up what she had discovered about the JFK assassination. Janney graduated from Princeton University in 1970, where he studied American History under Distinguished Professor Martin Duberman, and went on to earn a doctoral degree in Psychology at Boston University in 1981. In 2002, he completed an MBA degree at Duke University's Fuqua School of Business.

What are your memories of November 22, 1963, and the assassination's immediate aftermath?

I was sixteen years old and a sophomore in prep school in New Hampshire, and my most vivid memory is walking over to the chapel when we were told about Kennedy being shot because there was going to be a prayer service. This was an elite Episcopal boarding school, so they were encouraging everyone to take their most profound issues to God. I was disturbed but not truly aware of the severity of what had taken place.

It certainly became a moment etched in my consciousness given everything that subsequently occurred, but I do remember having a phone call with my parents shortly thereafter, and they were very upset, or at least my father was playing at being very upset. I didn't begin to see the enormity of it until I came home for Thanksgiving vacation a few days later, but I had incurred a football injury that fall, so my knee was all swollen, plus I wanted to get my driver's license . . . so these were the things in the foreground of my experience at the time.

And, of course, the operating cultural picture was that Oswald did it, and there was no discussion of what took place that Sunday when Oswald was killed. I remember sitting and watching a rerun of Ruby shooting Oswald with my father, maybe a day later, and his head was spinning with disgust that this was allowed to happen. Let me say I've never seen or come into any information that suggests my father was in on the inner circle of what I truly believe, based on volumes of evidence, happened, which is that the CIA was instrumental in this assassination taking place.

What was it like growing up in a CIA family?
Working for the CIA was a glamorous profession for those upper-crust, blue-blood, WASP families that were wealthy to begin with. A lot of these men came back from WWII, including my father. He was a highly decorated Navy pilot who won the Navy Cross. He and George H. W. Bush flew the same planes, and my dad would boast that "George got shot down, but I didn't." And ultimately, when George became head of the CIA, my dad worked for him. We were all friends—the Angleton family, the Meyer family, the Bradlee family—all in the same social circle. So as the children of these people we all hung out together, which is how I became best friends with Mary Meyer's son, Michael.

It was a very privileged upbringing, and as CIA brats, we were living in a dreamworld. We thought our fathers were James Bonds in one form or another. Every time a new James Bond film came out, we would traipse off with our family to see it because Ian Fleming was a cultural hero in my father's eyes.

The only person who challenged my worldview was our maid, Corine. She and I became extremely close, mainly because both of my parents were alcoholics. One of the things I learned about alcoholism is it erodes your capacity to feel as a human being. Intimacy and empathy become eroded, so my relationship with my parents wasn't particularly deep or intimate. When my parents would go away, Corine would take me and my brother to her little shack in Nanjemoy, Maryland, which was a predominantly African American community. It was a wonderful awakening for me because I saw a whole different side of what life was like for a very large segment of the population.

When did this glorified image of your father and the CIA start to crack?
Coming out of college, where I had one major awakening after another, it became earth-shatteringly clear I'd been lied to about the nature of what my father did for a living and what his work really entailed. I became more political and an ardent resister of the Vietnam War. I went to a lot of demonstrations and got teargassed and arrested, which was extremely upsetting to my parents, who just didn't get it. But I knew on a very deep level I was on the side I wanted to be on in terms of what my own emerging morality was dictating to me.

During my undergraduate years from 1966 to 1970, my relationship with my father eroded badly, and it was never resolved to any degree. My father became increasingly dependent on alcohol, and he smoked constantly. He started having heart attacks in his mid to late 50s and died at 59. It was clear to me he had been depressed from a clinical point of view for several years, and he wasn't looking forward to retirement. He was despondent and possibly coming to terms with what his life had been all about once he got out of the Navy.

In a classical and conventional sense, my parents were very well educated, but my mother's illness, which was more than just alcohol, precipitated her going into psychoanalysis four days a week for at least six to eight years. My father was smart enough to realize if she was doing it, he better do it, too, so he also went into psychoanalysis.

I'm not a big fan of conventional psychoanalytic psychotherapy or psy-choanalysis because I think it's a very limited focus from a mental health perspective in terms of helping people confront the deeper issues of their lives. But, nonetheless, I realize it was what was available at the time. I think both wanted to save their marriage and our family. So, they both went into psychoanalysis and didn't get divorced like several other people in their milieu did.

It was a part of my awakening of growing up in a CIA family because I was willing to look at the other side, the alternate reality of what the truth was regarding what the CIA was doing. I had some wonderful professors at Princeton. One, Martin Duberman, turned into a lifelong friend. He and I really developed a significant connection. He was my thesis adviser, and he challenged me on several things and forced me to think in ways I'd never been asked to before. He was a "lefty" and academically one of the most brilliant and wonderful people to talk to, but my relationship with him and what he challenged me to do made my undergraduate experience one I'll always treasure. I emerged from college a very different person, and it forced me to grow up in certain ways very quickly.

Was this kind of personal and emotional dysfunction among CIA employees—and by extension their families—during the Cold War common?

Allen Dulles recruited most, if not all, of the high-level CIA people who had immediate access to him, and almost all of them were very well-to-do, Ivy League, blue-blood guys. Many of them were WWII veterans and real heroes in one capacity or another. They came out of the war understand-ing they never wanted to see another world war again. Nobody wins with nuclear weapons, so they had to develop a different type of strategy to stay on top as the world's superpower, and this meant doing whatever had to be done. They didn't give a damn who was in their way or who they needed to take out.

It became their modus operandi, and it forced these men to violate parts of their own morality. Frank Wisner[1] was driven to suicide because of all the damage the CIA had done in any number of incidents in terms of killing many innocent people. It really got to him, and the reason it didn't get to some of the others the way it did him was because they became anesthetized, and alcohol enabled them to shut down a certain portion of their consciousness, their guilt, and continue to carry out orders.

I think we always tend to underestimate what war does to those who experience it.

My father told me a story about when they would come back from dangerous combat missions during WWII, and the first thing he and his fellow pilots wanted to do was drink. So, when they ran out of alcohol, they would sneak up into the aircraft carrier's torpedo ready room and siphon off torpedo fuel and make a crude distiller so they could get blitzed.

This became routine because of the level of fear and terror they had to face, sometimes daily, in terms of when they got into large battles, such as the Battle of Leyte Gulf.[2] I have all my dad's letters he wrote to my mother, and in one letter he talks about just having lost his best friend, and he's very upset about it, but it's clear he's going to maintain an even keel and do whatever he has to in order to get through it.

The point I'm making is that alcohol became the drug of choice to maintain a certain disposition that allowed these men to deal with combat and later engage in the almost constant treachery the CIA was involved in, including overthrowing democratically elected governments and assassinating leaders of other countries.

When did Mary and Cord Meyer's son (and your best friend), Michael, have his fatal accident, and how did that affect you?

Michael was hit by a car and killed just before Christmas in 1956. I was nine years old, and it was incredibly traumatic for me. I had a tremendous grief reaction to his death, and it created mental health issues for me because my parents didn't know how to manage the enormity of that kind of loss. One of the people who *did* know how to manage it, ironically, was Mary Meyer, who I became increasingly closer to after his death. But my relationship with Corine, our live-in maid, really saved me. Without her in my life, I daresay I might very well have ended up taking my own life or being institutionalized.

Cord and Mary Pinchot Meyer as newlyweds in 1945. (Source: Bettmann via Getty Images)

What are your memories of Mary Pinchot Meyer?

Mary was like no other adult I knew as a child. She was qualitatively different because she *listened*. Adults of that era basically looked at kids and said, "How are you? Now get out of my sight." Mary was quite present, and when she asked you a question, she did so in a way you knew she sincerely wanted to hear about what you had to say and what your experience was. It was clear she was someone who was much more real and present than anything or anyone I had ever known, except maybe for Corine, who I felt was the same way.

When Michael and I would hang out at his house, Mary, who was often in her little studio painting, would come out and see how we were doing. She was present and connected. I felt safe and cared for in her presence. For lack of a better word, I felt "loved" by someone who was very loving by nature, and she wasn't a drinker, which is important. She had many opportunities to descend into alcoholism in her life, but she didn't.

This was a woman who, as an artist, wanted to deepen her artistic sensibilities, so she did what many other avant-garde artists were doing at the time. She explored Reichian therapy as a therapeutic technique, and when LSD came on the scene in the late 1950s and certain people in Hollywood were talking about how great it was, she was right there in line to do it next. She was a fearless explorer of herself, and nothing was going to hold her back from that.

On top of that, in all the conventional ways, she was beautiful. She brought a lot of men to their knees when she was around them. She was, in many ways, out of the mythic literature in terms of what it meant to be a goddess in that era.

I remember one anecdote that came to me by way of Scottie Lanahan Smith, F. Scott Fitzgerald's daughter, who was a very close friend of my mother's. They were roommates at Vassar College, and Mary was in the same class as them (1942). Scottie tells the story of when five or six couples got together, and they were hanging out drinking, and eventually they got bored, So, someone came up with the idea for the women to rank the men in the room on a piece of paper based on who they would want to sleep with and for the men to rank the women in the same way.

Well, when they unfolded the pieces of paper, all the men had Mary as their top choice, and all of the women had Cord as either their last choice or second-to-last choice. Scottie told me, "You could only imagine what kind of fight Cord got into with Mary on the way home that night." Apparently, he was very upset, but the point is Mary was the kind of person you wanted to be around and get to know.

What inspired you to write *Mary's Mosaic*?

Mary was murdered on October 12, 1964, and when I came home from boarding school that Thanksgiving, I wasn't aware she had been killed. My mother kind of casually announced it at the dinner table that Wednesday evening. I vividly remember that whole scene because as she was talking, my father didn't say anything. In fact, he was vacantly looking off into space, as if purposely not saying anything. I was bludgeoned by what my mother was telling me, and it precipitated a very uncomfortable night for me. Mary's death started to eat away at me, and I was never satisfied with the unresolved nature of it.

Fast-forward to 1991, when author Leo Damore was working on a book he was going to title *Burden of Guilt*, which was about Mary's murder. He had just written the bestseller *Senatorial Privilege*, which focused on what happened on Chappaquiddick Island with Mary Jo Kopechne and Ted Kennedy. So, he knew about Mary because he was very close friends with Kenny O'Donnell, JFK's primary adviser in the White House. I got to know Leo when he started working on *Burden of Guilt*, and I was driven to contact him because I knew what he was attempting to do was important.

Fortunately, Leo was very receptive to me and knew my father was one of the pallbearers at Mary's funeral, so we eventually became close and spoke for hours at a time. Leo was able to get the inside line on who Mary was in the White House because he was able to tap into what O'Donnell knew. He was a fearless researcher and wasn't easily intimidated, and he knew, given what O'Donnell had shared with him, the enormity of JFK's attachment to Mary and why it was so important to JFK. And this just confirmed everything I knew about this woman and made me want to help Leo in any way I could.

When Leo allegedly committed suicide in 1995[3] and it was clear he wasn't going to get the book done, two writers came forward: John Davis, a respected Kennedy researcher who knew Leo and wanted to take up the mantle, and a young writer named Nina Burleigh, who actually came to interview me for her book *A Very Private Woman*.

From my point of view, in the end, she wrote a terrible book, and everyone who knew Mary thought it was trash and was very disappointed in it. John Davis, on the other hand, simply stopped writing his book. Jimmy

Smith, a former assistant district attorney and friend of Leo's, asked him about this, and Davis replied, "I decided I wanted to live." What Smith took from this, as did I, was that Davis's life had been threatened.

That had to be a serious motivator to write the book.
For me, personally, there was no turning back; I had to write the book that still hadn't been written. In 2006–2007, I reached out to Leo's chief research assistant and asked him about Leo's research. He still had it, so I flew down to Washington, met with him, and offered to buy the research for $5,000. He agreed, so I packed all of it into two suitcases and flew home. It got extremely serious for the next five years because that's what it took, putting everything else aside. I worked on it sometimes ten, twelve, or fourteen hours a day, six days a week, flying all over the country to interview people.

Were there any startling revelations you made during your research that made you second-guess your decision to write the book?
My first interview was a former CIA guy named Victor Marchetti, who had worked for my dad. He knew who I was, so we went to lunch at his club, and he allowed me to tape-record our conversation. I told Victor what I was up to and asked, "Victor, do you think the CIA is going to be upset with me?" and he looked at me in a funny way and said, "No. They'll just do it." I realized what he meant was they would simply kill me. He was telling me I damn well better know what I was getting involved with.

I went home after lunch and was visibly shaken for several days. I was also engaged at the time, and I literally nixed the engagement. I told my fiancée, "Look, this is dangerous, and were we to stay involved and have a family, I would never forgive myself if something were to happen to you." This was the first of a number of commitment checks I had to make in order to proceed. I took this on with the understanding I was going to get to the bottom of this if it was the last freaking thing I ever did, so I continued to do years of research and stayed on it.

What I wasn't prepared for was when it became clear to me in 2010 that my own father had been involved peripherally in the conspiracy to murder Mary, and the reason I say this is because it was my father who called Ben Bradlee[4] on the day of the murder, at about 2:00 in the afternoon, and casually told him there had been a murder on the tow path and asked if he had seen Mary Meyer, which precipitated Bradley looking into it.

But this was all a planned move on the part of the agency because Ray Crump had been apprehended by 2:00 that afternoon, the coroner was at the murder scene, and the police started calling people to find out who the victim was. They didn't know yet, but they had a lead because one of the gloves she was wearing had the "Meyer" name tag inside of it. So, they started calling all the Meyers in Georgetown and by process of elimination got to Mary's house, where of course nobody was there.

Coming to the realization that this was a CIA-sanctioned murder must have been a bit overwhelming for you, considering your close ties to some of the players.

This entire operation was orchestrated by the CIA; they were in control of everything. And this realization threw me for a loop. I was very despondent and emotional, and I was smart enough to know what was going on with me. So, I started meeting with a psychotherapist, who I already had a relationship with, sometimes twice a week, because I needed to resolve this and continue with the book. Particularly after my lunch with Victor Marchetti, I would go to bed at night in abject terror. I would shake violently and have episodes of acute anxiety and terror.

After the book came out, I had three former CIA people get in touch with me because they felt I had solved a major mystery. And independently of one another, because they didn't know one another, they all told me they were surprised there hadn't been an attempt on my life. I think I'm out of the danger zone at this point because it would be suspicious to take me out now that the book is out and there has been some notoriety around it. The thing about the agency is they don't want to bring attention to this subject matter, but before the book came out, believe me, my safety was on my mind.

In 2012, CNN called to interview me about the book, and they tried to ambush me during the interview by reading a letter from the CIA saying the book was utter nonsense, it never happened, he's got it all wrong and something about me getting JFK's relationship with Mary all wrong. It was terrible, but I walked into it unprepared and tried to cope the best I could. What this told me was the CIA was well aware of what I was doing and was trying to discredit me. They don't want to get into another situation like when Oliver Stone's movie came out, because they were caught with their pants down and were unprepared for the firestorm that took place.

Why is it important to understand who Mary Pinchot Meyer was as a person, and especially as a woman, living in that era?
Mary was, in many respects, a very private woman, meaning she wasn't looking for glory and notoriety. She was a serious person and increasingly a more serious artist, and if you look at what took place, one of Mary's roles in her lifetime was to make an alliance with two possible major leaders of our country post-WWII: Cord Meyer and JFK.

It was no accident she met JFK when she was fifteen years old. When his eyes met Mary's, it changed his life. At first, she wasn't particularly impressed with him; he was superficial and on the make at that time, and he didn't have a lot of depth to him. So, they were acquaintances; I wouldn't say friends. She was much more intrigued by Cord because he was kind of a visionary at that time of his life. He was being set up to be potential presidential material, but he blew it and succumbed to depression, alcoholism, substance abuse, and basically sold himself to the devil when he met Allen Dulles, who seduced him to join the CIA. Cord lost his soul at that point in his life and never recovered it. JFK went the other way, from rather superficial to a man of substance, but he never got over his initial attraction to Mary in 1936.

The whole thing seems incredibly synchronistic, and almost fated, in a way.
It was haunting how the universe set things up circumstantially and kept the two of them connected. Mary, being who she was and on the vanguard culturally, particularly with her interest in psychedelics, realized she might be in position to not only turn a president away from the Cold War toward world peace, but also be a major force in potentially instigating

certain instruments of world peace. This is the apex of their story and how they were able to fall in love with each other.

Let's talk more about the significance of the relationship between Mary Meyer and John Kennedy, okay?
Their relationship was a relationship of redemption for Jack. We're talking about a man who was extremely wounded in the arena of intimacy with women. Understandable considering his mother, who was a no-show. The only real relationship he had with a woman before Mary was with his sister Kathleen, and that relationship taught him that women could be a lot more than just sex objects, that they had personality and brains and any number of profound gifts they could give, particularly to men. Jack was able to experience some of this with his sister, who died tragically in a plane crash in 1948.

He respected Mary like he respected his sister, but with Mary, there was also a strong sexual connection. She increasingly came to be someone who was safe and whom he could trust. She had no ulterior motives. She didn't need or want his money or status because she had that growing up, and she wasn't going to put up with any nonsense from him. She wanted connection

Mary Pinchot Meyer at President Kennedy's 46th birthday party on May 29, 1963. (Photo by Robert L. Knudsen/Wikimedia Commons)

and real intimacy, and I don't think Jack had ever been with a woman who was that well integrated as a person and who could offer him so much.

Increasingly, Mary became more and more powerful, not in a manipulative way, but in a loving way, in his life. This connection really afforded him the beginning of an immense period of healing for himself, and the tragedy was that neither of them was able to consummate it. He told Kenny O'Donnell he wanted to divorce Jackie immediately after his presidency to be with Mary. That's what he was looking forward to, and I daresay it would've taken place.

Would you say she became a positive influence on him both personally and politically?
After the Cuban Missile Crisis in 1962, Mary was instrumental in helping JFK examine why he had to turn away from the Cold War and define what kind of president he really wanted to be. What was he willing to stand up for? Given what the stakes were—nuclear war and the obliteration of civilization—it was becoming increasingly clear to him he could never let anything like the Cuban Missile Crisis happen again.

He was also becoming much closer and trusting of his relationship with Nikita Khrushchev. They were writing secret letters back and forth and confiding in each other, and it was becoming increasingly clear where Kennedy was going, which was away from a Cold War mentality and toward world peace. Later that fall, he told a group at the United Nations he was planning for the United States and the Soviet Union to go to the moon together, and had that taken place, it would've been the ultimate symbol of the end of the Cold War.

For Mary's part, she had, by all conventional standards, a brilliant intellect, and she was also a quasi-Bohemian at the time. After divorcing Cord, she really came into her own as a woman and an artist. And nobody knew she was having this incredible relationship with the president and seeking out people like Timothy Leary because she believed psychedelics were one of the most important tools we had at our disposal for making people's minds—and particular the minds of men in power—larger in the sense they could grasp a bigger picture of all the different dimensionalities of life on this planet.

Their relationship was transcendent, especially for Jack, and I think the fact that he and Mary did a mild psychedelic journey together—I don't think it was LSD but psilocybin—opened him up a little bit more, and this was a few weeks before what I believe to be one of the most important presidential addresses ever given, which was the commencement address at American University on June 10, 1963.[5]

What do you think triggered Mary's determination to expose the truth about the JFK assassination, and did this determination get her killed?

When JFK was assassinated, it precipitated a huge explosion in her, especially after the Warren Commission Report came out. She needed to get to the bottom of what had taken place, and this led her back to her former husband, Cord Meyer, and the godfather of her children, James Jesus Angleton, who was the embodiment of evil.

So, when she put the pieces together and realized there was a cover-up taking place, she couldn't live with herself and had to go public with what she knew. I submit that's what she was on the verge of doing, but the CIA was keeping close tabs on her, and they realized "either we take this woman out, or we have a huge problem on our hands."

During Kennedy's presidency, the CIA was trying to undermine him at every possible turn, starting with the Bay of Pigs in 1961. He was very much aware of this and was fueled on by Mary, because she knew about some of the inner workings of the CIA because of her marriage to Cord, who was right up there at the very top of the CIA and part of Allen Dulles's main coterie of henchmen.

Mary was also not blind to the fact that Jim Angleton, the godfather of her children, was also part of this cabal. When she got involved trying to find out what happened in Dallas, she had access to people like Kenny O'Donnell and Dave Powers, who were in Dallas that day and knew the shots came from the grassy knoll. These men knew the FBI was cooking up a story that made no sense whatsoever, but, of course, they had to change their testimony and wouldn't go public with what they really knew because the FBI was putting a lot of pressure on them, and they didn't want to rock the boat.

Was Mary able to figure out the deadly "game" that was being played, especially because she knew so many of the players quite well?

Yes. Mary got hip quite quickly to the fact that not only had there been a conspiracy to take out the president, but there was now a full-fledged conspiracy to cover it up, and she became increasingly paranoid about why her friend Phil Graham, the executive editor of the *Washington Post*, had allegedly committed suicide in August 1963.

One of the points I try to make in the book is the CIA and the national security apparatus knew if they were going to pull off the assassination in November, they had to control the media, and Graham was already upset with the fact he had been so cozy with the CIA in the past because he felt the agency was thwarting the real truth of history. He was having second thoughts about where his allegiances were because as a member of the Fourth Estate, his job was to act as a watchdog and hold these agencies accountable, not propagate their agenda. If he had still been alive after Kennedy's assassination, he would have listened very closely to what Mary had to say about a cover-up.

Understand that Angleton had her phones tapped, and the agency had another CIA agent's wife try to discourage her from going public because that's what she was planning on doing after she read the Warren Commission Report. At that point, she knew it was a complete cover-up and realized the thing she needed to do as a citizen was try and wake people up to this fact. But the agency wouldn't allow that to take place, so they eliminated her.

What exactly do you think Mary was able to piece together regarding the JFK assassination?

That the CIA was running the entire operation and Allen Dulles was the project manager. I think she had enough conversations with informative people who were either there or knew about it who basically gave her the keys to understanding why it happened and why it was necessary because of what the stakes were.

And I think she would've been able to lay it out in such a way that a portion of the public would've really grasped what she was saying, and this would've opened the doors to checking it out even further. The fact it was coming from an insider, someone who was with JFK the last three years of his life, knew the intimacy of what was taking place within the national security apparatus, and knew what JFK was really worried about and up against, would have made her accusations extremely powerful and fact-checkable.

It would've been explosive, and, of course, there were people who would've tried to shoot her down. But she was fearless and wouldn't have backed down, and she would've taken on anyone in a debate about what she had discovered—*and* at a critical moment when the cover-up depended on enough high-level people willing to say Oswald was the lone-nut assassin. She would've fueled everyone's doubt about what had taken place.

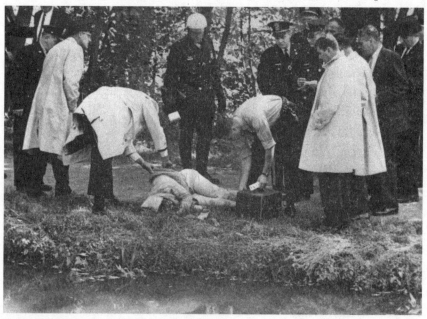

Mary Pinchot Meyer was found shot to death on October 12, 1964, along the Chesapeake and Ohio Canal in the Georgetown section of Washington, DC. Her murder remains unsolved. (Source: Bettmann via Getty Images)

Do you agree with that assessment?

Absolutely. The CIA ran the whole thing, and the crowning jewel of this statement is knowing where Allen Dulles was on the weekend of the assassination. The disgraced CIA director was at Camp Perry, the CIA's most secretive facility in Williamsburg, Virginia. What was he doing there? This is a revelation David Talbot mentions in his book *The Devil's Chessboard*, one of the most critical books ever written about the Cold War. *The Devil's Chessboard* and James Douglass's *JFK and The Unspeakable*, in my opinion, are the only two books you need to read to understand the Cold War and what happened to JFK. It's all there, very tightly summarized and extremely well researched.

How might Mary have gotten this powder keg of information out to the public?
I think she would've found a venue to begin to come out and make some very serious media statements as to who she was and what her relationship was with the president, and this alone would've caused a huge ruckus. And Mary would've done it in a way to put a huge damper on what the Warren Commission Report was all about.

Remember, we were at a critical moment in our country's history, when the national security apparatus *had* to find a way to convince millions of people the Warren Commission Report was accurate, and Mary would've created a huge shitstorm because she wasn't some floozy; she was a substantial person who happened to be very forthright . . . a well-educated woman from a prominent family who wasn't going to stand down. She was going to stand up, knowing she was very likely going to take an incredible amount of crap for putting herself out on the table and revealing what she knew.

She wasn't naive, but I don't think she anticipated this would lead to her death. She may have, but I think if she knew something like that was coming, she would've acted more quickly. The bottom line is she was a substantial human being who couldn't be easily dismissed by prominent people in the media or within Washington's social scene. She was a force to be reckoned with, and it would've been a huge disaster for the PR campaign surrounding the Warren Commission Report and their desire to put this thing to rest.

Did Cord Meyer know about the CIA's decision to eliminate Mary, and if so, why was he so willing to let it happen . . . or even encouraged it to happen?

You don't see a lot of information related to Cord's involvement in any of this, but did he know about it? Of course, he did. I conducted some critical interviews with people who knew Cord. Charles Bartlett, the Pulitzer Prize-winning author, was good friends with both Cord Meyer and John Kennedy. He told me the relationship between JFK and Mary was a dangerous one and that JFK told him he was in love with Mary. Bartlett and a couple of other people all agreed Cord never got over losing Mary, even though he treated her very poorly in many ways. I think he was utterly devastated that she left him and started this affair with JFK. He knew about it, and it infuriated him.

And JFK never liked Cord, either. When a young John Kennedy, writing for the Hearst newspapers, asked Cord for an interview at the 1945 United Nations Conference in San Francisco, Cord turned him down, and Kennedy never forgot it. So, the two of them weren't pals to begin with. In the aftermath of the Kennedy assassination, Cord knew what was going on and knew what Mary was up to because his close friend James Angleton was informing him of what Mary was saying on the taped phone calls. And again, if Mary had been able to speak out and share what she knew with the public, it could've been very injurious to Cord, possibly even criminally.

According to what Bob Crowley told Gregory Douglas, when the moment came, Cord was all for it; he didn't blink twice. It was Angleton's meeting, but Cord certainly didn't put up a fight to save her, and this was the mother of his remaining two children.

What were the Crowley-Douglas conversations, and why are they important to this story?

What's important about this is that Robert Crowley, who joined the CIA in 1947 and achieved the rank of assistant director of clandestine operations, realized he was coming to the end of his life and wanted to get the truth out. In 1993, he contacted this kooky character, a historian named Gregory Douglas, who was about to publish his first book on Heinrich Müller, the former head of the Gestapo who became a secret, longtime asset of the CIA. Crowley supported Douglas's work on Müller, so they forged a relationship and had a series of long telephone conversations, which Douglas recorded.

I never got the actual tapes, but I did get some of the transcripts, and people ask, "How do you know he didn't just make it up?" And that's a legitimate question, but there are specific details in these transcripts related to Mary Meyer that Douglas couldn't have made up because he couldn't have known these things. Crowley told Douglas he actually saw and read Mary's diary, which Angleton kept in a safe, and he told Douglas what was in it. He said Mary had what happened in Dallas all figured out, so the CIA had to take her out. This isn't a slam dunk, but there's enough credible evidence there, certainly that I saw, that further legitimizes the CIA's guilt in the Kennedy assassination.

Many people will have a hard time believing the CIA could murder an American civilian mother of two, but what in the psychological makeup of CIA operatives during the Cold War made them capable of doing just that?
One of the ways to look at it is that these guys were in a cult; the CIA was a cult. In fact, it was the title of one of Victor Marchetti's books—*The CIA and the Cult of Intelligence.* They know everything, and nobody else knows anything because they alone have access to the truth, and at some level, they think this legitimizes them to make decisions that run counter to everyone else's system of morality—because they're saving the country from Communism or some bullshit like that.

When you get involved with cult-like behavior, people do crazy things, and in the case of many of these CIA guys, throw in the dimensionality of alcohol, where their connection to a deeper sense of morality becomes eroded in terms of their human faculties. They lose certain dimensionalities of their personality in terms of being able to have intimacy and empathy.

And when you get to Cord, who was already infuriated with Mary and never really took responsibility for himself or engaged in a self-introspection, where he could have resolved certain issues in his own being, you have a higher level of lawlessness. Anything goes. We can kill whomever we want, including a sitting president or a civilian mother of two. These people look at a national security threat as the most important thing in the world.

In the book, I talk about what James Angleton said in a 1985 interview he did with author and producer Joseph Trento for Trento's book *The Secret History of the CIA*.[6] In the interview, Angleton confessed about always being the skunk at the party, but he also told Trento that JFK and Mary Meyer were madly in love and had something real. Angleton, being the intellect he was, wasn't stupid, and he understood the relationship between JFK and Mary was indeed something very special and rare. But even so, he went ahead and took her out . . . a year after he had taken out the president.

What have been the ripple effects of the JFK assassination and the "collateral damage" deaths of individuals such as Mary Pinchot Meyer?
In the context of the other major assassinations in the late 1960s, it really has completely upended, on a very deep level, the structure of our democracy. Finally, when people got up the courage to go back and really look at what had taken place, it was clear there was a type of political suppression that was, and still is, very ruthless.

If JFK had lived, I believe the Vietnam War wouldn't have escalated, there would've been a growing alignment with Russia, and nuclear weapons would eventually have been eliminated. Now think about what this would have meant for the military-industrial complex, which was building up these weapons. The JFK assassination changed the trajectory of where this country went. We were so close to heading toward world-peace ventures, and this was totally eliminated when he was killed.

Do you think Bobby Kennedy knew what really happened?
Bobby Kennedy knew very quickly what happened, but he couldn't go public with it. The evidence is overwhelming he didn't believe the Warren Commission, and the fact he wanted to bring back his brother's points of view as to where he wanted to take the country would've been a disaster for the CIA. As it was, the House Select Committee on Assassinations was onto them, and if the CIA wouldn't have been able to manipulate that effort, it would've been made extremely vulnerable. I know my dad was seriously sweating it at that time, and the stress of the HSCA really took a toll on him; all the CIA guys were sweating it.

And then you had Martin Luther King Jr., who was equally as vocal in his own way, pounding home this idea that the United States was the most violent country on the planet and what we were doing in Vietnam made no sense and was imperialistic. Now couple that with the anti-Vietnam War protests and cultural schism in the country at that time. It was a pivotal time in our country and around the world, and I think world peace ultimately lost when JFK was killed.

What bothers you the most about the official narrative of the JFK assassination?
Just the mere fact Oswald was caught on a Friday and assassinated two days later on live television. Give me a freaking break, and millions of people were having that same thought, but you didn't see the *New York Times* come out and say, "We better look into this." Instead, the mainstream media reported it as mere coincidence. Only a few individuals back then had the courage to come forward and say, "This is complete nonsense in terms of what you people are trying to pull across the American public." It's just outrageous, but here we are, fifty-five years later, and the official stance is still "Oh, yeah, Lee Harvey Oswald killed JFK." It's such horseshit that it infuriates me every time I talk about it.

Why is it critical younger generations know who Mary Pinchot Meyer was and understand why she was murdered?
I'm sure you've heard the phrase "He who does not understand the past is destined to repeat it." One of the things I'm so upset about is what has happened to education in this country since Nixon. It was Nixon who started the ball rolling on destroying the high quality of public education we were reaching in the late '60s and early '70s. He didn't want any more snot-nosed, educated kids disrupting America's little imperialistic wars around the world. And the Republicans who followed him, including Ronald Reagan with Iran-Contra, felt the same way. This has been one of the most disappointing things to witness.

And now, of course, we have a growing number of people, millions of people, who buy into this QAnon nonsense and other propaganda because they have no critical-reasoning faculties. They don't have the kind of education that allows them to understand some of the diametrically opposed forces that have shaped our country, so they fall prey to any conspiracy theory that comes along.

There's very little critical reasoning in terms of what's getting taught in secondary education today. Most high schools have dropped civics at this point, so people are graduating high school not understanding how government works. This is what I see as one of the biggest pieces of tragedy here.

It's important for younger generations to know about these things so when it starts to happen again, they can begin to make connections and draw conclusions, understanding exactly what took place in the past, not the propaganda they grew up with and are surrounded by. I was so fortunate to go to a college like Princeton and have the teachers I had because they confronted me and gently pointed me to other points of view. That kind of educational/academic experience was a cornucopia of treasure I can never forget. But very few kids get that kind of exposure anymore, and that's not by accident.

So, the "dumbing down" of America is deliberate?
There's a whole power structure in this country that doesn't want you to know the truth about the genocide of the American Indians and its involvement in the institution of slavery. So, we're living in a country where there are these secrets, and until these secrets are exposed and reckoned with, we can't really evolve as a people. The Germans came together and confronted the horror of the Holocaust and all its implications. They had the courage to really look at themselves and say, "We really screwed up, and we can't allow this kind of thing to ever take place again."

And this is the kind of look in the mirror we need to have in this country. But you have these very powerful institutions like the CIA that are determined not to let out all the documents about the JFK assassination—which would clearly point to the fact that it all ends up at the CIA's doorstep—even though this is exactly the kind of thing we need to take on as a country . . . to accept and forgive and move forward from.

We don't need to abolish the CIA; we need the CIA because we need to have intelligence gathering, but we need to come to terms with our past mistakes and misdoings, including state-sanctioned murder. The fact is the power dynamic ran amok in the CIA in the 1960s, and there's ample evidence the CIA was involved, to one extent or another, in all the major assassinations of that time, and we're not going to move forward as a nation in terms of understanding the true meaning of democracy until we look at our real underbelly.

How have the sum of your experiences—being the son of a CIA operative, Michael Meyer's death, Mary Meyer's murder, your pursuit of the truth regarding Mary's murder—shaped you as a person and your perception of your purpose in life?
Being a student of meditation and metaphysics, I believe part of my life's purpose was to take on this story should it develop. In other words, I came into this life and was born into a particular family that positioned me perfectly to take this story on.

I don't think it was a foregone conclusion when I was born in 1947 that Kennedy was going to be assassinated and these events would play out, but it was quite ironic that I was born into this family and my best childhood friend was Mary Meyer's middle son. First, he was killed, and that opened the door to a much deeper relationship with Mary because she was the only one who could reach me in terms of my grief, which she shared with me. Were it not for her, I don't think I would've been able to take the steps I did to deal with the grief reaction I ultimately dealt with somewhat as a child but much later in my childhood.

In college, I was introduced to the books of Carlos Castaneda and realized mind-altering substances were sacraments and, if used responsibly, could potentially allow people to take great leaps in their consciousness, understanding, and personal evolution. As a young psychologist in the 1980s, I was part of a secret group in the Boston area that used MMDA (ecstasy) for couples and families in crisis. Today, MMDA is on the cutting edge of treating people with PTSD, trauma, recovery, and these kinds of issues. It's coming back as one of the best tools mental health must deal with these things in ways pharmaceuticals cannot.

So, when I began to open up in the way I did—starting my meditation practice, getting committed to esoterica, and seeing how useful some of that information can be—I started to have these little visitations from Mary. I could feel her, and she would talk to me in certain ways. I feel Mary and I are somehow kindred spirits, and when I decided to write the book, the universe started to provide for me in a way that just blew me away.

The process was difficult, but I had help, and a lot of that help was on a spiritual level. This has been my experience; I can't prove it in an empirical sense, but I'm not certifiably crazy. This is my story and a large part of how this came to be.

I could never have done this without this other level of dimension or reality—let's call it the spirit dimension—becoming a growing, integrated part of my own being. I desperately needed it to get to the conclusion I arrived at. The CIA can most definitely render you impotent on this 3D plane in terms of having any impact that's going to thwart their power.

The only thing that could ever possibly get to them would be an enlightened citizenry, which President Eisenhower implored in his parting words to wake up and realize what was happening. In the late 1950s, there was a growing industrial/military/intelligence complex taking over the country, and if citizens didn't understand this and rise up, this power complex would be exceptionally successful. Unfortunately, Eisenhower was correct.

What is the most important message you would like to share regarding Mary Meyer?

From my point of view, having known this woman, known her family, and having had a personal connection with her, this was an extraordinary human being who happened to be a woman and an intelligent person who understood at the core level that personal evolution was the only game in town when you came to life on planet Earth.

She was courageous in regard to her own development and awareness and wanting to expound upon that, and this is what made her curious about psychedelics and their potential to have a positive influence on the human mind. She wasn't afraid of being alone and not being married in a culture that shunned single women of her age. She was a forerunner of the women's movement, in her own quiet way, because she saw what was possible.

She initially thought she could help Cord Meyer have a remarkable life, that is, until it became clear he was too deep into the cult of the CIA. And then Jack Kennedy came back on her radar, which I believe happened by intelligent design. I believe positive forces can set up conditions whereby if enough well-intentioned people are willing to see and fight for a better way, great things can happen. But oftentimes negative forces are also on the march, so there are these battling forces throughout human history. And what we saw, looking at this particular era in our history, was a birds-eye view of how this battle played out.

Mary was a profoundly good force who was trying to help the world realize the futility of a Cold War mentality and turn toward the possibility and pursuit of world peace, and John Kennedy felt the same way. Unfortunately, in the end, they were eliminated by these negative forces.

How do you feel today about having completed the book and getting it out to the public?
There were some profound challenges in taking this on, especially with the understanding there was no turning back. I was determined to get to the bottom of this, and if I died today, I would die with a smile on my face because of having at least written this book. I'm 73 and in good shape, so I'm going to keep working on getting a film made about this until it's abundantly clear it isn't going to happen in my lifetime.

CHAPTER 11

CHANA WILLIS

Chana Gail Spainhouer Willis is the daughter of Freddie Philmon "Phil" Spainhouer, who served in the US Navy from 1941 to 1963, rising to the rank of master chief, with a specialty in Photographic Intelligence. Before his death in 2014 at 91, Spainhouer confided in his daughter that he was involved in the Kennedy assassination before, during, and after the event. Specifically, he was ordered to do some filming that day and was stationed behind the picket fence on the grassy knoll in Dealey Plaza on November 22, 1963. A 1983 graduate of Texas Tech University who also attended Abilene Christian University, Willis is the recipient of the Texas Governor's esteemed "Yellow Rose of Texas" Award, which recognizes outstanding Texas women for their significant contributions to their communities in the preservation of history, the accomplishments of the present, and the building of the future. She is currently writing a book about her father's life and experiences as an intelligence officer, much of which contains what he wrote during his lifetime and retirement years.

What did you think your father did for a living when you were growing up?
I knew he was a professional photographer who started his career in the US Navy, then worked for an aerial photography firm that processed agency and government film, then for the Dallas Police Department, and finished his career as chief of photography at the Dallas Fire Department.

I remember trying to play around with his cameras, equipment, and briefcases all the time. That's why he gave me my own Brownie box camera when I was five. Mom said, and he admitted, that he'd been a playboy around the world, and I knew he had a life as a bachelor until he was thirty-five years old. When mom met him, she was twenty-one and thought he looked like debonair Hollywood star Errol Flynn. She got pregnant, they got married, and they celebrated fifty-six years of love and roller-coaster moments.

His saying was "I didn't want to drag a family around when I had a Navy career. I joined when I was eighteen right after Pearl was bombed." During the war, he got a "Dear John" letter from his gal back home, and it broke his heart.

Did his behavior ever strike you as odd?
Growing up, I never understood why dad was so outgoing at work, yet in the evenings and weekends he was so reclusive, strict, and easily angered. Once we were on vacation, and I asked him the wrong question about his work, and he told me to "shut up." Don't get me wrong, my dad loved us, but he was authoritative in his family life because there was so much he didn't have control over in his work life.

He later told me that when "they" told him to be at a certain place, he needed to be there. Period. He often transferred those frustrations to putting a lot of pressure on the family. He told my mom on many occasions, "When you need to be ready, be ready, or I'm leaving you behind." And he did. We were going on vacation one time, and she wasn't ready . . . and he left her at home.

What kind of photography did he do for the Navy?
It was aerial photography but also photo intelligence. He built cameras and camera lenses for U2 spy planes. He showed the pilots how to trigger the cameras to take pictures based on formulas he computed for altitude, speed, humidity, and time of day. He was given meritorious service awards for being part of leading the photo recognizance in VAP-62[1] during the Cuban situation in the early 1960s.

We lived in Florida for a while because of the Naval Air Station Jacksonville's proximity to Cuba. He told me he would put his pants and

A young Freddie Philmon "Phil" Spainhouer in 1941. (Photo courtesy of Chana
Gail Willis)

shoes by the bed, and he trained the pilots to blow the jets' burners over
the house when they were returning from their missions in Cuba so he
would know to get up and race to the photo lab on base, mix and warm
up the chemicals to process the aerial film. They would make mosaics out
of the 9"x9" negatives and piece a larger aerial together on a wall. Then he

and the team would help identify where the missiles and missile launchers were located.

Even after he left the Navy, dad was an asset. He had a little piece of film and a frame with astronaut Neil Armstrong on it. I asked, "What's that?" And all he said was, "They only had one chance to process that film and get it right the first time. That tiny piece of negative was on the moon, and they wouldn't let me keep any more of the film."

Was he with Naval Intelligence?
Yes. I have a document of when he was in Naval Intelligence, ONI, and the pictures of the guys in his class and the secret ratings they were given. Dad had something called a "cosmic" clearance. He showed me pictures he took at missile testing, of ships, and his certificates and awards during conflicts and missions, including Korea, photo recon over Cuba, and more.

I asked why his current copy of his DD214 (military service record document) didn't have any of these awards or duty locations listed in it. He said when he went deep, they striped all the info off the form. A military officer walked up to me once at Camp Mabry Army Base in Austin, Texas, and told me they knew I was trying to finish dad's book and that his DD214 wouldn't be updated to reveal this info until after he died.

Was there ever a moment you realized your father might work for the CIA?
It was 1973 . . . I was thirteen and my brother was fourteen, and this is when it really dawned on us. We went across the Texas border into Mexico to look at all the little shops. We were there for about an hour when my brother came up to me and said, "We've got to get back into the States NOW."

I noticed my dad's tan skin and ruddy complexion, and he had sweat beads coming down the side of his face and above his lip. I asked, "Why?" And my brother said, "Because he didn't get permission to leave." I stood there staring at him, "What?" My brother whispered in my ear, "CIA." And I thought, "Okay. I'm confused. What's going on?" Once we got back home, Dad told us that because of his photo intelligence work in the Navy, and agency work, he had to get permission wherever he went.

He also told us anyone who was in as deep as he was would never admit it and take that secret to the grave, and if someone bragged about being with the agency, they *weren't* with the agency; they were liars. Dad scared the dickens out of us.

How do you think your father found himself working for US Intelligence?

Ruby Houston, my dad's mother's sister-in-law, was an OSS (Office of Strategic Services) civilian asset during WWII. She worked for R. L. Thornton at Mercantile National Bank on Main Street in Dallas for over fifty years. I remember visiting with her and talking about her "duties."

Dad went into the Navy in December '41 and was a gunner and boat-swain man. When he got out on leave in December '45, after the war, he went to SMU for two semesters and went back in the Navy in '47. I found out later that's when the OSS converted to the CIA. In trying to connect the dots, I think his gateway into the agency was through his Aunt Ruby. She had no kids and took Dad under her wing.

Mom confessed a few years after Dad died that he was once arrested when in the Navy. As she sat there puffing her Pall Mall cigarette and drinking her sweet Texas tea, I gulped in astonishment and said, "What the hell? How did dad rise to the rank of master chief with THAT on his record? What did he do?" She said it was early in his career and involved a ring of five guys counterfeiting ID cards. He got thrown in the brig for thirty days but somehow got it off his record. So, I talked to some folks and figured they set him up, or he really did it and got caught, and getting it "cleaned off" was his gateway setup into the agency.

Aunt Ruby had another nephew, Jesse Ray Houston, who was also in the military. Dad and Jesse Ray were cousins and close childhood friends. Jesse Ray became president of a bank in Garland, Texas, which is where Dad said he immediately went after he left Dealey Plaza on the day of the assassination.

One day Dad got a call and was told they found Jesse Ray's body in a hotel in Dallas. I guess each person who was involved, or who was forced to be involved, dealt with the aftermath of the assassination in different ways. Dad said Jesse Ray drank. Dad was easily angered, stubborn, often overbearing, reclusive, and obsessive with writing.

It sounds like you discovered things about your father slowly, over the course of many years.

Dad told me the story in pieces, like a quilt. He did the same with my mom and my brother. So, I had to piece all of it together over the years. For some folks, it was like having a curbside view of something. For me, it was being in the water and dealing directly with the ripple effects.

It was a process over time that eventually culminated with my dad telling me a lot once he was retired and much older. I went to school at Texas Tech, and I remember him driving me there and dropping me off on the sidewalk. I asked him, "Aren't you going to help me move in?" And he said, "No. I didn't get permission to leave Dallas." I instantly remembered our two-hour jaunt into Mexico near the border years before. It was certainly a weird way to grow up, and I didn't know other kids weren't raised this way.

I'd sit at his knees on the living-room floor and ask him to tell me stories of his Navy years. In 1971, he gave me my grandma's tin bread box full of more than 400 letters he wrote home during the war. At first, I loved the postage stamps, but then I was mesmerized by his stories from 1941 to 1958. As I got older, I'd pull out a letter and reminisce with him over it, and then I'd go jot down notes so I'd remember details. As an adult, I interviewed him and recorded a lot of stuff. It took me thirty years to build up the guts to ask him point-blank about the day of the assassination.

When did your father start telling you specifically about Dealey Plaza and the JFK assassination?

In 1976, when the House Select Committee on Assassinations came to get materials from the Dallas Police Department, my father was conveniently positioned there to decide what they got. He took the negatives and made prints, and he begged them to allow him to make an extra set of copies of some of those prints. I found them in his closet one day.

There's a photo of Oswald's arrest, the police report of J. D. Tippet being killed,[2] the boxes stacked on the sixth floor of the Texas School Book Depository, the 6.5×52mm Carcano rifle and Jack Ruby's arrest. I still have them. They're 8"x10" black-and-white prints, and when I found them, my dad sat me down and explained what they were. He told me the boxes in the window weren't stacked like that at the time of the assassination; they rearranged the boxes for the photo shoot according to how they thought they were stacked. He also showed me where they'd placed the gun.

I remember when we moved to Dallas . . . it was November 4, 1963. And the reason I remember is Mom and Dad both were almost savant with dates and numbers. They [Naval Intelligence] had arranged for us to move into a furnished home about five miles from downtown. Mom and Dad both told me the story of someone named "Joe" showing up at the door a week later, around November 11, and handing dad a piece of paper. And he said, "This is where you go to work next week." That was about eleven days before the assassination.

The week of the assassination, my dad was couriering plans in these big, round film canisters for aerial film through Love Field Airport. "That's the closest I came to getting caught," he said. "The airport security wanted to look inside, but I said it would expose the film." These canisters were the size of round oatmeal boxes. I remember asking, "Daddy, what was in the canisters?" He said, "Film." I looked at him and asked, "Is that all?" Silence. I pressed, "What else was in the canisters?" He said, "The plans." I replied, "For Dallas, for JFK?" And he said, "Yes." Then he turned his head away and looked out the big bay window of our living room toward the woods. I went to the bathroom, threw up, and cried.

Then he told me Lee Harvey Oswald was on his team and never fired a gun that day. According to my father, Oswald DID handle a gun that day, but he NEVER fired one. The team of operatives he was on was told they were part of an operative photo intelligence exercise to protect the president. When they realized the truth the week before the assassination, Dad said, "one person on the team committed suicide and another one went crazy."

I can't speak for Oswald, but evidence does point to the fact he knew about the assassination and tried to warn the FBI about it. I think my father, and the other members of this team, were manipulated and put into place for various purposes, and whoever was caught would be the patsy. That wound up being Oswald.

The grassy knoll, where Willis believes her father was "stationed" on the day of the assassination. (Photo by Andrew Lichtenstein/Corbis via Getty Images)

I tell people to look at photos from around Dealey Plaza that day and look for my dad's car. He was driving a 1957 fantailed gold-and-white Dodge Coronet. He admitted to being down there.

It's like he told you certain things, but you knew there was so much more he could share.
Now that I know more, I wish he was still alive and I was brave enough to ask more questions. All that time my mom thought he was going to work at Texas Instruments, where he was embedded. Most of the time he got home in time for dinner, but he also worked late a lot, and sometimes he'd have to go in after we all went to sleep. With a briefcase handcuffed to his hand, he was taking flights out of Love Field to Boston and getting home the same day before dark. It was enough to drive him crazy, but he was following orders and never really knew the true purpose behind what he was doing.

No one person knew all the components; they just carried out their assignments. They told my dad only what he needed to know. He told me how they would sometimes courier things in vegetable and fruit delivery box trucks, unknown to the drivers, who were being used as mules. "Third box of tomatoes, fourth row back, under the second one." Sometimes, the drivers knew. Code words of vegetables and fruits were their favorites.

So, your father was part of a US Intelligence team on an operative photo exercise, and he had orders to be at a certain location in Dealey Plaza on November 22 to film something. How did this play out?
He eventually found out what was really happening, and he wanted out, just like some of the other members on his team. But they told him the same thing they told Oswald. And when I say this, you can look back at photos, and you'll know why Oswald looked the way he did. They said, "Oh, you don't get out. If you try to get out, you're dead, your wife is dead, and your kids are dead, and we might even get your parents." And this can scare a man. My father had an entire career with these people, but if he didn't follow those orders, it was over for him and his family, so he did what he was told to do.

The one time he took me and my brother down to Dealey Plaza, which was after I found those photos, we walked behind the picket fence. He just stood there and took deep breaths. That's when I knew he was standing next to one of the shooters that day, filming the assassination. He asked me to not ask him details.

His job was to film something, get to his car, and drive from the Texas School Book Depository through downtown to Highway 78/Garland Road to the First National Bank, where his cousin, Jesse Ray, worked as bank president. I'm guessing he handed the film off to him, or he handed it off to someone while he was still downtown. My mom, then twenty-six, was ironing in the living room watching TV when she saw the news coverage of the assassination. She tried to get my dad on the phone, but all the lines were busy.

For years, she told me he was at work at Texas Instruments. Eventually, I said, "Momma, I think you lied to me. I want the truth because I got it out of Dad before he died. He told me of his involvement in Dealey Plaza in 1963."

She said, "I never really got a hold of him that day, but I knew he was down there. I was afraid to talk about it and didn't know your dad told you. He seemed to have told you a lot more over the years than I knew." I replied, "He told me that, too, and said he didn't want you knowing more because he feared for you."

It's like she was in denial because she knew about the threats. Dad told her about them, so she was scared, too. And they threatened Oswald the same way. "You do this and that, and if you don't, you're dead, your wife is dead, and your kids are dead."

Did he ever tell you exactly what he filmed?

No, but I've been told several men have seen the "other film," not the Zapruder film, and they believe it to be Dad's work. One day, years later, Dad sat in the living room and told me, after going over some fire department death-scene photographs with me, how to look for evidence in photos, and how "the government had this bullet that, when it was fired into the head, exploded and made a big hole in the backside, just blowing the brains out." And he held up his hand near the side/back of his head with his fingers spread out. Then he looked out the big sliding glass doors into the woods—like the time I asked him what was in the canisters—and just stared, saying nothing for a long time. I'll never forget that glassy stare.

Was your dad certain about what he told you about Lee Harvey Oswald?

My dad was adamant "Lee never fired a gun that day." Oswald was Naval Intelligence, and he was also a company guy. His marriage to Marina was orchestrated—the double-spy thing. Oswald "defected" to Russia in 1959 and returned to the United States in 1962, When a person renounces their citizenship and moves to the Soviet Union, *especially during the Cold War*, they're going to grill them when they want to come back to America. Oswald wasn't arrested; he wasn't even interrogated. He was simply "debriefed."

The point is, what my dad said about Lee rings true when you realize, based on what has come to light about his ties to US Intelligence, he would've been a willing participant in this "photo intelligence exercise," manipulated to be where they told him to be that day . . . and the perfect patsy.

Apparently, the plans for the assassination were on pieces of paper wrapped up in film canisters and in the film negative, and those had to be taken from Point A to Point B, which is when dad said he came closest to getting caught. That was the moment I realized he wasn't only involved that day, but he was involved before, during, and after the assassination . . . and not by choice.

I suddenly understood, and it wasn't until I met Saint John Hunt [see Chapter 9] I didn't feel so alone. It was the first time in my life, at age fifty-six, I met another agency kid with skin in the intelligence "game." I suddenly didn't feel alone in telling Dad's story for history.

I want to clarify that US Intelligence agencies share assets; thus, your father was with Naval Intelligence *and* an asset for the CIA, correct?
Yes. There's another "off the books" agency I can't mention, and I honestly don't know if they exist today, but back then Dad told me exactly what building they were in. He told me several times before he died that he was in the Navy *and* the CIA. I thought his agency work was only for a few years before he got out of the Navy, but I realized that when he went back in 1947, he was also with the CIA . . . plus the other agency that's not on the books. But he never wrote about that, and I was told never to mention it.

Also, the Navy didn't always know, nor did the corporations he worked for in his civilian life. Nobody was supposed to know he was with the CIA. He knew Oswald through Naval Intelligence. I asked him specifically, "Did you know Oswald?" And he shook his head up and down, "Yes." Oswald was part of his team; there were three teams, but not everybody knew what the other team was doing. "That information was on a need-to-know basis," he said.

Hearing this from your father must have been mind-blowing.
I just know what I lived growing up, and the revelations . . . and being scared witless and told, "Don't talk." My dad sat there one Christmas, two

years before he died, and pounded his fist on the table. He said, "Little girl, I never thought you were writing this stuff down, figuring it out and piecing it together. People like you . . . they don't live very long."

And in my brain, the thought bubble went over my head, but I didn't say it. We were looking right at each other, and I thought, "What the hell?! Did my dad just threaten me? Or is he warning me?" I didn't know which it was.

The secrecy must have taken a real toll on him.
The emotional impact of all these things really changed him. He said he was often scared to death. There were some hard years in our family because of it, very hard years. What I'm sharing is what Dad told me, along with all the photos and documents, and his voice recordings. It is what it is, and he asked me to finish his writing and tell his stories if I wanted to.

I don't think people realize the collateral damage associated with this. Here were these guys, thinking they were patriots. Your father really thought he was fighting the good fight.
Exactly. They had no clue they were being used and manipulated. And if they got a clue, they were threatened. When the operation was disbanded after Dallas, Dad begged to get out, and with his skills—photo processing and manipulation—he couldn't get out. When I was a teenager, he taught me photo manipulation in a lab directly beneath the Dallas Police station where Ruby shot Oswald. I remember going there to learn how to process film. He was teaching me how to make *new* negatives out of spliced pictures and manipulate pictures. I still have all his cameras.

I wish I had asked him more questions. I shouldn't have been in shock so much and should've kept following through more. As he got older, it was easier to redirect him and dig deeper. I did ask him one day, "Who was the ultimate person behind the assassination?"

He paused a long, long time and said, "It was LBJ." That's what he thought, anyway.

Can you summarize what you know about your father's involvement in the assassination based on what he told you?

I know he was in Dealey Plaza that day carrying out certain orders, film-ing *something*. I know he had some documents in film canisters. I know he was ONI and CIA. He told me about where he went immediately after the assassination. He also confessed to carrying plans through Love Field Airport and knowing Lee Harvey Oswald, and Lee being "on his team." I know his demeanor and how it changed afterward. I don't know exactly where in Dealey Plaza he was, but I'm surmising from his conduct when we visited there that at some point he was by the picket fence.

Afterward, was it just knowing and not being able to say anything?
I've never asked anyone if they believe me because it's my dad's story. And you can't change the facts of someone's life. Everything he told me, he backed up. I'm flipping through all this stuff, and it includes his security clearances, photos of the places he'd been, the letters he wrote home with postmarks. He wrote it all down and saved a lot of stuff.

Your father played the "company game" well, but he must've known that at any time, if they wanted to, they could get rid of him because of what he knew. Is that accurate?
Yeah. We grew up hypervigilant, always. That's why he had me learn how to watch people. I didn't know other kids *weren't* raised that way. I found out other dads of my friends *weren't* taken to NorthPark Mall and taught how to watch people. It was like a game as people walked by. What do they do for a living? What did they do today? Where do you think they're going? How old do you think they are? Watch their hands, their eyes. What kind of car is that on the highway? Make, model? Dad said, "If there's anything I've learned in life, it's to be VERY observant . . . and persistent."

When he died, he had this on his wall: "Press on. Nothing in the world can take the place of persistence. Nothing is more common than an unsuccessful man with talent. Unrewarded genius is almost a proverb. The world is full of educated derelicts. Persistence and determination alone are omnipotent."

How did your mother deal with all of this?
She had her bingo, and he had what he wanted, which unfortunately involved flirting around. They had some hard years, and I think a lot of it

was his philandering because of the stress he was under, still being watched and all. She's in her mideighties now and has fond memories, despite the tough years. She's sweet as can be, and very well read, artistic, and talented. Since he has died, I've had some good conversations with her because he often monopolized family chatter.

When did you first start talking publicly about this?
I always felt alone growing up, not being able to talk about it. And I didn't talk about any of it until about two weeks after he died in 2014. It was the first time I spoke publicly. I was scared to death. I hired a bodyguard because I didn't know what would happen if I talked. Occasionally, I'll get contacted by someone and told I'm talking too much, or I'll get a message from someone on the street who's passing by me. I honestly don't know how much of my life has been a manipulation. I figure, as Saint John Hunt and others have spoken out, the more sunshine on facts and stories, the better, even with all the disinformation characters out there spreading lies.

Why share his story?
It isn't so much about trying to convince people of my dad's story. When people ask about the book, I say the book isn't about that day in Dealey Plaza. If you're going to read it, if I ever get it finished, it's not about that. It's about my father's life story, being raised by Texas pioneers who carved homes out of the hillside in the late 1800s, to his skills in making camera lenses that fly in satellites around the world today.

It's his entire life story that tasks the next generation with owning the system we have and being in tune with what's going on with our government, and to participate. Because when we don't, there are people out there who are going to run it the way they want—for money and for other reasons, from the drug cartels to children being traded in the sex-slave industry. Citizens should and must participate in government entities and raise their voices. Silence is compliance.

I don't want to try and convince anybody of anything regarding my dad's life . . . but this happened. There was no way out. I speak up because I want people to be engaged in their government's process because if they don't, it could collapse. And the story needs to be told to learn lessons from history. They say every generation has its own war, and if you don't understand history, you're going to repeat it.

Have people been supportive of your efforts?
All of us have a system of belief and denial and acceptance of things in our lives of what we remember. For me personally, I get raised eyebrows. Some people are supportive and believe, and others doubt. I have no dog in this fight and feel no compulsion to convince anybody of anything.

I'm neither a "Lone Nutter" nor "Conspiracy Theorist," as there are all these researchers digging into statistics, ballistics, and logistics. I'm on the fence and getting poked by the barbed wire of experience. I lived this from the inside, with my family, watching it eat away at a man the latter part of his life. It was torment, and other than Saint John Hunt and a few others, I don't know of anyone else who has walked this walk. It's Dad's life story, his story for history, on paper, between two pieces of cardboard.

Do you worry about your safety?
Yes and no. I sometimes get concerned, but I refuse to live in any kind of fear or paranoia. I live life looking at the windshield in front of me and not in the rearview mirror at things behind me. I don't wait on life to be hard because I choose joy and productivity.

My dad said that when I found out about his involvement, he worried about me most of his adult life. If your child was being watched by your bosses for something you were involved in, it would take a toll on you. I've known two occasions when I was followed, but I don't let that affect my life. Never have. Never will.

One time I talked about my dad's life and came home from church, and our child's pet rabbit had been removed from its cage and decapitated with a knife, and the headless body was put on the curb so we'd see it when we got home from church. The kids were devastated. I got the point but moved on.

There have been little weird things my whole life, and now I have the answers as to why those things happened. Dad said they were warning signals that I was talking too much. Now I'm recognizing the life I lived growing up wasn't the normal life of an American kid, and not everybody's dad did what my dad did.

I've got boxes and boxes of photos, his cameras, his military orders, the things he wrote . . . and it's a part of our history. I can't sit on it when it needs to be shared with the American public. His life and the history of that time frame of men belongs to all Americans, not just me. Let the chips fall where they may when the story is told.

My children all know the story, and I need my dad's stuff to stay with at least one of them just in case something happens to me. A lot of it is scanned and on a terabyte drive, which I've given to twelve different people. If they're thinking about doing something to me for talking, I know how this game works. Something happens to me, and twelve different copies of my father's stuff get sent to various media outlets.

Did your father keep any of those film canisters from that particular "exercise"?
I found two film canisters in my father's barn, and there was still film in them. And I got a call from someone who told me they knew I had found the canisters. I also got a call to warn me the Justice Department could seize them, so I removed the canisters from my property. The canisters were the same size my dad talked about couriering the intel documents, but they were in a barn attic for forty years in the Texas heat and were damaged beyond repair. But the fact someone knew I found them was unnerving.

Do you believe your father was a true patriot?
Dad grew up in Liberty Grove as a cotton-picking farmer. His family has Dallas pioneer roots going back to the late 1840s. He told me he was picking cotton one day with his siblings in the Texas heat when he looked up and saw two planes flying overhead from the Dallas Naval Air Station. And he thought, "By golly, I'm going to be in the Navy someday."

My goodness, Dad loved his country. He said he saw and did things for America he never imagined he would get to see or do when he was a farm boy in the late 1920s. He was a loyal patriot and loved the flag so much he put it up most every day on the flagpole in our front yard. He wanted radio stations to play the national anthem every day at noon. He watched Walter Cronkite fervently.

Did he manage to keep his level of patriotism his whole life?
He told me if he ever went under anesthesia, there needed to be an operative present in case he said something he wasn't supposed to say. When he had stomach cancer in 2008, he had emergency surgery, and afterward he was put into an ICU room with four other people, and he started to talk under the morphine. To everyone else, it must've sounded like the rants of an 88-year-old man on drugs, but he was talking about things that didn't need to be heard by others.

So, I called my congressman's office, gave him the code phrase and said, "I don't know who my dad's 'hammer' is, but I know he checks on him every year. My dad just had surgery, and he needs to get out of this ICU room and put into a private one before somebody takes him half seriously." And within two hours he was moved.

As time went on, they simply forgot to debrief him every year. When he was ninety, he said, "Little girl, I'm going to die soon, and they've forgotten me." I asked him what he wanted me to do, and he said, "I want my last debriefing so I can die in peace." I said, "Daddy, are you asking me to contact the congressman? And he said, "Yes."

It was very difficult to get an operative or asset to fulfill dad's request. Even the congressman's office had difficulty. I said Dad would talk to NO ONE unless they knew his code name. Finally, after a few months of many phone calls and side meetings with politicians at their "town halls," we had success in the request.

A female operative showed up at the house. She knew everything about our life as a family, and she apologized for not giving him a debriefing in five years. She said they thought he had passed. One of the phrases they use when your intelligence career is over is "It's a beautiful day, isn't it?" And you say, "Yes." . . . and you're done. They've released you. He wanted to hear that. He wanted to know he had done his duty for country and served to keep our liberties free.

Any final thoughts?

I don't know if there's any honor in my dad's story because he was so tormented by being involved. It's not honorable to say my dad was involved—despite his low level of involvement—in the plan to eliminate President Kennedy. Frankly, that's quite embarrassing and upsetting. Who would want to walk up to somebody and say that? But there's more to the story because he was manipulated and didn't have a choice.

When you're under a lot of pressure not to share what you know with anybody, and then your daughter asks you a million questions over the years and is able to connect the dots, it must be awful. When I figured it out, the look of terror on his face sent chills down my spine. He was terrified . . . terrified for me and not just himself. I'll never forget that look. I became physically ill. It was a defining moment in my life with him.

CHAPTER 12

KRIS MILLEGAN

Kris Millegan is a writer, researcher, and publisher whose father, Lloyd S. Millegan, was in the Office of Strategic Services (OSS), Military Intelligence (G2), and later the CIA, rising to branch chief, head of Intelligence Analysis for East Asia. His father told him some things he didn't quite understand in the late 1960s, but it sparked an interest that led to more than thirty years of research into the subject of CIA drugs, clandestine operations, and secret societies. Millegan's publishing house, TrineDay, arose as a vehicle to get suppressed books wider circulation. He is one of the authors of *Fleshing Out Skull and Bones: Investigations into America's Most Powerful Secret Society*. He is a prolific songwriter with two songs in *National Lampoon's Last Resort*. He currently resides in Oregon.

What triggered your involvement in this work?
Two things. First, I was fourteen years old and in ninth grade when the JFK assassination happened, and our teacher announced it. Then we got a call over the classroom loudspeaker asking me to come to the principal's office. I got there and my paper boss was there because I was a paper boy, so I got taken out of school and put on the street corner selling newspapers. That only happened twice in my life—once when Kennedy was shot and again when Oswald was shot. It was a traumatic time.

Second, my father was in US intelligence. He never talked about it at home. A couple of years earlier, he asked me what I thought of the

Vietnam War. I was a teenager and gave him a flip answer. I said, "Oh, you have a sack of hand grenades and some rice paddies, and you throw the hand grenades and win it for the good guys wearing the white hats." He said, "Well, we have to have a talk." That talk came years later.

In the late '60s, I was growing my hair long. I started college, then dropped out and started a record store. One day while at home my dad said, "You know they're trying to opiate your whole generation." I'd never heard the word "opiate" before, but I understood what it meant. I said, "I just smoke a little pot." I'll never forget it. He responded, "Well, you're just making money for *them*." The way he spat that word out, I knew he didn't like *them*.

In 1969, the day before my twentieth birthday, I went to my parents' house. I figured we were having cake and ice cream and doing birthday stuff, and my dad said, "It's time to have that talk." With him was D. F. Fleming, an emeritus professor of International Relations at Vanderbilt University who wrote the two-volume history of *The Cold War and Its Origins, 1917–1960*. He took me into my little brother's room and sat me down. He didn't say hello or anything, he just said, "The Vietnam war is about drugs, and the secret societies are behind it." So, I'm thinking he's talking about the mafia, and then he added, "Communism is all a sham. The same secret societies are behind it all. It's all a big game." It didn't make any sense to me. As a kid I'd been stuffed under my desk at school because the Russkies were going to bomb us.

My dad proceeded to tell me all about his intelligence career, and then Dr. Fleming and my dad started this conversation about how they were playing out a "lose scenario" in Vietnam and involved in creating this report for Eisenhower. They said the things we were doing in Vietnam represented one of the scenarios they talked about, and then they started talking about psychological warfare.

This must have been a little unnerving for you to hear.
Yes, but I went on with my life, and a couple years later I was reading a girlie magazine called *Gallery*, and it had stories about the JFK assassination. I'd always been interested in that, so I read those articles. They were also starting to publish articles about the subject I call "CIA drugs," which

is what my dad had talked to me about. I remember reading one article about the JFK assassination in which they talked about the various groups believed to be responsible, including the mafia, the CIA, and a bunch of others. There was a throwaway line referring to the possible involvement of secret societies, and that brought back the conversation I had with my dad again.

I thought, "Gee, is that what dad was talking about? What's going on here?" So, I started to research CIA drugs.

I remember telling somebody about my research and what my dad told me, and this guy said, "You're a conspiracy theorist." Now this was in the 1970s, so I asked, "What's a conspiracy theorist?" I decided to take on conspiracy theory as an independent discipline. My way of researching is reading books, so I went into every bookstore I could find—religious, feminist, mainstream, and fringe—and asked to see their conspiracy section. All of them had at least one book, so I started collecting them. They're what you would call screeds (long discourses or essays) that were essentially formula books. I could find a book that blamed one conspiracy or another on the Jews, another on the Masons or the Mormons or the hippies or the secular humanists—any group you could think of.

I started thinking there was something strange about the synchronicity of it all. I would get to the bibliographies, get those books, read them, then go to their bibliographies, and soon I was into books about banking and social history. The hardest thing to find was books about secret societies, but finally, in late 1988, I found Anthony Sutton's book, *America's Secret Establishment: An Introduction to the Order of Skull and Bones*. And suddenly I understood what my dad was telling me way back in 1969 because it all started to make sense.

Please describe Skull and Bones for the readers.
Skull and Bones, also known as The Order, is an undergraduate senior secret student society at Yale University founded in 1832. It's known for its powerful alumni, including Prescott Bush (father of George H. W. Bush), Averell Harriman, George H. W. Bush, and George W. Bush. At this point my dad was ill, and he died in early 1990 of pancreatic cancer, so I never got to ask him what he was trying to tell me.

Yale alum and Skull and Bones member George H. W. Bush served as CIA
Director from 1976 to 1977. (Photo by David Hume Kennerly/Getty Images)

I kept reading and looking into all these interesting things, and I started doing some writing on Skull and Bones right before the Internet came along. I tried to touch base with Anthony Sutton and couldn't find him anywhere, but when I posted some of my Skull and Bones writing on the Internet, he saw it and got in touch with me. *High Times* printed some of my stuff, and I started an email list on the Internet called CIA Drugs and got a lot of different researchers on there.

Did this lead to you starting your own publishing company?
Yes. A friend of mine, Daniel Hopsicker, came to me one day and said, "My book has been in New York for over two years with an agent and nobody's going to print it." After hearing him grumble about that for a while, I finally told him, "Well, I've got a computer, and they say I can make a book, so come on out and let's see what we can do." Together, we published his book, *Barry and the Boys: The CIA, the Mob, and America's Secret History*.

At around the same time, Anthony Sutton told me his publisher was going out of business, so his book was going out of print. I told him, "Anthony, that can't happen. It's never been in hardcover. It's never been in libraries." So, I borrowed $5,000 and started a little publishing company, and we put out *America's Secret Establishment*, then *Expendable Elite*, and then a book fleshing out Skull and Bones. There were a lot of books circling New York, and suddenly, they started coming my way, all these different authors.

Then Ed Haslam [see Chapter 6] called me up and said, "I've got this book, *Mary, Ferrie & the Monkey Virus*. I have some new research and I'm tired of self-publishing, so let's see what you can do." I said let's do it, and we produced *Dr. Mary's Monkey*. He also told me about Judyth Vary Baker [see Chapter 7]. The first time I heard her story, I was like, "No way. She'd be dead." As everybody else in her circle *was* dead, murdered. We spent about two years doing research on her story and published her book, *Me and Lee*.

What kinds of challenges did you encounter while doing your research?
The challenges we've had with Hollywood really stand out. I've had several people want to make *Dr. Mary's Monkey* into a film, as well as *Me*

and Lee, and they get stopped every time. I was working with a gentleman who was the executive producer for the TV show *24*, and he saw how they were using *24* as psychological warfare, so he looked around to find some real, honest stories, and he found our company. He wanted to make a number of those books into movies, so he started bringing in Academy Award-winning directors and such, and we'd sit around a big table and talk.

One of the projects was with Nick Bryant, author of *The Franklin Scandal*, the true story of a nationwide pedophile ring that pandered children to a cabal of the rich and powerful. So, Nick was in L.A. talking about the project with some film people, and they got this computerized phone call that said, "We're really glad that you and Nick are working together." The producer had a way of finding out where the phone call came from, and it was from a Boston FBI office. Then they got another computerized phone call sourced from the Seattle FBI office. He called me another time and said, "I can't shake this white SUV that's been chasing me all around town." Another time he called me and said, "Well, they're trying to get me fired. There's this rumor going around I'm out on Sunset Boulevard selling Oxycontin at night."

It went on like this, with all kinds of weird stuff happening to him. Eventually he gave me a call and said, "I've got to take a sabbatical for two weeks. Somebody met my wife on the street corner and told her, "If your husband doesn't stop what he's doing, we're going to kill him, and then you. What are your children going to do?" I told him to go take his sabbatical. He called me back two weeks later and said, "Well, I guess we're just making Will Ferrell movies now."

I also worked with the people who had the *Terminator* franchise. I was sitting there with them at the Four Seasons in Beverly Hills, and they said they were going to make a $126 million blockbuster movie on the Bilderberg Group.[1] The contract was already signed, but I said, "You know, you might have some political problems with this." And they responded, "Once we get the latest *Terminator* movie out and the video game, we'll have enough money in our pockets, so it won't make any difference." They went to Spain where the author was and announced a $126 million blockbuster movie on the *True Story of the Bilderberg Group*. Well, in less than six months, their company was bankrupt, the contract was invalid and there was no movie.

Have you ever feared for your life because of your research?

Yes, but not for very long because it's all much bigger than me. One thing that's happening is we're getting a lot of help from ex-military and ex-intelligence people. Sometimes it takes them twenty years to figure out why they were there and why they were doing the things they were doing. I know some of them have told those who would harm us, "These researchers are just writing books, and if you come after them, just wait until you see what we have to say."

What have you concluded about the Kennedy assassination based on your research?

I've come to a personal conclusion about the JFK assassination "crew." At the bottom you have J. Edgar Hoover and LBJ. They were so blackmailable you could make them do whatever you wanted them to do. And then you have the consigliere, Allen Dulles, the first CIA director to be fired (by President Kennedy) for insubordination.

I first read about this in a book titled *The Defrauding of America* by Rodney Stich, a Navy pilot during WWII. In 1993, a former deep-cover CIA officer, Trent Parker, told Stich a CIA faction was responsible for the murder of JFK. Parker said his highly secret intelligence unit, called Pegasus, was shadowing J. Edgar Hoover, who didn't think his phones could be tapped, but they were, so Parker and his team recorded phone conversations of plans to assassinate Kennedy. Parker told Stich the "crew" involved in these conversations were "[Nelson] Rockefeller, Allen Dulles, [Lyndon] Johnson of Texas, George H. W. Bush, and J. Edgar Hoover."

David Rockefeller and Averell Harriman were on the outside helping these guys, and I believe Edward Lansdale wrote the assassination script. Harriman, by the way, was a member of Skull and Bones, an East Coast Establishment insider, and Prescott Bush's business partner in Brown Brothers Harriman, which made loans to and had business dealings with Nazi Germany in the 1930s. In fact, the company had its assets seized in 1942 under the Trading with the Enemy Act. Harriman was a high-level, behind-the-scenes man of power who interacted regularly with those in secret societies and the intelligence community. Lansdale was all CIA and a pioneer in clandestine operations, political-psychological warfare, and manipulation of governments. Kennedy didn't make him ambassador to Vietnam in 1961, a position Lansdale coveted, but he did make him the head of Operation Mongoose, the covert plot to overthrow Fidel Castro.

I've done a lot of research on Lansdale and, in fact, have a connection to him. In 1936–37, my father was an exchange student at the University of Shanghai in China and started working with the State Department informally. They asked him to gather information of interest to them. In 1939, he graduated from college and was supposed to go to school in Switzerland, but there was something going on in Europe at that time, so that didn't happen. He got as far as Washington, DC, and was soon in the basement of the Library of Congress working under Archibald MacLeish, who was Skull and Bones, cooperated with COI [office of the Coordinator of Information], and later joined OSS. They gave my father the Philippines desk and told him to become an expert on the Philippines.

The COI became the OSS, and while my dad was in the OSS he got drafted. The OSS guys put him in the military on General MacArthur's staff because they didn't trust MacArthur or his chief of intelligence, Charles Willoughby. They wanted my dad to report on them and put him into G-2 (Army Military Intelligence). The guy my father was working under died, so he started working with the guerillas. He went into Manila way before the American troops and helped the guerillas set up their government. He put a bunch of the Japanese collaborators in jail and sequestered the puppet government's library and their papers. The Japanese government sued him for that, while the American government gave him the Legion of Merit. MacArthur had been raised in the Philippines, so when he got to Manila, he found a bunch of his childhood friends in jail. My dad was responsible for jailing them, so MacArthur said, "Get rid of Millegan."

They moved my dad out of the Philippines to become the head of research and analysis for the invasion of Japan, so they had to get somebody who was in both the OSS and G-2 to take his place. That somebody was Ed Lansdale. My dad had been working with him in psychological warfare during World War II. My dad was still in the CIA in 1956 and did a trip to Vietnam. He met with Lansdale and wrote a report, and soon Lansdale was recalled. My dad came back and there was obviously a power struggle because Lansdale stayed, and my dad was soon out. He left the CIA softly in 1957, and by 1959 he was completely out and moved our family to Oregon.

Averell Harriman was a member of Skull and Bones at Yale, an East Coast Establishment insider, and Prescott Bush's (George H.W. Bush's father) business partner in Brown Brothers Harriman, which made loans to and had business dealings with Nazi Germany in the 1930s. (Photo by: FPG/Archive Photos/Getty Images)

Wasn't Lansdale, who used psychological warfare in both the Philippines and Vietnam during the Cold War, an expert at regime change and scenario planning?

Yes, and for my money, he wrote the script for the Kennedy assassination. Fletcher Prouty, who served as chief of Special Operations for the Joint Chiefs of Staff under President Kennedy and who was the model for "Man X," played by Donald Sutherland, in Oliver Stone's film *JFK*, said, "The hit is the easy part. The escape must be quick and professional. The cover-up and the scenario are the big jobs. They, more than anything else, prove the Lansdale mastery."

You've got to play a whole bunch of people so they don't come for you afterward. The conspirators get these individuals to think they're carrying water for the operation, but all they're actually doing is carrying water for the mud. There are assassins out there who have worked for the federal government, and when you talk to them, many say they were in Dallas that day. Most of them had nothing to do with the operation, but it puts mud around it and puts a hand on their shoulders saying, "You aren't supposed to talk about what you did, and how are you going to explain why you were in Dallas that day?"

It wasn't as if somebody woke up in March 1963 and said, "Let's kill the president." It's my opinion the Kennedy assassination is a long-range psychological warfare operation. The planning started before Kennedy was elected, the assassination was a mass trauma hit on the American population. It's part of the psychological warfare the secret societies engage in. For me, it wasn't a CIA operation, or a Secret Service operation, or a military operation, or a mafia hit. It was a secret societal operation that used all these different pieces to pull it off and cover it up.

It seems like secret societies are very much an elitist thing, wherein a privileged few attempt to control the many. The men you just mentioned were all known to have an enormous sense of entitlement based on their blue-blood upbringing and Ivy League educations. Would that be accurate?

Yes. Through my years of research, I've found that secret societies run the world through a leviathan of three levels, and each level has three parts. The top level is mining, metal, and money. If you control the mining, where the metal comes from and on which the money's supposed to be based, you're in a pretty good position. I've found they hold that level very tight. I knew one author who could affect that level. I resisted publishing his book for many years. When I finally published it, he was dead in seven days, a hit-and-run in London. And this was no unsubstantial guy. His attorney was William Pepper, the attorney for the family of Dr. Martin Luther King Jr.

That's very disturbing.
It is. The middle part is a very active level—drugs, guns, and oil. It creates all the big slush funds, and where this meets the road is media, because they've got to control the story. Also, movies and music, because they've got to control the culture or it will bite them on the butt. And then there's "magic," the ability to hoodwink us to make us think something else is happening and their use of mass trauma rituals to scare the heck out of us and keep us in place. They have iron control at the top, but as it goes down their control is less and less. My feeling is we can flip this thing one day and actually have a *real* world to live in.

The fact that a small group of individuals can control billions of people like that is horrifying, especially when it's all about control and power. They're not exactly doing these things so all of mankind can thrive. It's quite the opposite, isn't it?
It's as nefarious as it gets.

Let's switch gears. What was Oswald's role in the Kennedy assassination?
He was Naval Intelligence who got loaned to both the CIA and the FBI. He had a file folder that moved around. Every intelligence operative has a file folder with information in it, and this folder goes with him to the loaned agencies. Every six months there's a review to determine if the loan is working, and it must be renewed. Oswald was an intelligence operator who was doing his job.

Realize this was a very well-thought-out plan, with a script, to confuse and control individuals like Oswald by having them participate in some way or giving them knowledge about something that could get them in trouble. With military people, the collaborators looped them into some little thing they look back on and realize they could be accused of being part of the plot, so they just shut up. So, there was a script written to game them, to play them into position so they could control them. The Cubans were lied to and told to do certain things, and they did them. You see this in Watergate and the JFK assassination.

Also, in these types of ops, you don't have a single shooter; you always have a team. The shooter hits his target, then drops the gun and walks.

Another guy cleans up the scene and leaves. That's how these operations are conducted. Lee Harvey Oswald was a patsy.

What have been the ripple effects of the assassination, good and bad?
I see very few positive ripple effects. The main negative effect is we lost any semblance of our republic, of our democracy. We've been living in that psychological warfare hellhole ever since. There's a very good book out of sociology called *Elite Deviance*, by David R. Simon. He talks about scandals. From 1850 to 1950, there were two major scandals, and then starting in 1950 there has been scandal after scandal after scandal, and it's pretty much always the same group of people. The Kennedy assassination has given these shadowy forces way more control, and they've been continually ratcheting up their control.

It *is* a positive thing we have knowledge of these people in the shadows, but what they're doing is perpetuating evil. One of the Skull and Bones famous songs goes, "We're poor little sheep who have been led astray, bah, bah, bah." They come from a hyper-Calvinist background. They believe that along with an elite in heaven, there's an elite in hell. That's where they get the ability to do that evil. They're absolutely nuts, and they're making the world nuts.

When you do these types of things, it creates all these ripple effects, and they've worked very hard to create "warring" sides. They give the right honest things to carry, and they give the left honest things to carry, and then those honest things get debased by having them fight each other. So, the Kennedy assassination is part and parcel of a program of psychological warfare that has been perpetuated upon our population, and upon the entire world.

Why does the JFK assassination still matter all these years later?
We lost our country, and that's very important because it's one of the main points of the psychological warfare. And if we own up to it, we can get past it and get our country back. We're still moving toward a more perfect union. When they wrote and ratified the Constitution, people were slaves, so we're still working on it.

What would you want younger generations to understand about the JFK assassination?

It wasn't simply an assassination. It was a decapitation of our president, and of our government. The world you live in today is a lot different because of that act. You don't have the freedoms you had then. I was raised in the 1950s, and we went out and played until dark, until Mom said, "Hey, come on home." Now parents get in trouble for having their kids play on their own. The world has changed a lot, from the freedoms and the expectations you had for your life, what you could do, what you could become, what our world could become, and how we treat our brothers and sisters here. It's changed a lot, and not for the good.

Is there anything about the case you've never been asked and want to comment on?

The ties between the perpetrators and the drug trade. I don't get asked that a lot because many people don't enjoy my take on it. They like to blame the CIA, the military, and all these other people. I get marginalized because of my thoughts on this. Most people don't like to think about the connection with the secret societies because it's unsettling. You just had that reaction a few minutes ago, right? "Disturbing" and "horrifying" I think you said.

Is there anything you'd like to add?

I tend to agree a great deal with Fletcher Prouty and his understanding of the dynamics of the case. It was right on. And again, the crew was Hoover and Johnson, Allen Dulles, George H. W. Bush, Nelson Rockefeller, with David Rockefeller and Averell Harriman off to the side, and Lansdale writing the script.

Bush's motivation was about rising in the hierarchy of the secret societies. To achieve that meant committing certain acts. If you aren't born into a secret society, but want to join it, you must supply them with black-mailable material so that once you're in, you can be controlled. Bush had been involved in intelligence since the 1940s, and he was a paymaster for many of the Cubans. Why did Hoover send that memo to the State Department's Intelligence & Research Bureau, dated November 29, 1963, advising of a briefing given by an FBI agent to "Mr. George Bush of the Central Intelligence Agency" on November 23, 1963?[2] It was to cover Hoover's butt and show Bush he knew about it. Bush made his bones in the assassination, through his participation in the shadows, and it moved him up the hierarchy.

You've given readers a lot to chew on, Kris, but when you think about it, it's not all that surprising, especially when you realize that narcissism, elitism, and sociopathic behavior are all part of the human condition. This is kind of becoming a theme for this book.

When you see these individuals for who they really are, it's not surprising at all.

PART 4

TWO LITTLE GIRLS

The American Dream has run out of gas. The car has stopped. It no longer supplies the world with its images, its dreams, its fantasies. No more. It's over. It supplies the world with its nightmares now: the Kennedy assassination, Watergate, Vietnam.

—J. G. Ballard
English novelist, essayist, satirist, and short-story writer

CHAPTER 13

TONI GLOVER

Toni Glover, PhD, was born in Dallas, Texas, on February 14, 1952. On November 22, 1963, she was an eleven-year-old living in the Oak Cliff neighborhood of Dallas who begged her mother to take her to Dealey Plaza to see the presidential motorcade that was scheduled to drive through downtown. Standing on a concrete pedestal at the corner of Houston and Elm Streets in Dealey Plaza, Glover, known as the "Girl in Blue" because of what she was wearing that day, witnessed the Kennedy assassination firsthand. Seeing the president's death, which connected emotionally to her troubled childhood, had a traumatic impact on her life. Now an associate professor of English at the University of Scranton in Pennsylvania, she has come to terms with her past but still struggles with the raw horror of what she witnessed.

How did you end up in Dealey Plaza that day?
I begged my mother for weeks, and I got very manipulative about it. I was certain I could get extra credit at school if I went and saw the president, and I would constantly come up with other good reasons why I needed to do it. The school district said we would be excused if we missed school to go see him. That morning I was up at the crack of dawn sitting on the roof of our house, waiting for the kid to deliver the newspaper so I could see the final route.

I thought of every detail, but I had no idea what I was going to wear, which was important because my main goal was to have President Kennedy notice me. I just stood in my room and started crying because all my clothes were piled up on the floor. I was a total mess. In the end, I chose to wear one of those dress shorts that looked like a skirt, and I put on knee socks because a new girl at my school wore them, and all the boys fell in love with her. So, I put on knee socks, but I didn't have the calves for them. They kept sliding down my legs, and I was constantly bent over pulling them up . . . I can't tell you the number of times I pulled them up running back and forth from Main to Elm waiting for the presidential motorcade.

Did you have any other concerns?
I remember it was cold that morning, but it warmed up by noon. We didn't know what to do with our coats when it got warm because we didn't want to put them on the ground. And if you left it over your arm, you couldn't clap. It was a dilemma, so I decided to put mine back on so I didn't have to worry about it.

So, you wanted the president to look directly at you when he passed by?
Yes . . . and he made eye contact with that smile of his, and you could've knocked me over with a feather. At first, I was devastated because he was on the other side of the car, but he and Jackie were very good about waving at individuals; they didn't just do the queen thing. Jackie was on my side, and I caught her eyes, those big brown eyes. She was something else. The last thing the president looked at as they turned the corner on Elm was a row of women lined up right on the curb. That's the last thing he was looking at before he got shot.

Where were you standing, exactly?
I was standing on a pedestal at the corner of Houston and Elm, right across the street from the School Book Depository. There were reflecting ponds in that area, and at the end of those was a cement fence with square holes in it, and at the end of that fence, there was a pedestal about four feet by three feet. I climbed up on it, and I somehow convinced my mother to do it with me.

We were standing on this pedestal, so I could see the presidential limo come from Main onto Houston. We were screaming, and then they turned onto Elm. For a second, they went behind part of a pillar, and then they came out and "boom!" President Kennedy's head exploded right after they came back into view. My eyes were on him when it happened.

Leading up to the motorcade coming into view, what was the atmosphere like?

We were about to see the movie-star president and his wife, so everybody was nervous and excited. You talk to people you don't know whenever you're like that. I would jump off the pedestal, leave my mom sitting there, and run down to Main to see if I could see them. They had the corner of Main and Houston blocked off, and there was a policeman standing there. I was like, "Oh, oh, oh!" and he would just say, "Relax. Relax." When I couldn't see them, I bent over with my arms hanging loose and groaned. I couldn't really see down the street unless I stepped out into it, but it was blocked, so I waited until the police officer's back was turned and then tip-toed out. He turned back every time and said, "Back on the sidewalk."

This happened like ten times because I kept running back to Elm to tell my mom and the crowd of people there, "I can't see him yet! I can't see him yet!" and they'd all be disappointed and do a collective "Oh!" This one guy had a seizure. I was going to help him, but adults jumped in and called an ambulance. The ambulance got there a few minutes before the presidential limo came. We were all thinking they were going to reroute it, but they didn't. They came around the corner a few minutes later. But I kept getting in the street, and the police officer kept telling me, "Back!"

He probably got a kick out of an eleven-year-old girl trying to do that.

He did, but one thing that made me gulp was he had a gun on his hip. My dad was mean, just cruel, and one day when I was four or five, he got mad at me, and he came out of the bathroom with a big gun in one hand and my kitten in the other, and he said, "Toni, you want me to kill this cat?" I just started screaming and crying. He was in a towel because he had been in the shower, so my mother came up and yelled, "John! What are you doing? Get back in there!" But before he did, he threw the cat and killed it, just squished it. So, when I saw the gun on the police officer, I was scared.

I'm sixty-eight now, but until recently, fear ran under my skin. There was this low electricity running through my veins, and things would make it ramp up, and I'd be terrified. To deal with it, I became a comedian and made fun of everything. In my family, we had a lot of gut-level laughter because we were covering up gut-level pain; there was a real dichotomy going on. So, at eleven, I thought President Kennedy could change all of that if I could just get him to smile at me. Of course, even if he wasn't shot that day, nothing would've changed, and I'd eventually come to realize that. But instead, I was devastated right then and there.

I went back to Dealey Plaza as an adult, and one of the things I did was get up on the pedestal and film, with my phone, coming down Houston and turning the corner and turning down Elm. Because I was five feet off the ground, it put me way up. It was a great vantage point, and I had a good view of everything.

Walk us through those moments from when they came into view until the gunshots rang out.
There really weren't very many people there. There was one row on the curb, and we were way above them, which is probably why we got attention. The view was unbelievable, and when they turned the corner, the limousine flashed in the sunlight because they were coming from the shadows of the tall buildings. When they turned onto Houston, there was a gleam or reflection from the car. They were smiling and they were there, and it was amazing, absolutely amazing. Jackie looked at me first, and then he swung around. In my mind, he locked eyes with me. Everybody was so happy, and then six seconds later his brains were on the street.

When they made that left turn onto Elm Street, they were now moving away from you, correct?
Yes. They were moving away down Elm Street toward the triple underpass.

Can you explain what happened next?
I didn't recognize the first shot as a shot, and I'll bet you most people didn't. A lot of people looked because there were eight police Harley Davidsons around the car, so maybe the noise was from one of the bikes. The second

one I knew was a rifle, having grown up in Texas. I definitely thought, "Oh no. That was a gunshot." So, now I'm spinning and turning, and the third shot and the gray spray coming from his head happened at the same time. I was far enough away that it looked gray to me.

Toni Glover watched as President Kennedy was struck by the fatal head shot. (Source: Bettmann via Getty Images)

Did you realize at that moment what was happening?
Your brain denies everything, so I turned to my mom and said, "Mom! Someone threw fireworks in the car and the police are really mad!" Back then they had a firework called an M-80, and it was probably very close to a bomb, but when it went off, gray paper went up and exploded, so my mind immediately went to that.

Did people start to become frantic at this point?
No . . . because very few people could actually see the car when the fatal shot occurred. Only those who were on Elm Street could get a clear view of it. Most of the people were on Houston, and once the motorcade turned

the corner onto Elm, they couldn't see anything. I saw it because I had a high vantage point and happened to turn around in time.

The word came up the street, and people were trying to find out what was going on. There were gunshots, but was there any problem? Were the gunshots directed at the president? There were three or four cars behind him, and they were all coming around at the same time as we were trying to figure out what happened. There was a lot of confusion.

I ran over to a police motorcycle that was parked on the side of the schoolbook depository and was trying to hear what the radio was saying without getting too close. I heard "gunshot to the head," or at least I thought I did. I just wanted to get my mom home, so I went back and said, "I think it grazed his head or something. I'm not sure, but let's get in the car and go."

How did your mother react?
She was upset. Everyone was upset because guns had gone off and police were in full respond mode. It became unavoidable . . . you eventually realized something terrible had happened. I seriously believe if we hadn't gone home and heard the quote "three shots rang out in Dallas," most witnesses couldn't have told you how many shots were fired because of the noise level and everything that was going on. I remember a rifle shot and then the last one, but I don't remember the first one. People ask me, "Was it bang-bang? Or was it bang-pause-bang?" And I'm like, "I don't know! I was eleven."

That must be frustrating for you.
Every human being there . . . we didn't show up with *tabula rasa* . . . we showed up with an emotional landscape created by our life experience, but I can tell you we left Dealey Plaza with terrible images and scars from that afternoon. For some of us, we had plenty of scars to begin with, so we didn't need more of them. I've talked to a lot of witnesses, and everyone brought their own world with them, and then that world was shattered. Everyone went from 110 percent euphoria to "Oh my god!" in six seconds.

So, now you just want to get home with your mother.

Yes. We got in the car, and I was worried about Mom, so we drove straight down Elm because Elm turns into the street that goes straight to our house. We literally drove over his brains. Today, every road would've been blocked off immediately, but they didn't block off Elm or Houston . . . they didn't block off a thing. We drove right through the crime scene.

Wait. Are you saying you drove past where President Kennedy was shot to go home?

We drove the same exact route the presidential limo did. Everybody did . . . a bunch of cars. If you look at photos that were taken two, four, or five minutes after he was shot, there are cars in the street going down Elm, right in the spot where it happened.

Three "tramps" were arrested for questioning in Dealey Plaza the day of the assassination. They were not detained and disappeared after release. (Photo by © CORBIS/Corbis via Getty Images)

What happened when you got home?

You must realize, we lived in the Oak Cliff neighborhood on North Hampton between Jefferson St. and Fort Worth Ave. The Texas Theater is on Jefferson St., a few blocks from where we lived. Another three blocks down Jefferson is a high school with 2,000 students in it, and as soon as the assassination happened, they told the students they could go home. So, three blocks from the Texas Theater, where they arrested Oswald, 2,000 students were let out of school with half of them walking down Jefferson. The rooming house where Oswald stayed was also only a couple of blocks away. So, I lived three miles from everything that happened after the assassination. If you look at a map of Oak Cliff, there's our old house, Oswald's boarding house, the spot where Officer Tippit was shot, the Texas Theater, and the high school.

So, we came home and were all in a grief coma for about a week to ten days. This was the first time there was 24-hour TV coverage of an event. I and my three siblings rolled up in blankets on the floor in front of the TV with my mother sitting on the sofa behind us. I remember getting up and getting a Dr. Pepper from the kitchen. I was popping the lid off it when I looked in the living room, and all the lights were out except for the light coming from the TV, and it was like my family's faces were ghosts because of the TV light. It was spooky to turn back around and know the entire world was curled up in a blanket in front of the TV. We ran out of Kleenex in the first hour of watching the coverage, so we all had our own roll of toilet paper sitting there.

Can you describe the emotional trauma of being there and witnessing something like that?

Yes. I can also describe how it impacted another witness who was also eleven years old that day and was standing on the corner of Main and Houston. Both her parents were alcoholics, but they were highly functioning alcoholics. She never really processed what happened that day, and today she's very reclusive. The Sixth Floor Museum at Dealey Plaza has conducted hundreds of interviews with witnesses, so they called her to do an interview, but at first, she said she couldn't do it. They finally convinced her to do a phone interview, but before she did, I called her, and we got to know each other. She's had a very hard time of it and has suffered from serious PTSD.

What about you?

I started trying to kill myself at fifteen, but I can't identify whether part of my disintegration was caused by that. But you never lose the image, and you never lose the butterflies of going from ecstasy to agony in a matter of seconds, so that's always there. I wrote a letter to Jackie Kennedy, but I never mailed it. I tried to sound intelligent, but then I called myself a "knuckleheaded girl" at one point. I told her I was going to be a brain surgeon so I could learn how to fix brain injuries. Thank God I was raised by wolves, so nobody gave me a stamp and envelope to mail that letter anywhere.

Can you clarify what you saw the moment the president was hit by the fatal head shot?

I just saw a gray spray, and then he immediately fell into Jackie's lap, and a member of the Secret Service detail jumped on the back of the limousine. I was fixated on it, and it all seemed like one motion. President Kennedy was in a brace, so he couldn't fall forward but instead fell sideways . . . and part of his head was missing. You can see photos of the limousine at Parkland Hospital with pieces of his brain all over the backseat. Apparently, when they got to Parkland, Jackie was holding the pieces of his head together. They started to take him in, but she wouldn't let them because she knew if she took her hands off, his head would fall apart. Secret Service Agent Clint Hill took his jacket off real fast and put it over Kennedy's head and said, "I'll take care of it." There are a million little stories like that.

What made you decide to break your silence, go to the museum, and confront your demons?

I went to the museum on the twenty-fifth anniversary of the assassination, but I chickened out. I went back on the thirty-fifth anniversary, but I couldn't go into the exhibit. I wasn't going to walk through that, but before I left, I went up to the security guard and said, "I'd like to speak to a historian because I was on the corner that day." He picked up the phone, and people came down to see me. A man said, "Hi Toni. Come with us," and took me into the office, where we had a long talk.

It was hard because at the time, all the windows in the curator's office looked onto Dealey Plaza. So, I was sitting there talking to them with the pedestal twenty-five feet from me, and I was trying to keep composed, but I started crying. I said, "I'm sorry," and they said, "No . . . it's okay . . . it just proves you're a witness. None of them can get through it without crying."

Did doing that help you?
I thought witnesses were probably dying, so maybe I should tell them what I saw. Turns out some of the people who were directly in front of me on the ground told the historians they thought the gunshots were fireworks. I had yelled about fireworks from up on the pedestal.

You went back for the fiftieth anniversary. What was that like?
I didn't have tickets to it, so I wasn't at the event itself. I was on my pedestal, which wasn't very far from the event, but I just walked around with people who were milling around Dealey Plaza. Those who were old enough to be alive at the time were still haunted by it. They had this concerned, painful look on their faces. We were standing in a place that was the scene of a horrific crime. I remember asking myself why I was there and why I wanted to remember it. I did a CNN interview that day and just cried my way through it. I kept apologizing for it.

What do you think have been the ripple effects of the assassination?
The immediate effect in Dallas was profound. At the time, we were hosting a lot of Mexican foreign exchange students. That Christmas, several of them came up, and they asked us where our guns were because they thought we would be wearing them. As far as they were concerned, everyone in Texas wore six-shooters, but they soon realized we didn't all carry guns. They thought it was going to be the Wild West when they got up here, and people across the world thought that. There was a song . . . "In the dusty streets of Dallas, he was shot down." Two years later, we went to a dude ranch in Colorado, and my mom said, "Don't tell them we're from

Dallas." And we didn't. If you didn't have to tell people you were from Dallas, you didn't tell them because everyone was angry at Dallas. Dallas killed Kennedy. We were really careful about that for a long time.

But then, in time, the Dallas Cowboys started to become a big deal, and it drew the city away from the tragedy of the Kennedy assassination. "Oh, look . . . there's something else in Dallas." In the late '60s and early '70s, there was something of a Renaissance that took place in Dallas, so that also eased the stigma.

What do think changed that day and is still affecting us as a nation?
Lack of security. The feeling that however permanent you think something is, it can fall . . . it can die . . . it can go away.

What about for you?
There was a delayed effect for me. Between the ages of thirty to thirty-six, I was in and out of hospitals. I tried to kill myself. There was absolutely no reason for me to be alive. Then I just started carving on myself and cut myself horribly for two years. Then I went back to school and was struggling there, but as I did better in school, I got a little better emotionally, but I couldn't finish school until I dragged this part along. Clinical depression is chemistry, and through trial and error we found the right chemistry. About every ten years or so, your body changes and you have to retweak the cocktail. It's a nightmare when you must do that, but I've been great for a long time.

Posttraumatic stress can be triggered in different ways, but being in Dealey Plaza that day and watching the president get his head blown off would definitely be considered a trigger.
People showed up that day with their emotional landscapes, and they were either able to deal with seeing something like that or they weren't. Everyone was affected differently. As different as we all are as individuals, there were that many reactions.

Why does the JFK assassination still matter all these years later?
I think it was an experience of extremes in many ways. The idea of Camelot[1] was suddenly dead. You're screaming and cheering, and then you're

devastated. We have this young, wonderful person leading our country, and then suddenly, we have this old Texan who happens to be an asshole. Lyndon Johnson really was an asshole. It's just extremes. Everything about it was a national tragedy.

There aren't a whole lot of things that constitute a national tragedy. When 9/11 happened, everybody said it was like the Kennedy assassination. National grief to worldwide grief . . . those two situations both had a visceral effect on the country *and* the world. And it's scary for the world when the United States gets knocked to its knees for any reason. Watching President Kennedy get killed or watching those towers come down, it scared the entire world, not just us.

Do you ever talk to your students about the JFK assassination?
What happens usually is a student will come in and say, "Were you at the Kennedy assassination?" And I say, "Yeah. How did you know?" And they'll say either their parents or grandparents mentioned something about it. So, I'll give them the link to the CNN interview and tell them to watch it, or have their parents watch it. There's not much else to it because why would I answer parents' horrific questions? You wouldn't believe what I have in my office. I have a baseball somebody asked me to sign, and people send me pictures of myself and ask me to sign them, and I'm like, "All I did was go downtown that day."

Well, you were witness to history. It's like being a *Titanic* survivor.
And I'm one of the younger ones. Many of the witnesses have passed on.

You were eleven years old that day in Dealey Plaza. What would you say to an eleven-year-old who experienced something like that?
It would depend on whether the eleven-year-old had a family. If they did, I would say sometimes things happen and you must rely on your family. You have to rely on people to take care of you, to hold you emotionally and physically until you're better. That's what you learn from something like that, from a tragedy that big. You can't belittle it, and I think I probably got through it because we were all going through it. There may have been variations on how deep or how permanent the effects were, but I

wasn't grieving by myself. I was in a household of people who were grieving, so I think I would say, and I would say it from a psychological perspective, "Don't try to be a hero. Don't try to go it alone." And if they don't
have a family, I would tell them to find a new family . . . find close friends
you can lean and depend on.

**I've been told there was a feeling of guilt associated with being in
Dealey Plaza that day. Is that true?**
Everyone who was there says, "Why didn't I look up? Why didn't I do
something?" But there was nothing anyone could do. There was no reason
to look up. I was looking up at people waving from windows, but this was
before the motorcade got there. I certainly didn't see anybody sitting at a
window with a rifle.

Any final thoughts?
I wasn't unusual in the regard of not coming forward as a witness right
away. There were several books that came out about the assassination,
and some of them talked about witnesses dying under mysterious circumstances, so it put a lot of fear into me. It was a fear that many witnesses
locked on to. Many people didn't come forward until thirty or forty years
after the assassination. Even today, most witnesses still can't talk about
what they saw without crying. I think it was Rose Kennedy who once said
something about time healing all wounds, but I don't believe that. Your
mind will cover them with scars, and the pain lessens, but it's still there.
This wound is so deep for the witnesses that when you start to touch it
again, when you start to talk about it, it just brings up a tremendous
amount of pain and emotion.

CHAPTER 14

PAT HALL

Pat Hall is the owner of the Oswald Rooming House Museum, located at 1026 N. Beckley Ave. in the Oak Cliff neighborhood of Dallas, Texas. Her grandmother, Gladys Johnson, bought the house in 1943 and lived there with her husband for years, renting rooms to single men. On October 14, 1963, a man identifying himself as O.H. Lee (a.k.a. Lee Harvey Oswald) took her only available room, paying $8 a week including refrigerator and living room privileges. Over the course of the next five weeks, Hall and her two younger brothers got to know him as Mr. Lee. On November 22, police officers swarmed his room after his arrest at the Texas Theatre, and Hall's grandmother endured an onslaught of reporters and other intruders for months after the assassination of President Kennedy. Hall, who moved back into the house in 2001 to take care of her ailing mother, experienced a steady stream of tourists who came to her front door and asked to see "Oswald's room." Over time, she realized it was important to tell people about the Lee Harvey Oswald she knew as a young girl and let people see where he stayed for five weeks leading up to the assassination. So, she decided to turn the home into a museum in 2011 and opened it to the public in 2013 on the fiftieth anniversary of the assassination.

Tell us about the Lee Harvey Oswald you knew while he was living at your grandmother's rooming house.
In 1963, I was eleven years old, and I had two younger brothers—Harlan, ten, and Michael, six. We lived with our mom in our own house, but we

were at my grandmother's rooming house all the time because my parents got divorced when I was nine, so we needed care after school. We would go to my grandmother's after school, get homework done, and wait for my mom, who was a photographer and artist, to finish work and pick us up. I don't remember the exact day we met Lee, because with eighteen roomers, there were people moving in and out all the time.

Lee was twenty-four years old when he moved in, and we knew him as a sweet, considerate, compassionate young man who loved children. He was the only roomer to stop doing what he was doing at the time and go outside to play with my brothers. Children can bond with someone within a few days, and my brothers bonded with him because he was so much fun and so nice to them. He didn't care what they wanted to do—baseball, football, jump rope, cowboys and Indians—he was happy to get involved.

As a girl, I didn't play with the boys or the men, but Lee was always very kind to me. I could tell he didn't like the way my grandmother tried to teach me. I was dyslexic, and today, experts agree Oswald was dyslexic, so he understood me more than my family did when it came to my struggles in school. For my grandmother, failure wasn't an option, and she didn't understand what my learning issue was. I had reading and math issue because groups of letters and numbers would flip their order. Lee had the same issue, and they didn't know he had a learning disability when he was in school, either, but he was really smart.

In his day, it was typical for little boys who weren't doing well in school to skip out, so he got a record for truancy, but he spent his time at the public library, where he taught himself how to read. He read constantly. His coworkers said every time he took a break from work, he would read. My grandmother kept four newspapers at the rooming house—two Dallas papers, a Ft. Worth paper, and a New York paper (sometimes the *Wall Street Journal* and sometimes the *New York Times*), and he read all four newspapers cover to cover every day.

So, every time I had a test coming up, my grandmother went over the test material and pounded it into my head. I wasn't reading, but I could memorize. She drove me to tears, and Lee always tried to get near me and say in a very low voice, "Don't worry about this. Just try and do your best, but don't ever give up." Most twenty-four-year-old boys wouldn't say this

to an eleven-year-old girl; they would simply ignore her, but Lee was a car-
ing person, and that's why the disaffected, loan-nut persona the media and
the government put out about him really bothers me. From what I knew
of him, that portrayal of him is a lie.

The Texas School Book Depository (upper right) is located approximately two
miles from the boarding house where Oswald was staying when President
Kennedy was assassinated. (Source: Bettmann via Getty Images)

Do you remember any other specific stories about him?

One day I got through with my chores and was watching some TV, and my
brothers were out in the front yard wrestling—not the best idea between
a ten- and a six-year-old. Mike got hurt, and he had a short fuse, so he
jumped up and plowed into Hal, and they started fighting. Before I could
get out there to stop it, Lee, who had been sitting on the porch, went out
and got them, brought them to the porch, and sat on the porch steps in
between the two of them. He said, and I'll never forget this, "Boys, I'm
going to tell you something, and never forget it. I want you to pay attention because it's important. You are brothers, and you have to take care of
each other and love each other, and never do anything that would harm
another human being."

He said this two weeks before the assassination. It's just not something a twenty-four-year-old says to two little boys he barely knows. Most adults would simply ignore them fighting, especially back then. I had come out and was by the screen door on the porch, so I heard every word of it, and I was really happy he was saying this to them. It was a good life lesson.

After the assassination, we were talking to my mother, and my brothers related this story to her, and she said, "I want you to remember this conversation, go over it again and again in your head because one day it might be very important." That's why I tell the story verbatim the way I remember it because my mom knew it was an important story to recall and share correctly.

I've been very vocal about inviting Marina and her daughters to come to the house and hear our stories about Lee. We have fond stories about him, and they need to hear them. Marina and her children were sequestered for almost two years after the assassination. Marina remarried to a man named Kenneth Porter, and the girls changed their last name. I just think Lee's daughters need to know what he was really like . . . and that whatever he did or didn't do, their father was a kind, compassionate person.

Did you ever meet Marina or anyone else associated with Oswald during that time?
No. He was always on the phone with Marina, but she never came to the rooming house. She was living in Irving with Ruth Paine[1] at the time, so he would go visit her and his daughters every weekend. He didn't drive, so he rode the bus there. He and Marina had lived in Oak Cliff in several different apartments before 1963, so he knew the neighborhood had an abundant amount of rooming and boarding houses. When he got the job at the Texas School Book Depository, he came over to Oak Cliff and got a rooming house near the bus line. I met Ruth Paine once but didn't have an opportunity to really sit down and talk with her. She also has fond memories of Lee, as well, even though she thought he was the lone gunman.

What do you remember about the day of the assassination and hearing that Oswald was arrested?
My brothers and I were at school that day, and our school didn't have enough TVs to put in every classroom, so they put the TVs in the hallways

for the teachers to watch. They went out into the hallway, watched a little bit of the news coverage, and came back into the classroom. It was "keep the kids busy" day as the news kept coming out. I looked through the door of the classroom and saw into the hallway, so I could see the mood in the school change. It was sad . . . doom and gloom. I knew something horrible must've happened. Teachers huddled together, hugged one another, wiped their eyes, then came back into the classrooms to check on us. After a while the principal came on the intercom and said the president had been shot and killed.

My mother's photography studio was directly across the street from the Texas Theatre, where Lee was captured. She actually saw him being arrested and recognized him as a roomer and someone who played with her children. She was already upset about Kennedy and now was even more upset about Mr. Lee being arrested. She came to pick us up at school shortly after the principal made the announcement, and she didn't say anything to us. We told her the principal told us the president was dead, and she simply said, "Yes, that was a terrible thing." When we got home, she unplugged the TVs and said they were broken. She didn't want us watching the coverage. When the news broke about Lee, she listened to the news when we were either outside or in bed, so we didn't know about what happened to him until Sunday.

What do you remember about Jack Ruby killing Oswald, and how did you react to that?
My brothers and I were watching one of our kid shows on Sunday, and a special report broke in to broadcast the transfer of Lee from the city jail to the county jail. So, we watched Ruby shoot him, and my brothers screamed, "That's Mr. Lee! That's Mr. Lee!" My mom sat us down and explained why Mr. Lee was arrested, why this was all happening, etc. She broke it down into terms we could understand. It came across very well, so I give her credit for that. My brothers were extremely upset about seeing Mr. Lee shot because they adored him.

I was upset, too, but I didn't have as close a relationship with him as my brothers did, but the bottom line is we saw our friend shot on television. Kids don't care about politics; we just knew it was a terrible thing.

Mom didn't let us go back to grandmother's house until the investigation was totally over, about two to three months later. People were at her house constantly. Photographers were camped out across the street, and my mom didn't want them taking photos of us coming and going. She told us to keep our mouths shut about the fact we knew Mr. Lee.

How did these events affect you and your family moving forward?
It was hard for my grandmother. On the night of the assassination, she received death threats, so the police left a contingency at the rooming house. There was a *Life* magazine reporter who took a picture of my grandmother next to the bed Lee slept in. She regretted letting him take it because the magazine featured the photo and gave the exact address in the article for the entire nation to see, and this was the bestselling *Life* magazine ever. For nine months she received hate mail and became guilty by association. People were so upset, and they were upset for several years afterward about losing their president, so they needed to vent. Luckily, my grandmother was a smart enough woman, so she understood it. She would shake her head and say, "Poor things. They'll eventually get over this." She felt it, but she didn't allow the tragedy to disrupt the family.

From the moment the authorities arrived at the rooming house on November 22, they wouldn't allow any of the current renters to leave until the investigation was completed. They had eighteen potential witnesses all in one place, so they weren't going to let them go anywhere. Once the investigation ended, my grandmother had a mass exodus of the renters who were being sequestered there. She kept running the rooming house, and over time, she started renting rooms out again. People reacted differently when my grandmother told them Oswald had stayed there because she was straightforward about everything, but she never knew how they would react. Some people were appalled, and others were excited to stay there.

In your opinion, what was Oswald's role in the assassination, if any?
Personally, I believe he was a CIA operative who was ordered to be a part of what was going to happen. When you look at his military record, he didn't have the expertise to do that kind of shooting. In the Marines, you can't

get out of boot camp until you're a sharpshooter. He had one day of good shooting and received a low score as a sharpshooter, so the Marines were never going to use him in that capacity. Instead, they send him to Camp Pendleton and put him in two training programs at the same time—radar school and Russian language school. Russian is the hardest language in the world to learn, but he aced both programs.

To me, he was always tagged for the CIA. I believe he didn't take a single shot that day, especially not with that rifle. I don't think he knew he was going to be the fall guy; I think he was told to make his way to the Texas Theatre, where he'd meet somebody who would get him out of Dallas. The more that comes out about J. D. Tippit, the more we're learning he did odd jobs for Jack Ruby, so I believe Lee came back to the rooming house to weaponize himself with his revolver. He then got in touch with his CIA handler, who told him to go to the Texas Theatre, where witnesses said they saw him moving around to different seats looking for somebody.

Ruth Paine's husband quoted Lee as saying President Kennedy was the best president we ever had. It just makes no sense he would try to kill a man he admired. What I've discovered over the years is the horror of his childhood. His biological father died right before he was born, and he spent the majority of his first five years with his two older brothers in a New Orleans orphanage. His mother remarried and got the boys back. Her new husband was very good to all three boys, especially Lee, but he couldn't tolerate the mother. Everyone I ever met who knew her said she was a real piece of work. It's my opinion she was probably bipolar— unmedicated and undiagnosed—so Lee had a miserable childhood just being her son.

He had a very disruptive childhood; she moved the family constantly, then add the dyslexia on top of that. That's why I believe these government agencies could manipulate a young man like Lee because he had a strong need to be accepted into an elite group like the CIA or FBI.

Do you think he was a complicated man?
Yes. He was a very complicated man. He had a profound love of children, and I think if he had been born in today's world, he would've been more

Lee Harvey Oswald, his wife, Marina, and their daughter June. (Photo by ©
CORBIS/Corbis via Getty Images).

than happy to work with children because he had the capacity to give of
himself. He had a lousy childhood, and I think his goal was to give his girls
the best world they could have. He played with my brothers for two to three

hours at a time. As adults, most of us are too busy and disinterested to do that, so he had a capacity for kindness and patience most adults don't have.

He had marks against him growing up, but he made the best of it. He was definitely a good man, a kind man. I can say, categorically, that the man I knew as a little girl would *not* be guilty of doing what he allegedly did in shooting the president of the United States. And that's why it's been such an injustice.

When people tour the museum, what do you tell them?
I take them to his room and the living room where all the renters hung out and watched TV, but we mostly just sit and talk about Mr. Lee, and I share my memories. I love meeting people and seeing their reactions. Some of them are very surprised because they come in with a mind-set of him being the lone gunman, but by the time they leave, they realize they want to do more research. Others come in thinking it was a conspiracy, so they leave wanting to do more research, as well, but everyone leaves feeling like they know the man a little better, especially on a personal level and as an actual human being, which is quite profound.

If the government opens all its documents, without blacklining everything, shows real proof Oswald did the shooting, and answers all the unanswered questions, I'll be the first one to stand up and say I was wrong, but I don't foresee that ever happening. And I can't, in good conscience, knowing Lee the way I knew him, say he was the lone-nut gunman. I just can't say it.

Why does the JFK assassination still matter all these years later?
I believe President Kennedy was the last president who was for the entire country. He didn't owe his loyalty to any special interest group, so it's important to remember who he was as a president. America lost its innocence when he was murdered because we were suddenly faced with the fact that people in our own government were so devious, they could actually do something like this and lie about it to protect "the little people." We have a right to know the truth, and they've been hiding the truth about this for almost sixty years. It's insulting to all of us, to every one of us. He was "our" president, not "their" president.

And Oswald was killed before he could tell us exactly what was going on; he never had his day in court. They didn't charge him with the assassination when he was alive; they did it posthumously. And our history books are watered down. The only thing our kids learn about the assassination is that Lee Harvey Oswald shot President Kennedy. Period. That's it. That's all that's said about it. And look at the turmoil our country is in right now. It's as if the lies and cover-ups have festered over the years, and this has taken a terrible toll on the country.

Do you feel you and your family are forever tied to the JFK assassination?
I feel tied to the assassination, but my children and grandchildren aren't. When I'm gone, that association ends. I'm glad my brothers and I knew Lee Harvey Oswald, knew a man who has been misunderstood all these years, and I'm proud I'm able to speak for him and say, "You've got it all wrong."

I've already lost both of my brothers, and at a very young age. They rarely spoke about Mr. Lee because they were traumatized much more than I was. They both got into drugs, and that's how I lost them. I still get people from my high school saying on Facebook, "Oh my god, I never knew you knew Lee Harvey Oswald." My brothers probably talked to each other about it more than they talked to me about it. When my parents got divorced, my mom had to work constantly, and sometimes we didn't see her for days, so I was the one who became responsible for my brothers, getting them to school, etc. I was more like a mother to them, not a sister they could confide in about something like that. At their funerals, people came up to me and said they called me "little momma" because they always thought of me that way. It would've been fun to know them as a sister, though.

But as far as Lee Harvey Oswald is concerned, I'm just honored I can speak the truth for him. At the very least, he has been misrepresented by the "official story." He wasn't a malcontent or a nut job. He was one of the kindest men I've ever known.

PART 5

THE DEEP STATE AND THE FOURTH ESTATE

I had no idea that my life would be turned upside down and inside out—that I'd be assigned to walk into what I now call "the buzzsaw." The buzzsaw is what can rip through you when you try to investigate or expose anything this country's large institutions—be they corporate or government—want kept under wraps. The system fights back with official lies, disinformation, and stonewalling.

—*Into the Buzzsaw*, Kristina Borjesson
Investigative journalist and news producer

CHAPTER 15

PETER DALE SCOTT

Peter Dale Scott, a former Canadian diplomat and English professor at the University of California, Berkeley, is a poet, writer, and researcher. Before teaching at UC Berkeley, he served for four years as a Canadian diplomat at UN Assemblies and in Warsaw, Poland. An antiwar speaker during the Vietnam and Gulf Wars, he was a cofounder of the Peace and Conflict Studies Program at UC Berkeley, and of the Coalition on Political Assassinations (COPA). His prose books include *The War Conspiracy*; *The Assassinations: Dallas and Beyond*; *Crime and Cover-Up: The CIA, the Mafia, and the Dallas-Watergate Connection*; *The Iran-Contra Connection*; *Cocaine Politics: Drugs, Armies, and the CIA in Central America*; *Deep Politics and the Death of JFK*; *Oswald, Mexico, and Deep Politics*; *The Road to 9/11*; *The War Conspiracy: JFK, 9/11 and the Deep Politics of War*; *American War Machine*; *The American Deep State: Big Money, Big Oil, and the Struggle for US Democracy*; *Dallas '63*; and *Poetry and Terror*. His research has centered on US covert operations, their impact on democracy at home and abroad, and their relationship to the JFK assassination and the global drug traffic. His encyclopedic knowledge enables him to connect the dots among the players, the organizations, and the unacknowledged collusions—the deep politics—of our often-troubled political system. He believes international public opinion, when it becomes powerful enough, will become the most effective restraint to the excesses and follies of particular governments.

What is the "deep state," and what does its complex network look like?

The deep state is best defined negatively, as the system and processes of political power not open, recognized, and controlled by law. In *The American Deep State*, I identified the deep state with what I had earlier called the deep political system, "which habitually resorts to decision-making and enforcement procedures outside as well as inside those publicly sanctioned by law and society." I noted how top-level Treasury officials, CIA officers, and Wall Street bankers and lawyers all think much alike because of the "revolving door" by which they pass easily from private to public service and back.

The term "deep state" (*derin devlet*) was coined in Turkey to explain the so-called Susurluk incident, a lethal 1996 car crash whose victims included the deputy chief of the Istanbul Police Department, a member of Parliament, and Abdullah Çatlı, an international heroin trafficker and killer recruited by the Turkish police for "special missions" and paid in heroin while he was officially being sought by the Turkish authorities for murder.

The term "deep state" can be misleading. States are far more structured than the deep state, which defies clear definitions, and would in fact be misrepresented by any clear definition. For example, Tom Hayden's[1] notion of a "state within a state" is too restricted: those with that inner power (such as the higher echelons of the CIA) exercise it not by their seclusion, but by their interactions with an outside overworld.

And Mike Lofgren's[2] metaphor of the deep state as an iceberg, though useful, risks suggesting a too solid or structural relationship to society. Unlike the state, the deep state is less a structure than a system, as difficult to define, but also as real and powerful, as a weather system.

And like a weather system, the deep state contains conflicting currents within it. The deep conflict in US society today mirrors a deep conflict between nationalist and internationalist elements in the deep state, as well. This conflict is not new but goes back for at least a century.

A closer antecedent for the term "deep state" would be "the establishment," as defined for England in a famous 1955 essay by Henry Fairlie, in which he said:

By the "Establishment" I do not mean only the centers of official power—though they are certainly part of it—but rather the whole matrix of official and social relations within which power is exercised. The exercise of power in Britain (more specifically, in England) cannot be understood unless it is recognized that it is exercised socially.

Fairlie was a Tory, and the target of his satiric essay was the Whig consensus, dating back to the first Hanoverian kings, that in 1936 had forced the abdication of King Edward VIII. But the Tories, the party of nostalgia for an imagined former glory, are also an enduring part of the British deep state, just as Trump's MAGA backers, the heirs of the John Birch Society, are part of America's.

However, what Fairlie described in the British establishment was only that part of it serving as a restraining rather than an activist force. The

Allen W. Dulles, who served the interests of America's corporate and war-making elites, was Director of the CIA from 1953 until 1961, when President Kennedy fired him for lying about the Bay of Pigs. (Source: Bettmann via Getty Images)

part, in short, that is distinguishable from America's deep state, currently concerned to impose and preserve American hegemony in the world.

What are some examples of deep-state entities?

Today, the deep state is partly institutionalized in nonaccountable intelligence agencies like the CIA and NSA, but it also extends its reach to private institutions like Booz Allen Hamilton and SAIC, to which 70 percent of intelligence budgets are outsourced.

And behind these public and private institutions is the influence of Wall Street bankers and lawyers, allied with international oil companies beyond the reach of domestic law. They, in turn, function increasingly with their foreign peers as part of a growing international deep state.

To preserve America's traditional constitutional framework, it is important to see how particular cabals—such as the Project for the New American Century[3]—have repeatedly used invisible powers and networks—such as Continuity of Government or COG and its so-called "Doomsday Network"—to prepare for unpopular wars.

The political concerns and activities of the deep state are the chief source and milieu of what I've elsewhere called "deep politics," or all those political practices and arrangements, deliberate or not, that are usually repressed rather than acknowledged.

The biggest difference between my description of the deep state and those by Mike Lofgren and Michael Glennon[4] is that, unlike them, I focus on the underreported influence in the deep state of both the overworld (e.g., Wall Street, big oil companies, and their law firms) and the underworld (e.g., mafia-controlled unions used for strikebreaking by tycoons like Henry Ford, world's leading international drug traffickers used and protected by the CIA both abroad and domestically, etc.).

I also emphasize the role of the media in reinforcing the parameters of the so-called "Overton window"—politically acceptable issues for debate. And finally, I see the influence of the deep state in "deep events"—those misreported and covered-up disruptions of our politics (such as the Kennedy assassinations, Watergate, and 9/11) that have contributed to the erosion of our democracy and the American dream of an open society.

The similarities and overlaps of these recent deep events are in fact the most compelling evidence I know for the existence, influence, and present corruption of the American deep state.

Deep states are the residues of past, hopefully anachronistic top-down power; but this doesn't mean democracies are now mature enough to dispense with them. On the contrary, a deep state might still be useful to help a large society generate a solution to disruptive crises like climate change.

Can you describe how the deep politics of the early 1960s played a significant role in the "why" of the JFK assassination?
A consensus developed among people with significant influence that JFK was threatening what might be called the deep status quo. Along with elements inside government agencies, they were able to develop a plot that the government, facing exposure of its secrets, could be relied on to cover up.

In *The War Conspiracy: JFK, 9/11 and the Deep Politics of War* and elsewhere, I argue that JFK's death wasn't just an isolated case, but rather a

The Vietnam War was an economic boon for corporate and war-making elites.
(Photo by Patrick Christain/Stringer/Getty Images)

symptom of hidden processes associated with the deep politics of the early 1960s. Central among the tensions within the deep state at that time was the threat of US foreign troop commitments to the gold standard still maintained for the defense of the US dollar. Kennedy's plans to withdraw troops from Vietnam, which were offensive to a powerful anti-Kennedy military and political coalition, were secretly annulled when Johnson came to power. The split between Kennedy and his Joint Chiefs of Staff, and the collaboration between Army Intelligence and the Dallas Police in 1963, are two of the several missing pieces that need to be added to the puzzle of who killed Kennedy and why.

What have been the ripple effects of the JFK assassination?

The ripple effects of the assassination include increased militarization, restrictions on constitutional rights and income disparity, as well as increased CIA involvement in domestic security, more foreign wars, and the use with impunity of further deep events, not unrelated—notably Watergate and 9/11—to sustain the long-term agenda of foreign military involvement that JFK was moving to redefine.

Since the end of World War II and the start of the Cold War, the US government changed immensely in both function and scope, from protecting and nurturing a relatively isolated country to assuming ever-greater responsibility for controlling world politics in the name of freedom and democracy. The Kennedy assassination was central to this historic reversal and cemented the Deep State's total control.

In *The War Conspiracy: JFK, 9/11 and the Deep Politics of War*, I explore the link between the assassination of JFK and 9/11, showing how both events were used to influence war policy. Events such as these drive war policy, especially in the case of Kennedy because he was actively directing a move toward world peace and the end of the Cold War when he was assassinated. These "domestic tragedies" have been used to manipulate our country's direction, and when we analyze the causes of war and the long-lasting effects that major events in American history have on foreign and military policies, we see that deep politics exerts a profound but too-little-understood influence on all of it.

What is the cost of conspiracy—the cost of a secret cabal of powerful men manipulating the public and shaping US policies for their own interests—especially over time?

The cost is extensive and includes trivialization of constitutional politics, the weakening of party-political control over issues of profound importance such as the military budget and global warming, increasing cynicism and disbelief in democracy, and eventually perhaps the risk of World War III.

Was setting Lee Harvey Oswald up as a patsy simply part of the deep state's playbook?

The careful selection of an intelligence-related designated culprit or culprits is a central element of planning for a deep event. Oswald was an ideal designated culprit because the plotters knew that the CIA's use of his name in a counterintelligence operation, just a few weeks before the assassination, would force the CIA to protect this embarrassing secret and help generate and participate in a cover-up.[5]

Is the United States still a democracy, or has it morphed into something completely different?

America as a democracy has always been deeply flawed, but over time it has also addressed some of its biggest flaws. Some believe our country's openness to major change could be a threat to democracy, but I think better to regard it as a cause for hope.

CHAPTER 16

DONALD JEFFRIES

Donald Jeffries has been a JFK assassination researcher since the mid-1970s, when he was a teenage volunteer for Mark Lane's Citizen's Commission of Inquiry. His first novel, *The Unreals*, was published in 2007. His first non-fiction book, *Hidden History: An Expose of Modern Crimes, Conspiracies, and Cover-Ups in American Politics*, was released in 2014 and quickly became a bestseller. In it, starting with the assassination of President John F. Kennedy, he chronicles a wide variety of issues that have plagued our country's history. His other nonfiction books include *Survival of the Richest, Crimes and Cover-ups in American Politics: 1776–1963* and *Bullyocracy*.

What inspired you to write *Hidden History* and take a deep dive into political mischief?
In the mid-1970s, I volunteered to help Mark Lane's Citizen's Commission of Inquiry. His book, *Rush to Judgment*, is probably still the biggest seller of all JFK assassination books. He was my hero, my mentor. I guess it's a certain personality, but those of us who become interested in the JFK assassination become obsessed with it. We get immersed in the minutiae. I had to read every book. I went to my library and got the twenty-six volumes of the Warren Commission Report. I didn't go through the exhibits because they were boring, but I read all the testimony.

I was mainly a novelist, and I talked a lot about the JFK assassination in my 2007 novel *The Unreals*, but eventually I tried my hand at nonfiction. I wrote *Hidden History* with a strong emphasis on the JFK assassination and many other issues, too. I think these things are tied together, but a lot of people in the JFK research community don't. They tend to think the JFK assassination was a stand-alone thing. I tell them our leaders didn't suddenly become corrupt on November 22, 1963, and then went back to normal afterward. This is standard operating procedure for them. Governments are corrupt, and ours is no different.

I was a liberal Democrat as a young man. My family loved the Kennedys. We were Catholic, so we were extremely proud of him being the first Catholic president. One of my first memories was watching the saturated news coverage of the assassination on TV. I was seven years old, and I remember my family watching all of it. None of them believed Lee Harvey Oswald did it, so I was asking questions at a very young age. In fact, nobody I knew bought the official story, and I never bought it, either.

I write about a lot of other things, but this is something you can't close the door on once you open it. I get very passionate about it, as people who know me for years will tell you. They get sick of hearing me, but fortunately I can write about it and talk to people like you who actually want to hear it.

Why is the JFK assassination the jumping-off point for modern conspiracies and cover-ups?
A lot of people told me when I wrote *Hidden History*, because I start the book with the JFK assassination, that corruption and conspiracy didn't begin there, and I knew that. That's why I wrote *Crimes and Cover-ups in American Politics: 1776–1963* as a prequel to *Hidden History*. It shows that political crimes and cover-ups didn't start with the Kennedy assassination but instead began with the birth of our nation.

But for people like me, for Baby Boomers, the JFK assassination was possibly the central event of their lives, and certainly of their childhoods, and especially those who were older than me and in high school and who were thinking about joining the Peace Corps because they were inspired by JFK and his idealism. For them, this was an earth-shattering event that had a huge impact on their lives.

There's this kind of hackneyed cliché that our innocence died with the assassination, but there's a lot of validity to that because it set the template for the 1960s. You can make an argument that on November 22, 1963, America was at its peak as a nation economically, culturally, and in the way the world looked at us. Ever since then, if you look at a graph, it's been a straight downward decline.

When you look at major events that have happened since, you can tie many of them back to the JFK assassination, because so many things are connected . . . the RFK assassination, MLK Jr. assassination, and certainly the Vietnam War. Oliver Stone got it right in *JFK*, and I'm glad he emphasized National Security Action Memorandum (NSAM) 263[1] in the film, because I believe that was the main reason JFK was assassinated. He was undoubtedly planning on withdrawing from Vietnam and wanted all troops out by 1965. Just imagine the 1960s if that had happened.

Everything would've been different. We wouldn't have had the anti-war protests and the rise of the counterculture . . . hippies may not have

McGeorge Bundy, President Kennedy's National Security Advisor, drafted National Security Action Memorandum (NSAM) 273, which completely contradicted JFK's NSAM 263, the day before Kennedy's assassination. NSAM 273 paved the way for military escalation in Vietnam. (Source: Bettmann via Getty Images)

existed. All of this was born from the JFK assassination; nobody talks about its impact, but that's what lit the fire on this stuff.

If you want a conspiracy, a conspirator, I've got one for you—McGeorge Bundy,[2] Kennedy's National Security Advisor. He drafted NSAM 273 the day before the assassination, and he had to have known this completely contradicted JFK's NSAM 263, which had just been written and implemented. NSAM 273 turned NSAM 263 on its head and paved the way for escalation in Vietnam. If you're not a conspirator, you don't do this because JFK is your boss, and he would've probably fired you for writing it. These are the things you see, and they're there for us to see. And when I say these things are connected, they are.

You've researched these crimes and cover-ups by our nation's leaders (and very powerful individuals) throughout US history. As a result, what conclusions have you come to in regard to the future of this country?
When we see what's happening today, where the country is literally collapsing, we didn't arrive at this point accidentally. I talk about it in the introduction to *Hidden History*, when you look at these series of events and disastrous decisions made by our so-called representatives, over and over again, the results aren't going to be good. Awful trade deals, terrible legislation that favors the few over the many, political and economic graft . . . all of these things. And it's finally reached a critical mass. In 1963 the infrastructure was still new because it was upgraded during the Eisenhower years, but it hasn't been touched since . . . in sixty years. So, we're literally watching it crumble today.

When you have these priorities, these senseless wars . . . and again, JFK was the only president in history who rejected the overtures of the military-industrial complex over and over again. They kept trying to get him and Bobby to go to war during the Cuban Missile Crisis. The president and his brother were the only ones who didn't want to go to war with Cuba. They were battling Cold Warriors like General Curtis LeMay, who may very well have been involved with the planning of the assassination. Kennedy's Joint Chiefs of Staff all wanted war, but he stood strong and said, "No. We're not going to war with Cuba, and we're also going to withdraw from Vietnam."

This contradicted everything about our foreign policy before him . . . and certainly since. His assassination led to things like our perpetual involvement in places like Iraq and Afghanistan. I don't think these things would've happened if JFK had lived because the country would've been different, and especially if Bobby Kennedy had become president after John. These men were classic liberal thinkers. They were a dying breed, and they don't exist today.

So, I think the importance of the JFK assassination can't be overstated because it led to all these things, which again are all connected. People tell me all the time, "You think everything is a conspiracy." And I say, "Well, I think our country is being run by conspirators, no question about it. This is what they do. This is how they do business. It's standard operating procedure. They don't know any other way."

Most people understand when I say that, but when others say, "That's going too far. I can believe this but not that," I tell them I never close my mind off like that. I understand how these leaders operate, so I don't put anything past them. I'm not going to automatically say I can't go there because it challenges my belief systems or makes me feel uncomfortable as an American. I'm going to look at it for what it is . . . a crime, a conspiracy, a cover-up . . . because this has been happening since the birth of civilizations and political systems.

How has the media failed as a watchdog, as a Fourth Estate that holds our leaders accountable, and did this start with the JFK assassination? JFK researcher Jim DiEugenio was the first one in his review of my book who said the underlying theme is a condemnation of the media. I write very critically of the media; I call it state-controlled media, and I believe the only difference between our mainstream media and the news agencies TASS and Pravda at the height of the Soviet Union is that Soviet citizens were astute enough to realize it was state-controlled media. Too many Americans believe that CNN and MSNBC actually employ investigative journalists. Many Americans refuse to believe these news anchors and reporters are talking heads for the state and are simply regurgitating whatever the intelligence agencies and government officials tell them.

We first saw this with the JFK assassination because it was the first event that warranted twenty-four-hour news coverage. Dan Rather was a local reporter in Dallas, and he got on television and lied about the Zapruder Film saying, when the American public hadn't seen it yet, that JFK's head went forward, which of course you realize is a huge lie when you actually watch the footage. And guess what, Dan Rather's career took off afterward. And then again, years later when he was hosting the CBS Nightly News, he editorialized against Oliver Stone's movie, *JFK, three* different times.

This was unprecedented, but it shows how important it was for the media to discredit him. He caught incredible flack because he was a big Hollywood director, and he got big Hollywood actors to appear in cameos, and this was something that was beyond the pale.

And this is where the left-right paradigm comes into play because you're going to get Sean Hannity on the right and Rachel Maddow on the left in complete accord on this. They're both going to rip Oliver Stone and attempt to discredit his film before it even hits the theaters. The left and the right will argue about transgender bathrooms all day long, but they all hate conspiracy theories. The CIA created the term "conspiracy theory" in a 1967 memo in order to counter criticism of the Warren Commission Report. That's how it became popular. It was a term created to slander anyone who doubts an official narrative or questions authority.

I remember having Jack Cashill on my radio show. Jack wrote a great, well-researched book titled *First Strike: TWA Flight 800 and the Attack on America*, and he told me we wouldn't be able to write our books if we had real investigative journalists doing their jobs. With all of the hidden history I write and talk about, the media dropped the ball on every one of these issues.

As far as the JFK assassination is concerned, the only reason we're talking today and I know anything about it is because of the early work of citizens like Mark Lane, an attorney; Shirley Martin, a housewife; Harold Weisberg, a retired chicken farmer; Sylvia Meagher, a research analyst; and Penn Jones, a small newspaper editor. These are the individuals who did the work. They're the ones who went through the twenty-six volumes of the Warren Commission Report. Nobody from the *New York Times* or the *Washington Post* did. Instead, these papers slammed these people.

Anthony Lewis was a reporter at the *New York Times*, and he wrote a book attacking Lane, Weisberg, and Meagher, calling them "the critics and scavengers of the Warren Report." Instead of doing his job, Lewis and other mainstream reporters simply attempted to discredit these early researchers, claiming they were alcoholics and saying anything to ridicule them and make them look kooky.

The media have dropped the ball on the JFK assassination and all these other issues, and they prefer not to be skeptical of our authorities at all. They're only skeptical of those who question authority. They're skeptical of the skeptics.

Why has "conspiracy theorist" become such a negative descriptor, especially when the acts of corruption and conspiracy have become so commonplace in American politics?
Back in the 1950s, people would use derogatory terms like "commie" or "pinko." It was a way to shut down what a person was saying if you were unwilling to hear it. If you said, "Well, yeah, he's a pinko," that worked with most Americans back then, but now, in the real world, there are more so-called conspiracy theorists because there are more people willing to question things to some degree. Unfortunately, there are still more people asleep, and we're not going to reach a critical mass until the numbers flip. So, using "conspiracy theorist" to discredit someone still works, and it also keeps people like me off of national television.

It's frustrating because you can't study this and come away believing Lee Harvey Oswald did it. You can't honestly do it. It's impossible. I'm sorry. I believe in freedom of speech. I'm a civil libertarian, but you can't come away with that kind of opinion if you look at the evidence, yet we have people like Howard Stern, who still talks about Oswald being the lone gunman. Richard Belzer, the actor and author, said something that's quite true: "Ninety percent of the American people believe there was a conspiracy to kill JFK, and the other 10 percent work in the government and the media."

Today they've managed to include just about any questioning of official narratives as conspiracy theories. Any questioning of authority is "Oh, that's a conspiracy theory." And that works on those who are still asleep, but those who are awake don't have access to the mainstream media. They don't have a platform; they're certainly not working there. And that's the issue . . . even if we became the majority, we still don't have that kind of power. So that's why using the term "conspiracy theorist" works to discredit anyone who questions anything at this point.

In your opinion, was Lee Harvey Oswald a patsy?
Yes. I believe Jim Garrison was the first one to come up with the idea—and I have no reason to believe otherwise—that Lee Harvey Oswald was an undercover intelligence agent, probably a low-level agent, who was told at the time of the assassination he was infiltrating a group that was plotting to kill Kennedy. And those were the people Oswald was interacting with—Jack Ruby, David Ferrie, Clay Shaw, and the anti-Castro Cubans. That was the group Oswald thought was going to kill JFK, but they were also being manipulated.

I think that's the most obvious reason why Oswald acted the way he did when he was taken into custody. You can see he was flustered and didn't know what he was supposed to say. He was waiting for his handler to tell him. I think that explains why he didn't just blurt everything out. Although at one point he did say he was innocent and just a patsy. Again, I think when you look at the evidence objectively, you have no choice but to walk away knowing Oswald was a patsy.

You talk about "body count" in *Hidden History*, and how it keeps rising as a result of these conspiracies and cover-ups. Why is it important we accept that powerful people are willing to do anything, including commit murder, to maintain and grow their power, wealth, and influence?
If you face that fact, you realize what kind of people you're dealing with, and you can call them out on their behavior. Certainly, some of these heart attacks at young ages . . . I mean these things happen. But when you look at the JFK assassination, there were only a couple of mainstream media reporters digging into it, and the only national reporter was Dorothy Kilgallen.

I recently wrote an article about her, and I didn't realize just how many articles she wrote on the JFK assassination. She was right there from the

beginning questioning the official narrative, and she was going to produce her own book, which would have been unquestionably a bestseller
because she was one of the most famous women in America. She was a
respected investigative reporter, a celebrated columnist of the *New York
Journal-American*, and a radio personality, and she was also a regular on
What's My Line?, a popular TV show at that time.

She socialized with celebrities and had inside sources nobody else had,
and she was the only reporter at Jack Ruby's trial to interview him, not
once but twice. And her death was beyond bizarre. There's no question she
didn't die the way they said she did, which was by accidental overdose of
barbiturates. And, of course, all of her source material on the JFK assassination, which she had been compiling for years, simply disappeared after
her death.

Reporter and TV personality Dorothy Kilgallen was uncovering what she believed
was a massive conspiracy and cover-up in the assassination of President
Kennedy. She was found dead on November 8, 1965, of an "accidental
overdose" days before leaving for New Orleans to meet with an informant. Her
research files were never found. (Source: Bettmann via Getty Images)

The other mainstream journalist, Jim Koethe, was covering the assassination for the *Dallas Times Herald* and had been invited to check out Jack Ruby's apartment the night Ruby shot Oswald. He was also writing a book on the assassination, but he was killed by a karate chop to the throat as he came out of his shower on September 21, 1964. I think it's safe to say that's the only death of that kind on record.

If it's outside of the mafia or the world of entertainment, you have to question it, because in the world of the mundane, the everyday, blue-collar worker world, nobody dies like that. They just don't. But when you're connected to a dubious event and its subsequent cover-up, these types of deaths are all too common. And while some of these deaths may have been organic accidents or heart attacks, there are way too many that strain credulity. The numbers are way too large, and the ways in which some of these people died, like Koethe, are just too strange.

Is it fair to say powerful people go to great lengths and justify anything in order to maintain their power?
Absolutely. And they're very similar to mafia figures. The mafia guys would go to mass right after they ordered a hit. The TV series *The Sopranos* served a purpose because it showed that these guys could lead fairly normal lives. They could be there for their families and interact with their neighbors and so forth. And the power the mafia had in its heyday was nothing compared to the power of the presidency of the United States. I think the evidence is overwhelming that other than a few individuals like JFK, who I believe had a moral compass, most powerful political figures are capable of justifying just about anything.

Take Operation Northwoods, for instance. This was a proposed false flag operation that originated within the US Department of Defense and the Joint Chiefs of Staff in 1962 that called for the CIA and other government operatives to both stage and actually commit acts of terrorism against American military and civilian targets . . . and blame it all on Cuba in order to justify going to war with Castro, even if it led to nuclear war. This is exactly what they were planning in the early 1960s, and JFK, to his eternal credit . . . if he had not been president, it would've happened because nobody else opposed it. Kennedy heard about this and was like,

"That's insane. I'm not signing off on that." And it was another nail in his coffin, but for people who say it can't happen, we had the Gulf of Tonkin incident in 1964, which did happen.

These false flag operations have been going on for a long time. The first one in this country started the Spanish-American War of 1898. The rallying cry was "Remember the Maine," but even establishment historians are now saying the Spanish didn't sink the Maine. Yet that's why we went to war.

Somewhere along the way we forgot what George Washington said about not getting involved in other country's affairs, and the Founding Fathers all agreed with him, but once we went down that path, we never turned back. In 1915, the British joined the false-flag party. The sinking of the Lusitania by German U-boats made headlines across the world at the time, but establishment historians now admit it wasn't as advertised and that it was actually perpetrated by Winston Churchill and the British Admiralty to draw America into World War I.

And whatever happened to Iraq's weapons of mass destruction? It's the same kind of propaganda, yet we fall for it over and over again. And other than JFK, all the other US presidents have gone along with it.

Talk about the power and influence of social hierarchy in this country and how we, as a society, laud sociopathic behavior, thus allowing powerful people to do bold and terrible things, such as assassinate the president.

In *Bullyocracy*, I talk about the bullying in schools and how the school systems enable it over and over again and always defend the bully rather than the victim. That's the basis of the book, but I also talk about a study done on psychopaths and the professions where psychopaths were most prevalent. They're all the most successful occupations—lawyers, doctors, politicians, CEOs, celebrities—not construction workers, file clerks, or fast-food workers.

Why? Because many psychopathic traits are the traits we most admire as a culture—charismatic, grandiose sense of self, lack of remorse or guilt, impulsivity, cunning, and manipulative. Al Neuharth, who founded *USA Today*, said he stepped on all kinds of people on his way to the top. You see this mentality in many CEOs.

I examined the backgrounds of politicians, celebrities, and business leaders, and in almost every case, the overwhelming majority of them were popular in high school. They played some kind of sport. Joe Biden was a football star. Donald Trump was a high school baseball player. A lot of presidents, including Richard Nixon, played college football, and most people don't play college football. Gerald Ford played football at Michigan. George H. W. Bush was a baseball player at Yale. So, these people were part of the "jockocracy," which is essential to the "bullyocracy." Rosie O'Donnell was a prom queen. Would anybody think that? Ruth Bader Ginsburg was a high school cheerleader. Peewee Herman was a high school wrestler. Woody Allen was a baseball and basketball player in high school.

So, my contention in *Bullyocracy* is that the people who run things in high school go on to run society. And that's why they have a vested interest in social hierarchy because it has served them very well.

These are attributes we celebrate, especially in the world of sports, where winning is the only thing. And it doesn't really matter if you cheat, as long as you win. That's why you see so many sports analogies in politics. Politicians love to talk about sports, and they use these analogies all the time because it's part of their makeup. They want to win at all costs. Honor, decency, and morality, on the other hand, are not traits our society lauds. When you have a society where the credo "nice guys finish last" is accepted by all as reality and a true altruism, what does that say about our society?

And this ties directly to political corruption and conspiracy and all the things we're talking about, because if you're willing to do certain things to maintain your hold in the social hierarchy in high school, if you're willing to go along with what the mean girls are doing, if you're willing to do that to keep *that* position, what are you willing to do to keep your position in Congress or as the CEO of a major corporation or as the head of the CIA?

Unfortunately, we don't have any Founding Fathers around today, leaders willing to sacrifice their fortunes for the sake of a principle. And that's the crux of the biscuit now . . . we don't have any statesmen. Nobody has any principles and everybody's for sale, and the psychopathic tendencies all bullies have are reigning supreme. How can I, or we, get ahead? And innocent people get harmed and trampled in the process.

Everyone believes in "the ends justify the means" and in "might makes right." And that's the message we get in the media. How many movies do you watch in which the leading actor *doesn't* punch somebody and get the girl in the end? This is the kind of immature mentality we have as a society now, and it's basically a high school mentality.

Why does the JFK assassination still matter all these years later?
It's the most obvious example of how the most powerful person, theoretically, in the country can be taken out without going to the ballot box. George Bernard Shaw had a great definition of assassination, calling it the ultimate form of censorship, and that's what it is. JFK was literally censored forever.

And it's important because of what happened afterward. People like Noam Chomsky and others try to pretend that nothing changed at all, which is ridiculous. Vietnam was obviously measurably different, and there were no more criticisms of the CIA until the mid-70s when Frank Church's committee came out. JFK was seriously considering abolishing the CIA. Imagine any president attempting to do that now? He called out US Steel and called the steel firm leaders "bastards" in response to them raising steel prices. He went after the oil industry and wanted to cut the rate of the oil depletion allowance from 27.5 percent to 17.5 percent, which would have cost the oil magnates hundreds of millions of dollars in profit. Nobody has attempted to do these things since.

We also need to consider what he represented aesthetically. He wasn't just this great-looking guy; he represented class. We had a very cultured, classy, well-spoken president, and it made America look better. And that's why it was such a culture shock to go from him to this crude inarticulate bumpkin in Lyndon Johnson, who was very much like a southern version of George W. Bush or Donald Trump, where he just couldn't put his words together; he sounded awkward and looked so insincere. To go from Kennedy to Johnson was such a drastic shock to the system collectively for Americans that it shattered our illusions, shattered our innocence, if you will.

It's like a math equation. When you have one of those huge, complex math equations on one of those big boards . . . if any of those numbers are wrong, the answer can't be right. So, if you start at the JFK assassination, the very first number is dramatically wrong. Any numbers that come after are all wrong based on the original wrong number, so the answer is going to be monstrously wrong. And that's the problem we have as a country right now; we can't move forward as a true democracy until we correct the past, which in this case means exposing the truth about the assassination.

There's also the domino effect, where exposing the truth about the JFK assassination leads to the truth about MLK, RFK, and Vietnam. I call the JFK assassination the mother of all conspiracies because it got the most attention and had the most impact outside of maybe 9/11, but because of all these subsequent events and all the chicanery and corruption we see today, the JFK assassination still had the most impact on this country and the world.

What would you want younger generations to understand about the JFK assassination?

I do hear from young people who are interested in the JFK assassination. There's a high school kid who emails me multiple times a day. He's always asking me questions about JFK and other events. It's really cool, really wonderful to see that kind of interest.

Young people need to understand the JFK assassination in the context of its time. The early 1960s epitomized the era coming out of the Eisenhower years, which looked really good in retrospect, with an infrastructure rebuild and a strong economy. The JFK years blended that Eisenhower innocence and the golden era of American prosperity with a new idealism he was infusing. Things like starting the Peace Corps and opening these ideas up to the world. He didn't want to force our idea of freedom on other people at the barrel of a gun; he wanted diplomacy to lead the way to a better world. He wanted the Alliance for Progress[3] in Latin America. He wanted African nations to rule themselves. He supported all these nationalist movements, which no other politician had ever done in his position.

So, it's imperative for young people today to remember who he was. He wasn't perfect. He wasn't Thomas Jefferson, but for a modern politician, he was pretty good. It's important we don't forget the things he was trying to do. And we don't say his death was insignificant because it wasn't insignificant; it had an enormous impact on what happened afterward. And we can still learn the truth about the corruption we see today simply by exposing the truth about his assassination.

Can we turn things around, or is it too late?
I would love to sound optimistic, but it's just impossible. I think things have gotten so bad, especially in 2020. I don't know what to expect anymore, but at this point, the only reason I hold out a ray of hope, and it's probably because I'm a big Frank Capra fan, is because I've always believed in a happy ending. That somehow good will triumph and we'll have a fairytale ending. That's still a part of me, even though I'm cynical because of my research and I believe corruption is everywhere.

Right now, it's hard to be optimistic, but I do hold out a sliver of hope that maybe Frank Capra's off set, getting ready to scream, "Cut!"

CHAPTER 17

JEFFERSON MORLEY

Jefferson Morley is an author and veteran of Washington journalism who has worked as an editor and reporter at *The New Republic, The Nation, Spin Magazine,* and *The Globalist.* He spent fifteen years at the *Washington Post* and washingtonpost.com, where he was World News editor. Morley's first book, *Our Man in Mexico,* is a biography of Winston Scott, an Alabama math teacher turned FBI agent who joined the CIA at its founding and rose to become the chief of the agency's Mexico City station in the 1960s. His next CIA book, *The Ghost: The Secret Life of CIA Spymaster James Jesus Angleton,* tells the story of a paranoid genius who was perhaps the most powerful unelected official in the US government. His forthcoming book about Richard Helms will complete a trilogy about the founding generation of the CIA.

Morley is one of the world's most credible authorities on the Kennedy assassination. He was the plaintiff in a Freedom of Information Act lawsuit against the CIA, which exposed the CIA's obstruction of Congress's investigation of the assassination. He is editor and cofounder of *JFK Facts,* a blog about the JFK assassination. His newest blog, *Deep States,* launched in 2018, monitors the world's secret intelligence agencies.

How and why did you first become interested in the JFK assassination?
I have a very faint memory of the assassination. I was in kindergarten living in St. Louis, and all I remember is everyone sitting around our

black-and-white TV set that weekend. I came to understand it was because
of the Kennedy assassination.

I eventually majored in American History and was interested in that
time period, but I was intrigued by the assassination from a "cultural studies" standpoint rather than an investigative one. I started reading JFK
assassination books and was thoroughly unimpressed because I felt I
couldn't judge the conspiracy question. That changed with Oliver Stone's
movie and the passage of the JFK Assassination Records Collection Act
in 1992. At that point, I'd been in Washington journalism for a long time
and covered the CIA's role in the civil wars in Central America, so I knew
people in the CIA and knew how to read CIA documents.

When the JFK Records Act passed, my big hesitation about the JFK
story—that there was no new information—was no longer true. There
was going to be a lot of new information, and I felt there would be some
great stories in that information.

I knew something about the CIA in Latin America and the history of
the people who were involved in Watergate and how they turned up again
in the 1980s. Basically, I had a sense of the history of CIA covert operations. Sure enough, when the documents started hitting the National
Archives in '92 and '93, I found great stories.

It was fascinating because we had never seen these kinds of operational
records, sensitive communications, and policy memorandums before. I
was looking for JFK stories that were new and not based on conspiratorial
speculation, and these documents provided that.

One of the stories I ran across was how James Angleton went to Mexico
City after the death of Winston Scott and took his published memoir.
I met Michael Scott, Winston's son, and we became friends. He began
sharing information with me, and I wrote a story about his father for the
Coast Style section of the *Washington Post*. That particular story eventually
became my book *Our Man in Mexico*.

**Did the *Washington Post* approve of you writing about the JFK
assassination?**
I arrived at the *Washington Post* in 1992, and the newsroom was very
embittered. I would say not unanimously, but largely, the feeling in the

workplace was Oliver Stone was a bad guy who was very irresponsible. I wasn't the only person in the newsroom who disagreed with this assessment, and when the new documents came out, I was like, "Hey . . . I think there are some good news stories here." They didn't encourage me, but I was right, so my stories got published. Was it popular? No . . . it wasn't popular. Did I care? No . . . I didn't care.

Based on your research, what have you learned about the CIA and its modus operandi, especially in the early 1960s?
A couple of things come across when you study the agency and the culture of the time. The first is the CIA enjoyed complete impunity back then, which is hard for people to understand today. There was no accountability. They could do whatever they wanted, and they knew they could do whatever they wanted. The structures of law we think were in place simply weren't relevant to the world of covert action. I also learned how agency operations were organized and run, how agency communications were structured and how they circulated. But I also approached the research from a strictly journalistic perspective because I never liked the conspiracy paradigm.

Conspiracy is a legal term appropriate for a law enforcement setting. I'm not a prosecutor. I don't know criminal law, and I don't know conspiracy law. I also thought it was a weird way of looking at a historical event. We don't judge our interpretation of any other historical event on whether one theory about it is true or not. We don't have such a binary approach to any other historical event. We don't say Watergate is important or not important because this theory is or isn't true. There's no controlling paradigm except in the JFK story, which was always weird and made me understand it's a unique story in people's conception.

The most striking thing to me was the normal rules of journalism didn't apply to the JFK assassination. Nobody was interested in new information except for whether or not it proved or disproved a conspiracy. I was interested in it for the story value of the secret workings of our government at the time, and especially the aspects of the Kennedy assassination we didn't know about.

I looked at the Kennedy assassination as an intelligence failure. And I mean that in the strictest sense—it was a failure of intelligence procedures for the president of the United States to get shot dead in broad daylight, ipso facto. There's no question about it. There's no theory about it. So how did that failure happen?

To answer that, we need to look at CIA operations at the time and particularly CIA operations around Lee Harvey Oswald because *that's* the key to understanding the intelligence failure of November 22, 1963. I launched my lawsuit against the CIA in 2003 because I realized, especially after 9/11, there wasn't going to be journalistic interest. The world had moved on, the Cold War was over, and we were in a new global paradigm.

I wanted to create a process where there'd be a paper trail so we could at least identify a body of records that might be relevant. My focus changed from doing this research to write a story to a longer-term approach of creating a paper trail, getting it to the community, and developing a fact pattern around these CIA operations to really understand what was going on, who knew what, and how that factored into the events that led to the assassination and all the investigations that followed.

As I did that, I realized I wanted to write about what the JFK story looked like to the men inside the CIA who were closest to it. What Win

James "Jesus" Angleton, CIA Chief of Counterintelligence, has been described as a sinister, powerful, and paranoid man who was at the heart of the CIA for more than three decades. (Source: Bettmann via Getty Images)

Scott thought happened in Dallas was infinitely more important than what I thought, and what James Angleton did before the assassination was infinitely more important than any theory I could develop about it. So, using these personalities, I tried to describe the world as it looked to them in 1963.

What have you learned about the operational failures of the CIA and people like Winston Scott and James Angleton as it applied to Oswald and JFK?

I came to the case in 1992 or 1993, when the JFK Records Act went into effect. And the JFK Review Board was in existence from 1994 to 1998, so a huge body of records came into the public domain during this time period, and we've learned a few things.

One thing stands out as a staggering revelation—the Warren Commission didn't know about the Castro assassination plots because Allen Dulles didn't tell them. Gerald Ford may have known, but there's no evidence that anybody else on the Commission knew about these plots. This is an astonishing omission because if Castro knew the CIA was trying to kill him, it may have been a motivation for him to kill Kennedy. And since Kennedy was killed, allegedly by a Castro supporter, why didn't the CIA look into that as a possible motive of an American enemy?

We don't have the answer to this question, but the CIA definitely didn't look into it. So, we learned that the government didn't want us to know the CIA was trying to kill Castro on the same day somebody killed Kennedy. Knowing this fact alone would've made the Warren Commission do many different things it chose not to do, so this is highly important. The eventual revelation of the Castro assassination plots in 1975 created an outrage in the press that forced Congress to investigate and led to the creation of the Rockefeller Commission,[1] the Church Committee,[2] and the House Select Committee on Assassinations.

We also learned the story of Oswald as a disaffected man of no real interest to US intelligence and law enforcement was a convincing but preposterous cover story. There are about nine mentions of the CIA in the Warren Commission, and they all stress that what the CIA knew was completely routine, and therefore the agency had no interest in Oswald, which is all rubbish. What we've learned since the '90s is that Oswald's CIA intelligence file before November 22 was quite extensive, and the CIA had been closely monitoring him since November 1959. He was being watched for four years before the assassination. The CIA took notice of his actions and was extremely interested in his politics, associations, and personal life, and they collected that information, which wound up in one place inside the CIA . . . James Angleton's office.

So, the intelligence failure of November 22, 1963, was much more profound than anyone could've guessed. If it's true President Kennedy was killed by Oswald—and I'm not saying he was, but let's assume for a moment he was—then the man who killed the president was being watched by the nation's top counterintelligence office for four years, and the CIA took no action to detain, deter, or disrupt him as he made his way toward committing that act. If the full extent of the CIA's preassassination knowledge of Oswald had been known in the '60s, Angleton would've lost his job, and he should've lost this job because the counterintelligence function is to prevent the enemy from doing damage. Oswald had lived in the Soviet Union and acted on behalf of a leftist group that was on the Justice Department's subversive list.

In short, we now know Oswald was the subject of serious intelligence inquiries for four years when he killed the president. The CIA hid all of this, and we didn't learn about it for thirty years. That's highly suspicious, but the defenders of the official story say, "Of course we knew all along the CIA was interested in Oswald." Well, no, we didn't know all along because it was withheld for thirty years, so don't say it's old news.

And as new evidence, what do we make of it? Why was this withheld from all of these noteworthy investigations? It wasn't until we could recreate the unredacted preassassination Oswald file in the early 2000s that we realized the CIA never briefed the Rockefeller Commission, the Church Committee, or the House Select Committee on Assassinations about Angleton's knowledge of Oswald. They've never acknowledged it, and it's still something you're not supposed to talk about inside the agency. If you try and get records related to it, you'll find a lot is still classified fifty-seven years later.

So, what have we learned?

We've learned the CIA was planning to kill Castro on the day Kennedy was killed. We've learned Oswald wasn't a lone nut, but instead was the subject of intense intelligence community interest before the assassination. And the third thing we've learned, as a result of my lawsuit, was there was a propaganda operation around Oswald triggered on the night of November 22, 1963. It was called AMSPELL,[3] and it involved the CIA's assets in Miami who were paid by CIA operative George Joannides[4] through funds provided by Deputy Director of Operations Richard Helms. The AMSPELL operation was tasked with publicizing Oswald's

As the CIA's Deputy Director of Operations, Richard Helms funded AMSPELL, a propaganda operation that attempted to link Lee Harvey Oswald to Cuba. (Source: Bettmann via Getty Images)

link to the Fair Play for Cuba Committee and linking the assassination to Castro. It was a classic propaganda operation paid for by the CIA. I've interviewed the men responsible for it, and they're completely aboveboard about what happened. I don't think they've said everything they know, but they've described those events with some candor.

The defenders of the official story come out and say, "Well, yeah . . . that's all true. CIA assets were linking Oswald to Castro on the night of the assassination, but that was an accident; nobody intended that to happen." Nobody intended for this to happen, but the CIA was paying this money for propaganda and political action, and then these events transpired, and they generated propaganda and engaged in political action.

You simply can't say it's implausible to say somebody wanted that to happen. It *did* happen, and it happened in that sequence. Is this proof of conspiracy? I never said I was going to prove a conspiracy, but it *is* proof there were CIA operations around Oswald that have never been acknowledged by the government. The AMSPELL operation is one of them.

What about FBI documents and its handling or knowledge of Oswald?
Another Intelligence program we've learned about is COINTELPRO, a counterintelligence program conducted by the FBI under the purview of J. Edgar Hoover from 1956 to 1971. But COINTELPRO was also under the purview of James Angleton at the CIA. The way Hoover and Angleton got into business was in the late 1950s, when Angleton wanted to start opening the mail of Americans overseas. He didn't want to have to produce a warrant; he just wanted to be able to do it whenever he deemed it was necessary, so he proposed this to Hoover, who was very nervous about the illegality of it. So, Angleton said, "It will be a CIA program, and I'll share the information we gather with you."

Angleton took responsibility for the mail surveillance and Hoover got the product. Hoover was perfectly happy because there was no political risk for him. Angleton, on the other hand, knew there was political risk. His aides came to him and said, "This is flatly illegal, and we have no cover story available to us." And Angleton said, "Go ahead. Let's do it anyway." And they started opening people's mail illegally.

At the same time, Hoover launched COINTELPRO to discredit and neutralize organizations considered subversive to US political stability. He wanted to go after the communist party, but by the late 1950s, the list of targets expanded, as Hoover perceived many threats—the Socialist Workers Party, Students for a Democratic Society, the Black Panthers, the American Indian Movement, and the New Left. Organizations and individuals associated with the civil rights movement were also targeted, including Martin Luther King, the Southern Christian Leadership Conference, the Congress of Racial Equality, and the NAACP.

Hoover wanted to spy on all of them, and under COINTELPRO, he could do it. And with Angleton's mail surveillance program, he had lots of private information on his targets. COINTELPRO used this information to spread rumors, generate negative press coverage, and disrupt the activities of antiwar and civil rights activists.

The way COINTELPRO worked was that domestically, the FBI took the lead, and internationally, the CIA took the lead. The FBI knew about Oswald and contributed a lot of intelligence to his CIA files, but because he defected to the Soviet Union, the interest was primarily with the CIA. One of the things we've learned in recent years is that the Fair Play for Cuba Committee, of which Oswald was a member, was also targeted for COINTELPRO tactics. These typically involved infiltration, psychological warfare, harassment via the legal system, illegal force, and undermining public opinion.

The CIA has made multiple deceitful statements to law enforcement officials, the Warren Commission, and the House Select Committee on Assassinations in order to hide these operations that involved Oswald, however peripherally. The net effect of the AMSPELL operation was to identify Kennedy's accused assassin with the Fair Play for Cuba Committee and thus the Cuban government. If the CIA didn't plan this outcome—if it was mere coincidence—why are so many of the records associated with it still secret? The agency could release these documents and prove there was nothing there, but instead we've had fifty-eight years of deceptive statements that are then walked back. "We didn't know anything about this," or, "We knew a whole lot and didn't care, but still somehow something happened." It's damage control.

So, who was running AMSPELL? It wasn't George Joannides, the agent whose files I obtained via FOIA litigation. He was a midlevel career guy, supercompetent, but not a leader, definitely not a rogue. He was a company man, diligent, hardworking, and kept his mouth shut. He was sent to Miami by Helms. Who did he report to? Maybe Helms, but as deputy director, Helms had worldwide responsibilities, so he most likely handed off the AMSPELL operation to James Angleton, William Harvey, or David Phillips. If there was a plot to manipulate Oswald and link him to Cuba within hours of the assassination, the individuals running the AMSPELL operation were the most responsible. Who intended to do that and why? It's a very interesting question and an open one. We truly don't know.

An insidious and tangled web of intelligence and counterintelligence operations seems to have been prevalent during the early 1960s, particularly where Castro and Cuba were concerned. Identifying these operations, the men who ran them, and how Oswald was weaved into many of them offers fascinating insight into what may have ultimately led to the assassination of JFK. What else do we know today about these operations that we didn't know when the Warren Commission Report came out?

In the 1990s, we also learned of the existence of Operation Northwoods, a proposed false flag operation against the Cuban Government that originated within the US Department of Defense and Joint Chiefs of Staff in March 1962. The Joint Chiefs wanted to provoke a war with Cuba, and they knew Castro's opposition in Cuba was too divided for a coup to work. They also knew going in and invading a country without provocation would look bad, so they needed a pretense. Operation Northwoods was that pretense, but it was rejected rather abruptly by President Kennedy. The Joint Chiefs wanted to have a discussion, and JFK said, "We're not having a discussion about a false flag operation."

A year later, in May 1963, the Joint Chiefs very quietly revived Operation Northwoods and developed a whole series of plans around it. The task was assigned to the J-2 Planning Staff. They came up with a dozen ways the Joint Chiefs could provoke a war with Cuba, but the paradigm was always the same, which is stage a spectacular crime against an American target and arrange for the blame for that crime to fall on Castro. And when that happens, the president will have the justification for ordering the invasion of Cuba. JFK knew his generals wanted to invade Cuba, and he knew he didn't. So, he ignored the Joint Chiefs, and the Northwoods plan was never implemented.

Yet on November 22, 1963, we had a spectacular crime against an American target, and we had a CIA propaganda operation—AMSPELL—to link the accused assassin to Castro and Cuba. Did someone adapt the Operation Northwoods paradigm to Dallas? The intellectual construct of staging the crime and arranging for the blame to fall on a particular country or individual is *not* a far-fetched proposition. It's not a conspiracy theory; it was the policy of the Joint Chiefs of Staff, and the CIA wholly approved of it.

In a CIA document from May 1963 that the Assassination Records Review Board uncovered, and I wrote about in *The Ghost*, Angleton took particular interest in the security assessment of the Cuban Consulate in Mexico City. Apparently, anyone who sympathized with the Cuban revolution could travel to Cuba undetected through the Cuban Consulate in Mexico City. Angleton identified the Cuban Consulate as a target of some interest to US intelligence and a key to Cuban foreign policy and its efforts to defend itself and project its power in the Western hemisphere.

Angleton's office had been watching Oswald since December 1959, when he returned to the United States from the Soviet Union, and all the FBI reports on Oswald were sent to the counterintelligence staff. In May 1963, Angleton became interested in the Cuban Consulate in Mexico City. In September 1963, the CIA targeted the Fair Play for Cuba Committee. Two weeks later, Oswald, the well-known defector and member of the Fair Play for Cuba Committee, apparently walked into the Cuban Consulate in Mexico City in an attempt to obtain a visa for travel through Cuba to the Soviet Union. His presence there was immediately reported to, no surprise, Angleton's counterintelligence staff.

Oswald was heavily implicated in multiple CIA intelligence gathering operations in 1963. When he walked into the Cuban Consulate on September 27, it triggered LIONION, a CIA photo surveillance program that took pictures of everybody going in and out of the door.⁵ When he was denied a visa and called the Soviet Embassy, it triggered the LIENVOY audio surveillance program, a joint espionage project between the CIA and Mexican government.⁶ When he was arrested on November 22, it triggered the AMSPELL program. The fact he was implicated in these operations isn't really debatable, but what does it mean? It certainly looks like there could've been an intelligence operation to manipulate Oswald, but the CIA won't comment.

In the whole time I was in litigation with the CIA—sixteen years—the agency never once said, "Mr. Morley, George Joannides had nothing to do with the Kennedy assassination. He didn't know anything about it. You're crazy." And they would've had plenty of takers in the press who would've said, "Yeah, Morley's nuts." I believe Joannides had preassassination knowledge of Oswald. He must have had given his position as case officer for the Student Revolutionary Directorate. The CIA never explained his activities at all. They never explained why—fifteen years after running Oswald's antagonists among the Cubans—Joannides was brought back to manage the House Select Committee investigation, during which he stonewalled them.

Joannides didn't say anything about what he was doing in 1963 even when asked direct questions about the DRE. The most plausible explanation is he was brought back to protect an operation in which he participated. His job was to protect CIA sources and methods, and the CIA could probably justify to itself that its sources and methods around Lee Harvey Oswald had to remain secret because America's safety depended on it.

You mentioned the litigation you initiated—*Morley v. CIA*—which continued from 2003 to 2019. Can you elaborate on that?
I ran across this story about George Joannides and how he funded the Cubans who had contact with Oswald before the assassination. Nobody ever knew about this before, certainly not the Warren Commission and not the House Select Committee on Assassinations. I found these Cubans in Miami. They knew Joannides and described him, and they had contemporaneous documentation of their dealings with him. There's no question

that he was brought out of retirement by the CIA in 1978 to stonewall the HSCA investigation.

So, I went to HSCA counsel G. Bob Blakey and HSCA investigator Dan Hardway and asked them, "Did you know who this guy was? Do you know what he was doing in 1963?" And they were dumbfounded. They were appalled and angry. They remembered dealing with this guy during the investigation in 1978, and they understood how he had stonewalled them and what bad faith the CIA had acted on. The CIA had deliberately sanitized a Congressional investigation into the murder of a president.

I tried to interest the *Washington Post* in this story, and the paper supported it. They funded a couple of trips to Miami so I could interview people. When I came forward with the story, nobody said it wasn't a story. Nobody said there were mistakes. Nobody said it was offbeat. Some people said it was conspiracy theory, but when I asked them to point out what in the story was conspiratorial, they couldn't point to anything other than the fact it was new information about the JFK assassination. Yet nobody at the paper wanted to go to bat and publish it.

Why? Washington is a company town where people believe in the government. Culturally, people want to believe the government works, and they don't want to believe their government is capable of something like that. There's a lot of avoidance behavior at this point. The story was very clean, well documented with on-the-record interviews, so there was no speculation in it. It had a strong public interest angle, meaning the CIA screwed a Congressional investigation. It was a good story, but because it was JFK, it was radioactive. Are there pro-CIA people in the *Washington Post* newsroom out to kill such stories? I'm not going to speculate. I loved working at the *Post*. I had great colleagues, but at the end of the day, it wasn't my call, and it didn't go my way.

I moved on, but I didn't like it, so that's when I filed the lawsuit. I thought, "If I do this, maybe they'll cover it down the road," which they didn't. I was personally engaged in the story, especially knowing the CIA screwed the HSCA investigation in 1978. They also tried to lie about Joannides to the Assassination Records Review Board in 1997. I didn't get the key piece of information about Joannides working with the HSCA until the Review Board was out of existence. If I had that piece of paper when it was in existence, they would've looked into it and declassified a lot of information.

So, I sued the CIA in 2003, and in 2004 they coughed up a bunch of documents, some of which were already in the National Archives, some of which weren't, and then they asked me to go away. I appealed and won. I received more documents from the CIA in 2008, so I had a real strong paper trail and body of evidence. That became the factual foundation for which I would build my whole understanding of CIA operations and the JFK assassination, and it's a firm foundation. We understand who Joannides was a lot better now . . . how he was running psychological warfare operations and how he wound up at HSCA. It was a small but very interesting piece of the assassination mosaic that connected Oswald to the CIA and demonstrated how the CIA monitored, thought about and manipulated Oswald.

What did you glean about men like James Angleton and other Cold Warriors from your research?

They were unanimous in their understanding of Communism's political implications, which meant that anybody who made common cause with communists was just as big a danger as Communism itself, and that drove the CIA and US government into bed with authoritarian, right-wing governments. That monolithic view of Communism and applying it to every society in the world, is what led us into the disaster in Vietnam. We held the view we were fighting Communism, and in some ways, it just wasn't based on reality. Men like Angleton and Scott were staunch anticommunists and prisoners of that ideology. They had complete impunity and a cultural respectability to do whatever they wanted to do. In the '50s and '60s, the CIA was the good guys. Journalists didn't question what they were doing because it wasn't the culture. Today it's a different culture, so agency officials can't act in the same way Angleton could.

When Win Scott got out of intelligence and into retirement, he said it was a big waste of time, and he regretted it. He wished he had spent more time with his family and his business. It was a strange, stressful life for these intelligence people. Other people went mad. Frank Wisner, one of the founding officers of the CIA, went off the deep end and committed suicide. In the end, Angleton was a terrible alcoholic, as were many of these guys. The secret life, the life of espionage and covert action, the life of false news and false identities, takes a huge toll.

In the course of doing my work, I've met a lot of CIA kids who are my age and talk about the trauma and the difficulty of growing up in a CIA family, so I always try and bring that kind of personal sympathy to it. I might not approve of somebody like James Angleton, because he was kind of a monster, but I try to understand them as people. I talked to many individuals who knew Angleton and thought he was a special, formidable thinker, and clearly, he had that kind of intellectual charisma.

Were you ever concerned about your career or your safety as a result of your research or the lawsuit? Did you ever think, "Hey, I'm ruffling feathers here"?

I never worried about myself. Was I ruffling feathers? Yeah, but I tried to minimize that. I didn't have a theory, so I wasn't trying to convince anyone of anything. I knew people didn't like it; it was unpopular in the newsroom. It was definitely bad for my career, but I thought it was a good story, and nobody ever came to me and said it wasn't. I felt it was important enough to pursue. The JFK assassination didn't define my career, but I was very interested in doing my books and establishing and completing the historical record of the assassination. I felt like that was an unimpeachable role. Did it cost me? Yeah, but it was worth it.

What have you concluded about the JFK assassination based on your research?

I wanted to withhold judgment until we get all the JFK records, but we still don't have 15,000 records, and I can't wait around anymore, so based on what I know, I think Kennedy was killed by his enemies within the US government, and the CIA assisted in that. Who were the intellectual authors of the crime? There are some plausible suspects who participated in Dallas, but I can't say anything definitive about who those people were. In the US government, they either came from the CIA or the military. I think the Joannides files could shed light on who was behind the propaganda operations around Oswald. But I feel very comfortable saying the

president was killed by his enemies within the US government. That interpretation is much stronger than "one guy killed the president for reasons
nobody knows," which isn't a very credible story.

The Warren Commission fallback is that Oswald was a leftist encouraged by the Cubans, so the crime has a political dimension driven by
those two parties. The biggest problem with the Castro conspiracy theory,
which is the only other one I give credence to, is the CIA never investigated it. Angleton, who was the biggest anticommunist around, could've
investigated the Castro connection. The CIA was trying to kill the guy,
so if they thought he might've been associated with killing Kennedy, why
didn't they investigate? That would've been the perfect justification for
getting rid of Castro, which the CIA and Pentagon thought was over-
due. And the reason they didn't investigate Oswald's Cuban connections
is because most of the leads did *not* go back to the KGB or Cuban intelligence. They went straight back to the CIA and FBI, and they didn't want
that to come out.

**Why is it important for younger generations to inquire about the JFK
assassination and learn everything they can about it?**
We live under a government that has a very large secret sector, and if you
want to understand how the US government works, you need to understand this secret sector, and not in terms of conspiracy theory, but in terms
of real political realities. The Kennedy assassination was the moment in
which those national security agencies had impunity and weren't held
accountable, and the consequences of that in terms of the Vietnam War
and confidence in government are huge. The Kennedy assassination,
whether you know it or not, if you're an American, has affected your life.

The counterargument is, "Well, it's a dead horse. We know everything
we need to know. Somebody would've talked by now," but the point about
the Kennedy assassination is it's a paradigm of what happens when secret
government prevails over Democracy. Why does the United States now
have endless wars? How did we end up in a situation where the country has been at war for twenty years? Something that was unthinkable
in Kennedy's presidency is now the norm. Kennedy had a "strategy for
peace," and he was assassinated. There's a connection.

Are you satisfied with the work you've done?

My lawsuit was the big shot at this. I didn't have support of a publication, but I was able to create a paper trail and have judges talk about what I'm talking about now. For me personally, I didn't get everything I wanted, but I'm satisfied with what I did. I turned up an aspect of the story that's indisputable, and it's there for people to take advantage of and extend further in the future.

PART 6

PSYCHOLOGICAL, PHILOSOPHICAL, AND SOCIAL PERSPECTIVES

"When suspicious incidents occur that alter the nation's objectives, disrupt presidential elections, provoke military action, or otherwise affect the national agenda, Americans tend to accept the self-serving accounts of public officials, seldom considering the possibility that such incidents might have been initiated or facilitated by the officials themselves. The role and function of the universally understood concept of 'agent provocateur' is grossly neglected in the idiom of American political discourse. This mass gullibility, which itself invites SCADs (State Crimes Against Democracy), is unlikely to change until SCAD detection and prosecution are improved."

—Lance deHaven-Smith, PhD
Professor of Public Administration and Policy
Florida State University

CHAPTER 18

FRANCES SHURE

Frances Shure is a retired business owner, Licensed Professional Counselor specializing in depth psychology, and adjunct instructor at Naropa University in Boulder, Colorado. She holds a BS (specializing in biology) and an MEd (specializing in vocational rehabilitation counseling) from the University of Texas, and an MA (specializing in community agency counseling) from the University of Colorado. Having long worked for world peace and a sustainable environment, she is the cofounder of Colorado 9/11 Truth, a member of the 9/11 Consensus Panel, and is listed with Medical Professionals for 9/11 Truth. She authored the groundbreaking series "Why Do Good People Become Silent—Or Worse—About 9/11?" These articles examine the psychological resistance to information that contradicts official accounts or strongly held beliefs, as well as the current state of our corporate media.

When did you realize the official 9/11 narrative was dubious, and in what ways does 9/11 echo the JFK assassination fifty-nine years ago?
On 9/11/01, I watched the collapse of the WTC twin towers on TV, horrified knowing there were thousands of people in those buildings. I found myself saying shortly afterward, "I don't think this could've happened without someone knowing about it and allowing it to happen." But I believed the official narrative that Osama Bin Laden and the alleged hijackers were responsible. Those words must've been a spontaneous

intuitive response since I'd been well trained not to believe in conspiracies. Once I read some of the facts that challenged the official theory—mostly from Nafeez Ahmed's 2002 book *The War on Freedom*—I realized our government wasn't telling us everything about the event.

I haven't studied the JFK assassination in detail. However, from what I've read, this is my understanding regarding the parallels of the JFK assassination and the attacks on 9/11:

1. Researchers found copious credible evidence that disproves the official narratives.
2. Officials engaged in a cover-up: The 9/11 Commission whitewashed the 9/11 attacks just as the Warren Commission covered up the JFK assassination.
3. Media propaganda attempted to quell public interest in the evidence that contradicted both of the official narratives.

The main difference is in the 1960s there was no Internet for the quick spread of alternative information or for researchers to work together.

What is a State Crime Against Democracy, and how did the success of the conspirators in covering up the truth behind the JFK assassination ultimately lead to subsequent SCADs?

The term State Crime Against Democracy (SCAD) was coined by Lance deHaven-Smith, a professor at Florida State University. He coined this term to give a name to illegal or extralegal actions of public officials or elites who subvert democratic processes and undermine popular sovereignty. Basically, they're crimes that attack democracy itself. He did this to encourage social scientists to investigate these high-level crimes by state and elite actors. By distancing themselves from the "conspiracy theory" meme, he hopes social scientists will be more inclined to study the patterns and characteristics of these events as they do with other social issues. The term lends legitimacy to an area of investigation, whereas "conspiracy theory" tends to shut down conversation on an area of legitimate concern.

When a bully gets by with violence, he's emboldened to commit more and bigger atrocities. Thus, when the perpetrators of the JFK assassination (a SCAD) felt they had gotten away with the murder of our president, they (or other bullies) would naturally feel confidence to pull off another, even bigger, staged event. This is true in any context, from the family to the corporation to the nation. By not addressing State Crimes Against Democracy judicially, we perpetuate and increase a culture of unaccountability.

What are some human psychological traits that make it difficult for individuals to question official narratives, even though those official narratives are blatantly false?
There are several . . .

1. Obeying and Believing Authority
Stanley Milgram, with his authority experiments,[1] and Philip Zimbardo, with his Stanford Prison Experiment,[2] clearly demonstrated that human beings have a strong tendency to believe and obey authority. We want to believe our authorities even if their narratives and actions are questionable. We feel safe if we trust our authorities, and we don't feel safe if we sense they're untrustworthy. To challenge their dictates can be downright frightening since authorities normally can wield great power if challenged.

We haven't been educated to be *aware* of our fear and yet act for what we believe is right. So, even if we see that authorities lie or act unscrupulously, we may ignore our perceptions or minimize their actions. We can tend to "go along to get along." This leads directly to another very strong human tendency, which is conformity. Prof. Solomon Asch demonstrated with his "conformity experiments" that over one-third of subjects will give a wrong answer when they clearly perceive the right answer.

2. Doublethink
All defensive human proclivities originate in fear. If we don't believe an authority's narrative, for example, but understand that to challenge that narrative might result in some kind of discomfort or punishment (ostracism by the rest of society, prison, etc.), we may develop the mental contortion of "doublethink," which is the ability to hold two contradictory thoughts in one's mind and accept both of them, using each one as it is appropriate.

The psychological profession doesn't recognize doublethink as a defense. It was coined by George Orwell in his classic novel *1984*. I've observed people indulging in this strategy when asked about 9/11. When I challenged a woman who was demonstrating doublethink in her speech, she said in an exasperated tone, "What am I to do?! I know 9/11 was a false flag, but I'm surrounded by the official narrative—my teachers, my friends, the news. It's everywhere!"

So, out of fear, we can become like chameleons, changing our colors to feel hidden and safe.

3. Denial and Cognitive Dissonance

Denial is the human ability to *not* notice what's obvious. We need our worldview to remain intact to feel safe or "right." So, if we're confronted by evidence that contradicts our worldview, we unconsciously keep it out of consciousness (denial), or we stay away from unpleasant thoughts or situations (avoidance). If we fail to deny or avoid the new evidence, we face the discomfort of cognitive dissonance, a state of disequilibrium and anxiety, which is uncomfortable. We can then try our best to find equilibrium by minimizing the importance of this information or by finding a secondary explanation for it. A third option, however, is to study the facts and change our worldview to reestablish equilibrium.

4. Conformity and the Spiral of Silence

The spiral of silence[3] was a most interesting study on conformity conducted by Elizabeth Noelle-Neumann in Germany. She learned that many people would make up their minds in the last hours of an election and "jump on the bandwagon" of the "expected" winner. In interviewing these people, she found that, again, fear persuaded them to "run with the pack" in order to be on the winning side, in order not to be seen as a loser and thus be avoided by their fellow humans. She concluded these "run with the pack" people had low self-esteem.

5. Groupthink

Groupthink is a dynamic observed by Professor Irvin Janis of Yale.[4] Conformity can help societies function more smoothly, but sometimes people in groups who are making decisions apply peer pressure to get the whole group to conform to a belief. This is a dysfunctional form of conformity that can result in bad decisions and an inflated sense of certainty. We can see this dynamic in small groups, large groups, or in whole societies. People will naturally fear ostracism from group members when peer pressure is applied to "get with the program," so to speak.

If fear of ostracism is involved, groupthink is a likely dynamic. Surely, this example would apply to any resistance to further investigating the assassinations of JFK, RFK, MLK, and Malcolm X.

People in truth, peace, and justice movements can also be subject to groupthink. Any group of people can become attached to certain theories, and if evidence comes along that contradicts that theory, the members of the group can try to ostracize those who hold different views, even if those views are scientifically validated.

6. Learned Helplessness

When animals or people are subjected to a perceived or real traumatic situation in which they are helpless, they can become conditioned to "learned helplessness." What this means is after such a trauma, they'll tend to react to any overwhelming event or information by not engaging, by not trying to escape or confront the new situation.

As a therapist who has helped people heal from very early, overwhelming trauma, I suspect some of these clients were conditioned to this state of learned helplessness, and I suspect when these traumatized individuals are presented with evidence that suggests 9/11 was a false flag event, they're triggered into that state of overwhelm, and thus don't want to engage with that information. I also suspect those who are passive and apathetic and don't want to listen with an open mind to evidence concerning the government's involvement with the JFK assassination may have this dynamic in their background.

7. Abuse Syndrome and Disassociation

When we have trauma that conditions us to passively accept abuse, we may see abuse by our government or authorities as normal and not confront it. This sense of powerlessness can result in shame and apathy, rather than constructive action. When our authorities abuse us, the memory of past abuse in which we dissociated may be triggered, resulting in dissociating in the present. We then may become "spaced out" and unable to respond from an empowered place. This is a physiological reaction that can't be healed by simple awareness. It takes deeper therapeutic work to resolve that early trauma.

In summary, if we have trauma that makes it especially threatening to confront official false narratives, we have a variety of defense dynamics that help us maintain our emotional equilibrium and keep our traumas repressed. If we're afraid of questioning authorities for reasons other than personal trauma, there are other dynamics that keep us superficially in agreement with the blatantly false official narrative. Examples are our human tendencies to believe and obey authority and to conform. In the end, fear motivates us to "go along to get along," rather than take constructive action against false narratives.

Chief Justice Earl Warren presents the Warren Commission Report to President Lyndon Johnson at the White House on September 24, 1964. (Photo by: Cecil Stoughton/PhotoQuest/Getty Images)

From a moral psychology perspective, what prevents journalists, attorneys, congressional representatives, and others with the ability to expose the truth from doing so?

The study of moral psychology tells us our brains are wired for well-being. Confronting official narratives could result in ridicule and ostracism from one's peer group and sometimes even one's family. This is especially true for highly visible people such as journalists, attorneys, academics, and congressional representatives. They especially are subject to character assassination and thus can become pariahs among their associates. As a result, their innate drive toward well-being will keep them from seeing the evidence (denial), or if they see the evidence, they'll conform to the official narrative to maintain their places in society.

Of course, there are always a few who choose integrity and truth over well-being—or perhaps I should say their internal well-being depends on being fully in their integrity. These individuals have learned to not let fear rule them and will, therefore, speak out in spite of the psychological punishment their associates wield against them.

How did the sacred myth of American Exceptionalism (especially in 1963) blind people to the truth about the JFK assassination?

Many if not most Americans will readily believe that assassinations of leaders are a reality in other countries, especially those we don't closely identify with, such as Latin American countries and communist-controlled countries. Our firm belief is America is an exceptional country where such things don't happen, and this blinds us to the evidence that points to a conspiratorial group that assassinated JFK, rather than a lone shooter.

Why can't some people separate themselves from their image of their nation?

First, we're educated by our society to identify with America and believe she is "exceptional." However, this dynamic can go much deeper. If we're raised since infancy in a way that we aren't recognized as a separate individual, we probably won't develop a strong, internal sense of self. People with a solid sense of self see themselves as unique individuals, capable of recognizing their feelings and needs, and confident they can meet those needs constructively.

If we haven't been able to develop this solid sense of self, however, we develop instead a "false self," an image that corresponds to what our parents needed us to be. We feel empty, and we fill this emptiness with objects our image can identify with, such as a beautiful spouse, big house, academic degrees, motorcycle or fancy car, wealthy or macho friends. We can also identify excessively with a political party, a religion, and even our nation. Since we have no real sense of internal self, these objects become part of our identity. Thus, anyone who criticizes any of these symbols is seen as criticizing us.

When confronted with the assertion that members of our government (authority figures) wittingly committed insidious and malevolent acts such as the JFK assassination, why is it so hard for us to believe?
In spite of the historical evidence of the atrocities humans have committed on other humans, we may "refuse to believe" that in our day and age and in our country, such atrocities aren't only possible, but likely. People who don't want to perceive these current atrocities in our own country very likely know about the brutalities of Alexander the Great, Rome, and various European empires. Likely they know about the genocides in Nazi Germany, Rwanda, and Indonesia, and even in this country with the Native Americans. So, this refusal to believe in atrocities such as the assassinations of JFK, RFK, Martin Luther King, and Malcolm X must have multiple reasons. The first being American Exceptionalism: "This doesn't happen in America." (And if I learned it did, I wouldn't feel safe.)

What these people haven't considered is that (depending on who you read) between 1 percent and 4 percent of Americans are true psychopaths, which means they have an organic brain disorder that prevents them from feeling empathy or love, and from having a conscience. While they look normal, they can manipulate or murder without remorse. Since gaining power is their main motivation, if they have the family background and enough intelligence, they can rise to the top of a corporation or nation. And if they live in a culture that values domination, rising to the top is much easier.

Other people who aren't true psychopaths are also incapable of empathy or love. They may have had inadequate bonding as an infant and so developed reactive attachment disorder. Some, due to inadequate parenting, developed narcissistic personality disorder or borderline personality disorder (according to some psychologists). Some people may have had brain injuries that limit their ability to feel empathy or love.

Also, our world history of genocides and the brutality of empires shows us normal people can also commit atrocities if the conditions are supportive. Milgram's authority experiments clearly demonstrated fully two-thirds of us would be willing to risk a person's life if an authority egged us on.

People have said to me regarding my 9/11 activism: "Think about what you're saying! What *monsters* could do such a thing?" Others have actually said, "I refuse to believe that many Americans could be that satanically treasonous! Someone would have talked!"

Claims of human violence on such a massive scale are sometimes incomprehensible to many of us who are fortunate enough to be gifted with a conscience and with empathy for others. But these statements of horror also reveal how much fear is provoked simply by hearing someone consider that 9/11 might be a false flag operation. These people wouldn't feel safe if they thought it could be true that 9/11 was perpetrated by elements in our national security state. For some of these people, their reaction would be the same regarding the JFK, RFK, MLK, and Malcolm X assassinations.

What was Operation Mockingbird and why is this critical to understanding the failure of the Fourth Estate to hold our government and corporate institutions accountable?

Operation Mockingbird[5] is popularly understood to mean the CIA's infiltration of our major media. The term was first used by Deborah Davis in her book, *Katharine the Great,* but Davis doesn't tell us who revealed this term to her. Nevertheless, since the Church and Pike Committees[6] proved the CIA had indeed used journalists for information gathering and disseminating propaganda, as well as planted agents inside the media, the term has popularly stuck to describe this operation.

Since much of the media are still tightly entangled with the CIA and the Pentagon, and very often press releases from these two entities are used virtually verbatim as "news," the media don't fulfill their Fourth Estate function of being a watchdog over power. Instead, the corporate media act as lapdogs and stenographers for these powerful entities and the White House.

Most Americans aren't aware of this fact, in spite of the Church and Pike hearings. However, Americans have nevertheless steadily lost trust in the media. Gallup polling shows the highest rating of 72 percent in 1976 due to the reporting on the Vietnam War and the Watergate scandal. That compares to 32 percent trust in 2016 that the media report news "fully, accurately, and fairly."

My study of the media demonstrates two reasons account for why investigative journalists can't get their important stories in the news.

First is the influence of powerful entities. Investigative journalists themselves have revealed these entities are the CIA, the FBI, the Pentagon, military intelligence, media owners (with conflicting political agendas), the White House, advertisers, powerful family dynasties, and extremely wealthy individuals.

The second reason investigative journalists can't get their stories in the news is the structure of the corporate media itself. Our global media have become subsidiaries of megacorporate conglomerates that contain many industries, including the manufacture of weapons for the military.

For example, General Electric used to be the parent company of MSNBC. Since GE is part of the military-industrial complex, how willing would MSNBC be to question regime-change wars? Could this be at least one of the reasons the station purged all of its antiwar anchors? Also, since advertising is one of the main revenue sources for these news corporations, how willing would any of the news agencies be to report on any wrongdoing of these businesses?

The price of stock shares is the bottom line for corporations, not information the public has a right to know. For this reason, the news agencies avoid controversial issues, such as the JFK assassination, and they instead focus on trivial and sensational stories.

What are possible solutions to the failure of the media to fulfill their primary duty—reporting the truth—so citizens can make informed decisions?

The corporate media won't change because they're mired in their bottom lines of price shares and repeating official press releases. They aren't committed to airing controversial information the public has a right to know. Nevertheless, enforcing antitrust laws and thus breaking up the huge media monopolies is the No. 1 priority for getting some variety in news as well as reducing their inordinate influence on government. This includes social media monopolies as well as broadcasting and print media. But solutions will come from the grassroots, not from authorities who benefit from the current "propaganda model" of the media, as explained by Edward Herman and Noam Chomsky in their scholarly classic *Manufacturing Consent.*

We must also work for and vote for representative and presidential candidates who don't take legalized corporate bribes, and who therefore support the needs of everyday people, rather than corporations. We must elect politicians who support antitrust laws and who value the "marketplace of ideas," rather than corporate/government censorship.

The English-speaking world still has some excellent investigative journalists, none of whom work for the corporate media. I'm thinking of Glenn Greenwald, Abby Martin, John Pilger, Michel Chossudovsky, Kristina Borjesson, Aaron Maté, Max Blumenthal, Amy Goodman, James Corbett, and Chris Hedges. One may not agree with everything each of them reports (or doesn't report), but they're generally good sources of in-depth information we all need to know. We must support them financially and by subscribing to their YouTube channels.

There's an apropos quote from Supreme Court Justice Louis Brandeis, who said the ideal remedy for exposing falsehoods is "more speech, not enforced silence."

Censorship and propaganda are two sides of the same coin. Propaganda can only survive with its partner, censorship, which allows falsehoods and propaganda to run rampantly unchecked. In essence, it's up to us to try to keep what we have left of the "marketplace of ideas," which is crucial to a democracy.

What have been the ripple effects of the JFK assassination?

The word "corruption" is much too weak to describe the abuse of everyday people by government and elite entities today. Whenever abuse or atrocities go unchecked, this empowers those in power to get away with more and bigger abuse and atrocities. It's the same in any group, whether this is a nation or a family. Bullies have to be held accountable, not for revenge, but to bring the social order back into decency.

I agree with the majority of the population who don't believe the Warren Commission Report, which concluded that Oswald alone killed the president. I do agree with the subsequent congressional hearings in the 1970s that concluded the JFK assassination was probably the result of a conspiracy. Of course, this conclusion was never covered adequately in the media.

Like any bully, the conspirators who assassinated JFK would be emboldened to commit more and bigger atrocities. Let's also consider what JFK is alleged to have been committed to. If it's true he wanted to get the United States out of the Vietnam War, then thousands of Americans wouldn't have continued to die in that war; and hundreds of thousands, if not millions, of Vietnamese wouldn't have continued to be murdered.

If it's true JFK wanted to disband the CIA—or at least its ability to perform covert operations—then millions around the world would still be alive. One has only to read John Stockwell's book *In Search of Enemies,* as well as other books written by CIA defectors, to learn of the CIA's atrocities around the world, especially in third-world countries.

And if it's true JFK wanted to replace the Federal Reserve with a national bank and currency, would individual Americans be in such inordinate debt today?

Why do we need to keep the JFK assassination relevant when we talk about the state of our current "democracy" and the future of humanity?

How did we arrive at the current political state of the United States? We call ourselves a democratic republic, which means "we the people" democratically elect individuals to represent us in Congress and in the White House. But anyone who looks honestly at our country will see that, in fact, an oligarchy chooses whom we're allowed to vote for. JFK was elected by the people. The fact he was assassinated by a secret cabal demonstrates there are deep state operatives who ensure their interests are protected, not the interests of the populace as a whole. Some will call these interests the "national security state."

This oligarchy existed before the assassination of JFK, but that fateful day of November 22, 1963, was a turning point when deep state entities gained significantly greater power over the politics and policies of the United States. The JFK assassination was a classical coup d'état, except for the fact it was done in secret and covered up by the same deep state entities. For example, Allen Dulles, who had been fired as CIA director by President Kennedy, was one of the prime planning suspects of this coup d'état. Nevertheless, Dulles was appointed by President Johnson to the Warren Commission.

Is there anything else you wish to add?
America can only limp forward as it carries the heavy baggage of its many State Crimes Against Democracy. Our nation is very sick from its secrets— open secrets that many know, but few speak of. When an individual enters a psychological healing process, the truth of past traumas and adversities must first be revealed and a grieving process take place before this person can walk as a free and natural being, free of the burdens of the past, free of secrets, and free of the somatic ills that result.

Can this be any different on the collective level, for a nation? I seriously doubt it. Truth and reconciliation are the sunlight needed for many of our past, dark secrets, including—but certainly not limited to—the genocide of Native Americans, the enslavement and abuse of Black Americans, 9/11, imperial wars and CIA covert actions around the world, and the assassinations of JFK, RFK, MLK, and Malcom X.

It's never too late to disband the CIA and ban imperial wars so we give our brothers and sisters around the world a chance to prosper and live free of US and corporate dominance in their lives. It's still early enough to work for justice—and thus accountability—so elites will not be tempted to commit atrocities against the populace again. Enough is enough.

CHAPTER 19

LEE BASHAM

Lee Basham, PhD, has authored numerous articles and book chapters on academic, media, and political responses to allegations of conspiratorial political manipulation. Basham is among the first philosophers offering a broad defense of the rational, evidential, and democratic legitimacy in Western-style societies of public suspicions of extensive and routine hierarchical deception. He has also earned a number of teaching awards. Basham is a professor of Symbolic Logic and Philosophy at South Texas College and the University of Texas, Rio Grande Valley.

What attracted you to the study of hierarchical deception and conspiracy theory?
For many years, conspiracy theory was a kind of a constant commentary of performance art. It was the sort of thing you did in a coffee house or café. It was a matter of reinterpreting the facts, such that you could detect a deeper pattern. Not total understanding because it's not an arrogance; it's simply a general pattern of suspicion. For example, when I was a child, it quickly became evident to me and my friends the police were somewhat corrupt.

And maybe the Santa Claus story had something to do with it, too. Following the insight of Brian Keeley, a professor of philosophy at the Claremont Colleges in California, we can speculate that conspiracy theory may be connected to the fact there's a global conspiracy against our children to guide and manipulate them into the belief there's a magical elf who can travel faster than the speed of light using flying miniature reindeer, only to eventually have them discover it was all a lie.

Part of the role of mythology with children is when there are these fantastical stories, a kind of a "wink, wink heads up there" because you're about to enter the real world, and you'll find out it has its own patterns of society-wide manipulation, deception, and delusion. Kids play with toys as practice for real life. They build houses and towers out of Legos, arrange dollhouses, take care of make-believe animals and babies, and strategize with toy soldiers. And then they're presented with the real world. And sometimes you think to yourself, when you look back at some of the mythologies we were taught, they have the same function. People don't consciously understand that's what they're teaching when they teach these things, but they *do* know they were taught this way, and as you were taught, so you teach. History repeats itself.

So, we're naturally inclined toward detecting deeper patterns in things because of our childhood experiences and human nature. I imagine, therefore, that parents play a big role in how we perceive things as we grow up.
I know my parents were skeptical of many things during the Vietnam War. I had the incredible experience of learning from both my mother's and father's sides of the family, which were very different. My mother came from a large, working-class family. She had eleven brothers and sisters. My father came from a first-generation wealthy family that also produced a wealth of skepticism, and in a very intelligent way. I learned quickly there were a lot of questions being asked, and it was a natural expected pattern.

My mother's side had all sorts of interesting suspicions, mainly focused on local politics. On my father's side, my grandfather held a prominent position in the northern Texas community of Wichita Falls. He was a self-trained mechanical engineer who ended up with more than one hundred patents with the Texas Oil Company, which is now known as Exxon. He had money during the Great Depression when nobody else did, and he gave much of it away, so he was somebody people listened to. His oldest son became an Air Force colonel. His second son, my father, became an engineer like him. And his third son—you can see the whole rainbow of possibilities here—became a prominent evangelical minister.

So, you had a lot of creativity there, and much of it was driven by my grandfather's relentless realism and willingness to question authority. On my mother's side it was the same thing. They were union people, and they knew the difference between somebody who was working for the workers and somebody working for "friends of management," which in itself involves conspiracy and betrayals.

What did you learn from being around this willingness to question authority?
Here's the general pattern I witnessed as a child: People are good liars. For evolutionary biologists, it's the basis of homo sapiens intelligence, and it's called "tactical deception." There's a huge literature there, coming out of behavioral ecology, and also from our friends in experimental psychology, in animal cognition. But tactical deception often involves cooperative tactical deception. So, what we learned as children, and what we learned in our family stories and these massive discussions, was that people plot.

Conspiracy is simply the extension of our ability to deceive, often for good reason, not for bad. Deception itself is morally neutral, as it depends on what your intentions and purposes are. But conspiracy is the group form—two or more people, simply deceiving. Now, deception can be by omission—you keep a secret. It can be by commission—you actually tell a lie. And this can be for good or bad purposes. This becomes really interesting when you study the course of politics in the course of state and international affairs.

What you pick up on, at least in my family because we were so talkative and willing to discuss anything in such a flagrantly open way, was that this is a big part of life. All of us have told a lie. All of us have asked other people to cover up for us. All of us are conspirators. Conspiracy theory is the natural response. If I can do it, they can do it. If I know how to do this with my friends when I'm five years old, then so can anyone else. When we're children we might make up a story about why we didn't keep curfew. I remember arguing with my parents about being home by dark, and I said, "But the streetlights were on, so it wasn't dark."

These kinds of evasions and cleverness were natural. We organized our stories when we ran around in a little gang, rode around on these little bikes and just didn't want to go home. So, we came up with an excuse like some lunatic had chased us, or we got lost, and we all agreed to it. Then we went back to our houses and our mothers called one another to see if the story fit. Same reason the police divide suspects to this day. It's a deeply human ability.

Once I saw this, I also noticed a systematic attempt in our culture to be beyond amnesiac about it, to be appalled by this in the sense that not only is this not a good thing, but that it just doesn't happen in corporate, national, or international politics. But, of course, it does. I ask at what point did our national or international leadership forget what they knew quite well how to do when they were eight years old? And the answer is they didn't forget at any point. They conspire just as we all do by nature, but saying this is a bold move in a society where if you call something a conspiracy theory, you must be crazy. But let's get real, people.

It seems like you've always had a pretty good understanding of human nature and the human tendency to lie, deceive, and conspire to achieve certain purposes.
Well, what happened was I started talking about conspiracy theory with people, and I gave some public talks on it. Then in 1999, Professor Keeley published a paper in the prestigious *Journal of Philosophy* titled "On Conspiracy Theory."[1] In it, he argued that, using the example of the Oklahoma City bombing,[1] we could distinguish warranted, evidentially justified conspiracy theories from unwarranted ones. The way his argument proceeded was somewhat flawed, but it's an eloquent paper to this day. It's one of my favorite papers on this subject.

At that time, I was attending the University of Oklahoma, which has one of the better philosophy departments in the country. Ironically, it was this far-flung center of reason on the buckle of the Bible Belt. I had subscribed to the *Journal of Philosophy* because it was this bigwig journal, and I was getting my PhD in philosophy, so it seemed natural I should. And here's this theory on conspiracy theory, and I thought it was interesting because I was where it happened.

Were you at the University of Oklahoma the day the bombing occurred?
Yes. I was teaching a course on symbolic logic, and when I left the lecture hall, a number of my former students were clustered outside, and they said, "Basham, have you heard? They've blown up the Federal Building." I didn't know what to do; we were all horrified. So, my girlfriend and I drove up there to help. You could see the building burning in the distance . . . giant clouds of smoke. Everybody was piled up on the interstate watching this spectacle.

We tried to sneak a route through because we wanted to dig amongst the rubble and hopefully help somebody, but they wouldn't let us get by. I still have a Ziploc bag with a big chunk of this strange fibrous insulating substance from the building. You can still smell the cordite, the explosive. This was blowing out into the streets, so I grabbed it, not as a vicious or cruel souvenir, but just out of helplessness.

The next day I went up to the philosophy department, where I was teaching, and the chairman came running out of his office and said, "The psychology department has been speaking with the Oklahoma City Health and Police Departments, and they need you in Oklahoma City." At the time, I was also with the experimental psychology and neurology departments, which are very different from clinical psychology, but they both fall under the rubric of psychology, and they wanted psychologists up there. So, I agreed and drove to Oklahoma City.

There was a large church where they did the notifications, which were extremely difficult. They seated us and had us break the news to families, whether their relatives were okay or not. We weren't allowed to say "attack" or "victim." We definitely weren't allowed to say "bombing." We were only allowed to say "event" or "episode." Our job was to stay as cool as possible, but it took a toll on people. There was a woman doing the same job as I who, after four hours of this, started hyperventilating and had to run for the parking lot. I went after her and had to yell at her before she snapped out of it and started to recover. They took her away in an ambulance.

The next day I ended up having a really bad experience. I went to one table, and an old guy started pounding his head on it. He'd lost family members. We were told not to touch anyone, so I put my hand on the table so he wouldn't injure his head. After a while he realized I had done this, and he looked up and started to cry.

So, there was my connection. Salience. Psychological, moral, and intellectual salience. I became interested in the reality because I had just experienced the reality of an incredibly tragic event. And the conspiracy theories being expressed in that community became important to me. There was a lot of what Keeley calls "errant data," facts that either contradict the official account or should be explained by it and aren't. There were a lot of problems with the official story.

I was there, and I had witnessed the caution, the intellectual and evidential care that went into discerning that the official story had numerous problems, and that there were more cogent and well-evidenced explanations. So, I felt not just emotionally and morally impelled, but also intellectually impelled, to write and publish a reply to Keeley's paper in the *Journal of Social Philosophy*.

So, that's how conspiracy theory got on the map in academia, at least in philosophy. The implications of the Kennedy assassination, and the fact that the truth was being buried, began to emerge to me after more general conversations with a close friend and fellow graduate student. We talked about the fact that coincidence, while real enough, is the first resort of the inattentive and irresponsible mind.

What is "information hierarchy?"
We live in a very strong, very steep information hierarchy, where very few people control what most people believe, or are expected to believe, or at least are expected to act as if they believe. These are all important distinctions, but behaviorally they come to the same thing. The hierarchy is made up of national governments, global institutions (cooperation between national governments), and what we call the mainstream media. The point of the hierarchy is to stabilize the lower levels.

In the usual model there's a pyramid with secrets held above, and the secrets have to be somehow sealed off. But that's not the case with the inverse model, which appears to be what's really happening. The real pyramid is inverted, from what we can tell from our research, our historical studies, and so forth. This is an empirical claim, and it's well evidenced.

In this situation, the secrets are at the bottom of this inverted pyramid, unchallenged and uninspected, so it takes little or no effort to keep them there. The few challenges that might effervesce them up into the larger population are easily sequestered and controlled. So, when I talk about information hierarchies, the hierarchy is of course one of control.

In the inverted pyramid, we can look at this information differently. In what I like to call the United States of Amnesia, we just forget, we don't care anymore. That was then, this is now. And it takes those rare individuals, like the researchers in this book, to drill down into those ancient archives, and those almost-lost memories, to find out what's going to happen next. Because history does repeat itself.

What is "continuity of narratives"?
Continuity of narratives is extremely important for a stable society. One of the standard arguments is there's a competition between government, nationalities, major corporations, and mainstream media. Mainstream media are always snapping at their heels trying to find out the truth, the whole investigative journalism motif. And that's true at a more trivial level, but when you're investigating truths that might be overwhelming to society, it could in many ways radically destabilize the political order the mainstream media depend on.

The political order is composed of national governments and their investigative entities, in our case the CIA, the FBI, and the intelligence community here in the United States. When you're involved in that kind of behavior, you have every motive to leave it alone because all you can do is create chaos. The standard argument, the public trust approach argument, is simple. It says, "Look, it's going to get revealed. You can't keep a secret." But that depends on the nature of the secret. And if the media, those who have some status as reliable information givers, promote this story that is contra to the very survival, the continuity, of the current government and economic system, the consequences will be tremendously bad.

So, the idea that there's a strong motive in the mainstream media to discover the truth and tell the people ends up being self-destructive. For the more important, more socially destabilizing, more absolutely necessary information people should know, you suddenly see a sharp drop-off in the probability it will be reported or even explored because it's a nonstarter. Stability is the more basic and easily discerned motive. You'll crash the society, economy, government, and social order if you reveal the truth.

And that's the problem of what I call "toxic truths." Some truths are too toxic to disseminate, and their potential toxicity is easily foreseen, therefore they won't even be examined. That's what I call the "Why look?" problem, and it applies powerfully to both mainstream media and national law enforcement.

Besides the Kennedy assassination, can you give some historical examples of this?
Pearl Harbor is obviously one of many historical examples. We now know the United States knew the precise locations within a few hundred miles of the Japanese armada that was going to attack Pearl Harbor. We also know, from Captain Arthur McCollum's memos to President Roosevelt, that we needed to institute a war. The war was very unpopular, so it was going to require a serious event that would radically reverse the largely pacifist-isolationist public opinion regarding another war in Europe.

The Tripartite Pact between the axis powers had recently been agreed to, so our government realized it wouldn't be difficult to tempt Japan into an attack. They also knew a new kind of naval warfare was afoot. This wouldn't be a battleship war, but instead would be an aerial war, which requires aircraft carriers. So, the military actually moved the aircraft carriers out of Pearl Harbor beforehand. We went to great lengths to not inform the fleet at Pearl Harbor that we had this information. We allowed the attack to sink a number of obsolete battleships and other cruisers and destroyers.

So, the day that lives in infamy was created by crisis, because when you live in a democracy, you can't by edict simply tell the people you're going to war, not when you live at least in a pseudo, semirepresentational democracy.

And it's not either/or; it's a matter of degree. How democratic are we? But when you live in such a situation, you have to recognize public opinion has to be carefully manipulated. It can't simply be declared to the

President Lyndon Johnson signing the Tonkin resolution, which gave him power to escalate the Vietnam war after the Gulf of Tonkin incident, in which it was alleged American vessels had been attacked by the North Vietnamese. (Photo by MPI/ Getty Images)

state's apparatus. You're more likely to generate crises to justify the plans of state and, in doing so, garner, unite, and rally the support of the population. Pearl Harbor is a great example of that.

The Gulf of Tonkin incident, too, is a great example of this. The very idea you would question the legitimacy of a surprise attack in the case of Pearl Harbor has only occurred in the last thirty years among historians. The Gulf of Tonkin event was used by Lyndon Johnson after the assassination of President Kennedy to justify a new level of involvement in Vietnam. This led to the death of millions of Vietnamese and Cambodians, as well as around 58,000 American soldiers.

There was a small blip with Tonkin, however, because there were a couple of senators who said, "Wait a minute. This stinks. It doesn't look good." But it took fifty years for the United States to finally say, as a result of Freedom of Information Act enquiries and digging by historians, "We always knew the attack wasn't real. The North Vietnamese speedboat Navy did not attack our major vessels more than one hundred miles off the coast of North Vietnam. We knew this was all nonsense, yet we didn't say anything because this is where we wanted our military to go."

Now, if you're in the middle of a war, continuity of narrative is extremely important. Mainstream media and national investigative institutions and agencies will maintain a continuity of narrative because that ensures the continuity of society. Thus, it took fifty years for the truth to emerge.

How do you relate those things to "conspiracy theory phobia"?

The phobia is closely related because when you question this pattern, first by identifying it and second by decrying it, you're met with phobia. Let me quickly define the term because this is important. Conspiracy theory is simply a theory that explains events past, present, or future in terms of reference to a conspiracy. Conspiracy is two or more people who have intentionally cooperated to create a deception, either by omitting facts, keeping secrets, or producing pseudofacts and false claims. Conspiracy theory phobia is the idea that we can't countenance these deep and difficult questions about our society and its political structure. To do so is fundamentally destabilizing. But more important, it's a political piety.

I think you can see there's this going back and forth, this tennis-ball mentality of the people who suffer this phobia, this fear of conspiracy theory and conspiracy theorizing and therefore of conspiracy theorists, which include all of us. Anyone who is historically literate entertains well-evidenced, well-established conspiracy theories as previously defined.

The problem is this political piety. You have to do something very difficult. You have to ask the Santa Claus question. Maybe there's no magic elf. They lied to me, and I believe in this society that is motivated just as much by technology and truth, by science and reason, as it is by lies, deception, hierarchy, and control.

Political piety is bred into us as children, but unlike with Santa Claus, most of us don't outgrow it, and something that attacks that piety invokes great fear. It's heresy, and we know what happens to heretics. We don't get to burn them anymore, but we get to isolate, cancel, and try to somehow diminish them into silence. And this is intellectually dishonest. This is evidentially incorrect. It's a fundamental block to progress toward a more productive democracy where information is spread horizontally. We have a well-educated, critical-thinking population that can filter it out on the basis of evidence and then direct the state. So, the question is, is it *our* government, or are we *their* citizens?

In moving into this area of study, what kind of challenges have you encountered?
Surprisingly few. The students are absolutely open to it. We're living with a new generation that doesn't find the term "conspiracy theory" pejorative. We've done psychological studies. I've interviewed hundreds of self-identified conspiracy theorists. I presented their theories not to say they're true or they're false, but to look at how we apply evidence, what we think, to thousands of students, and they're extremely receptive.

What about pushback from academia itself?
Among analysts, epistemologists (people who study questions of how we know things and how knowledge is possible), and also among philosophers and logicians, initially you get a smirk, but then you get, "Wow. That makes perfect sense. You're right." So, the conversion with the logical

and the evidence-driven people is supereasy. In a way, you're giving them permission for what they were doing in the back of their minds all along. You're saying, "You're not a bad person. You're actually a smart person, and you'd be a better person if you just accepted the reality that conspiracy is a normal feature of human life. If we did it as children, we're surely doing it at the highest levels of governmental power, especially in an informational hierarchy."

The only thing we're having trouble with is the social psychologists. Their bread and butter is conspiracy theory phobia. The government pays for it because questions about organized deception of the populace undermine the foundation of the government being the trustworthy expression of the will of the people. That fundamental piety also applies to the reliability of the media to watchdog the government. We know the cases of that reliability seem to decrease in exact proportion to the necessity of that reliability. That's the problem with toxic truth. The bottom line is social psychologists are being paid millions of dollars to pathologize people who question the idea that mainstream media and national governments might sometimes engage in some very significant damaging, even catastrophic, lies, deceptions, and organized deceit.

We've fought and largely won that battle, but we're still fighting it. We go to these huge international conferences, and you've got sixty-seven of them and three of us, and we steal the show because we're asking the logical, evidential, rational questions. We're not walking in with the presumption that if you're willing to entertain doubts about the truth of your society's dominant narrative, you're necessarily pathological in one way or another. In fact, you're quite the opposite. The pathology lies in those who would pathologize those who have important logic-based questions.

And there's an important irony in the conspiracy theory stuff that emerges when you sit down and talk to the social psychologists who have taken up arms against a popular doubt about certain tenets of our current narrative and are being paid millions of dollars to pursue their research. What they almost always do is start telling you about the conspiracy theories they think are true. The irony is palpable. It's the difference between the job and the person.

What have been the ripple effects of the JFK assassination?

We came out of World War II with an almost artificial, contrived sense of unity. We came together to defeat the greatest Mordorian[2] menace that humankind has ever faced—the totalitarianism of the Nazis, the brutality of the Japanese. In that period there was a great deal of respect, almost adoration of our federal government because many people felt like we had come together as a nation and saved ourselves.

To see this shattered so quickly with the Kennedy assassination, to see the sudden jerk back to the mentality of the 1920s and 1930s, of union-ism and class division, it wasn't just a stone in the pond. It was a big boulder in the pond of American culture, and those ripples multiplied as more and more lesser stones were thrown in. What does it mean to live in a unified, beautiful, freedom-loving, near-utopian culture when the presi-dent could be shot in Dallas? And the answers given about why and how it happened, and who did it, are increasingly, and with attention, absurd.

That caught on, and instead of the waves dissipating, they grew because this was a betrayal. If you have children or beloved pets, you don't want to be too perfect because that's fragile, that's something to be shattered. They have to see you have flaws, but there was a sense of perfection after WWII, at least in the political mythology. Certainly not in the actual social structure or the way the United States was actually working, but in that mythology, that crystalline perfection was extremely perilous. And the mere fact Kennedy could be killed out of nowhere by some lone-gun lunatic, and there were so many incongruities . . . people inquired upon that very carefully because they wanted to recover that crystalline perfec-tion. And in the end, they dramatically failed, and the crystal turned into sand. And that's where we are now.

The overreach, the ambition of the JFK assassination, was a huge miscalculation. It could've been managed in different ways. He could've been shamed out of his next term as president. There were all sorts of things they could've done, but the brutality of an organized public assas-sination was clumsy. And it also shows you the arrogance of the ruling class at that time because they were riding this wave of almost deification because of our victory in World War II and our seemingly insurmount-able power.

It's true at that time the Russians had also developed nuclear weapons, atomic fission bombs, but there really was no question who was on top of the Pax Americana.³ It was the United States, of course. So, speaking as an American, I think the shattering of that glass sculpture became an extraordinary mistake for narrative continuity, for revealing the information hierarchy, and for suggesting to people's minds there are toxic truths, and what makes them toxic is also why they need to know them.

I think the inception, that seed known as the JFK assassination, grew and evolved into a bunch of other issues, questions, and concerns. And once you realize they lied to you about JFK, actually and rationally, the question is always: what else have they lied to us about? And as rational, well-motivated, intelligent people who have to live in this world, naturally we started asking other questions, too.

What do young people need to understand about the JFK assassination and its effects?

Our youth are blessed with a fascination with conspiracy, but not a morbid one, a healthy one, because it's so close to their own situations. When you're in your teens and twenties, you live a conspiratorial life for the most part. You're doing things you're not supposed to get caught doing. They have also recently emerged from a time of relative tyranny, for instance in public schools and their family life. And when I say relative tyranny, I don't mean that's an unhealthy thing. I believe parents should have a certain degree of authority and guidance, but it's a tyranny, and it's naturally resisted.

These teenagers are deeply curious about where the roots of this lay. Why was it that we developed a society of healthy suspicion, and why is it so vehemently, vigorously opposed today? The JFK assassination is the answer to both those questions. It was the beginning, the Alpha and Omega, if you will. And that great circle we're traveling now, which starts with JFK, is the circle of radical information reform in our society. The development of a truly horizontal system of responsible information. The JFK assassination is the reason they care about the conspiracies they care about now. They wouldn't otherwise have that permission, they wouldn't have that ability, they wouldn't have that credibility. They wouldn't have the intellectual sense of knowing that if it weren't for JFK, they wouldn't have been part of this radical information reform.

And look what happened after JFK was assassinated: the '60s. Most of the values they hold now—sexual liberation, recreational drugs, a sense of reemergent tribalism—all of these things find their roots in the sudden shattering of normality, conformity, and confidence that JFK blessed us with. If any man needed to die, if there's ever been a figure representing a political crucifixion, it's JFK. JFK is our Jesus.

What questions would you want to ask other academics and participants in this book?
I want to address myself to our friends, the social psychologists. They're really the only ones in the way now. Funding be damned; they're failing. Why don't you do social psychology studies on why you're so averse to conspiracy theory? And I've been asking them that.

I'd ask historians how important conspiracy is in the development of history. That's critical. You can't be historically literate and not be a conspiracy theorist. You can't be family literate and not be a conspiracy theorist, because every large family is full of these little cabals and things going on. You've got some people conspiring and so forth, and other people are looking at that and wondering what secrets they're keeping. Boom . . . conspiracy theorist. It's totally normal.

If you get to talk to media personalities, talk to them about at what point is there anything beyond the pale, and how do you decide that? At what point would you *not* investigate a claim, even if you're presented with good evidence? And if they say there's no point, they're lying.

Just go out and talk to some regular people and see what their real attitude toward conspiracy theory is, and you'll find they're fascinated by it because they're intelligent. It's common sense. And most important, I'd ask yourself, why are you writing this book? That needs to be spoken to. I'm glad you are.

How might philosophers write about the JFK assassination a century from now?
I believe from a philosophical perspective what the JFK assassination shows is how easily manipulated our information hierarchy is, and how

important it is to overcome that structurally. This is the goal of epistemology. Find a way to not just talk democracy, but as the cliché goes, walk that talk.

Plato's *Republic* is about a giant conspiracy against an entire society. If you're a Platonist, if you don't believe power should be invested in people, in a platonic Republic, what you need to learn is that your *intelligentsia* isn't trustworthy. You've got to learn that only through a diffused, statistical, interconnected network can real social intelligence emerge. And that's exactly the same kind of diffused, statistical network that defines the human brain and defines intelligence in general.

If you want to be smart, you have to understand that the JFK assassination shows how stupid our society was sixty years ago. And hopefully we'll all look back on it one hundred years from now and say, "It wasn't a network at all. It was a handful of controlling neurons deluding an entire body politic."

CHAPTER 20

DOROTHY LORIG

Dorothy Lorig holds a master's degree in counseling psychology, a secondary school teaching certificate, and undergraduate degrees in social work and technical journalism. A fourth-generation western Coloradoan, full-time real estate agent, and part-time psychotherapist, Lorig is the mother of two grown children and lives in a small town in the mountains of western Colorado. She is a practitioner of Re-evaluation Counseling, a process for freeing humans and society as a whole from distress patterns so that we may resume fully intelligent functioning. Lorig has been on the steering committee of Colorado 9/11 Truth since 2006 and began learning about problems with the official narrative of the JFK assassination in 1985.

What attracted you to the process of Re-evaluation Counseling?
In 1994 I took a fundamentals class in Re-evaluation Counseling, also known as RC and cocounseling, a grassroots-developed body of theory and practice founded on the novel idea of regular people taking timed turns to listen to one another. It's effective for two reasons: 1) the process encourages and supports each person's natural healing system of talking, crying, laughing, shaking, and yawning in order to release emotional tension and regain clear thinking; and 2) it empowers clients by helping them get in shape to advocate on behalf of social change.

RC practitioners consider most human distress to be a product of mistreatment stemming from oppressions such as young people's oppression, classism, racism, sexism, able-bodied-ism, etc. RC theory rejects as dishonest, destructive, and oppressive the so-called "mental health" system and its constructs of "mental illness" and "chemical imbalances," as well as diagnosing/labeling, drugging, electroshocking, and incarcerating the people it purports to help.

I've been personally using this system for twenty-six years, and it serves as the theoretical and practical foundation for my work as a professional therapist. I was never attracted to the study of psychology as most people think of the term; I learned RC because I wanted to heal the places where I'd been hurt. I soon came to enjoy being in the "counselor" role and listening deeply to the person in the "client" role as much as I enjoyed being listened to.

This section of the book focuses on, among other things, psychological perspectives on the JFK assassination, which is why I'm asking you about your background and preferred process of psychoanalysis. To clarify, is Re-evaluation Counseling an alternative approach to conventional psychotherapy?
It's a body of theory unto itself, distinct from and often in opposition to conventional psychology. Cocounselors assume that instead of entering the world as blank slates, babies emerge completely intelligent, confident of their own power, and possessing a huge zest for life. One oppressive thing after another happens to us throughout our childhoods while we're completely dependent on and being controlled by much more powerful beings. We try to assert our voice and our power and are shut down over and over again. Helplessness isn't something we're born with, it's learned, and it comes in so early we don't know we've learned it. It seems like it's always been with us because we can't remember those early days when we felt powerful.

Can you provide a specific example of a culture that raises its children more in-sync with this theoretical foundation?
You can contrast our Western style "learned helplessness"[1] with the experience of Yequana babies. In *The Continuum Concept: In Search of Happiness Lost*, a 1975 classic manual for alternative child-rearing, Jean Liedloff

describes an Amazonian tribe and its nonoppressive attachment parenting practices.[2] After birth, Yequana babies continue to develop a strong sense of security and love by being held full-time by parents, other adults, siblings, and cousins. When they've outgrown the "in-arms" stage, they're free to crawl or walk anywhere they want without supervision; they can sit on a cliff overlooking a river or play with a sharp ax, and no one worries because tribe members are confident their little ones are intelligent and possess an intact capacity for self-preservation. Because the adults simply model desired behaviors and avoid bullying, bossing, or advising young people, these children never lose their inherent sense of power and competence described by RC theory.

The other part of this theoretical foundation is liberation from oppression. RC was developed by a communist labor organizer named Harvey Jackins in the 1950s, so from the outset it possessed a strong liberation component. Conventional psychology focuses on an individual's problems and aims to help the individual conform to society, including such practices as drugging to alleviate so-called "chemical imbalances" (a theory that has been completely discredited even within the psychiatric community, yet the drugging continues). In RC we consider how both the oppressor and victim ends of our various identities have shaped our individual distresses, and we work with other counselors to clear out these distresses and get ourselves in shape to organize to end oppression—every form of humans hurting one another—in the outside world.

How did you become interested in corruption and conspiracy on a national level and the psychological effects of national "tragedies," both individually and collectively?
On September 12, 2001, my grad school professor stormed into our classroom, incoherent with rage because our country had apparently just been attacked. He was too upset to teach using his lesson plan or to otherwise lead the class. All anyone wanted to talk about was 9/11, and several students were loudly taking a very anti-Muslim stance. So, I took charge of the class by using RC. We divided into pairs and used a timer to take turns listening to one another. We were all a mess, and we needed to vent and be listened to in an orderly, nonjudgmental way.

In the weeks that followed, although I didn't question the official narrative of the 9/11 events, I kept returning to the idea of motive; I believe a given human behavior is understandable so long as we know the reason(s) behind it. And the reasons on offer—"because they hate our freedoms" and "blowback for everything this country has done to them"—didn't sufficiently explain why foreign actors would sacrifice their lives and, given our government's well-known history of disproportionate retribution, place their families and communities at grave risk.

In May 2006, with the encouragement of my then-husband, I began to seriously research the mountain of physical and behavioral evidence that had been gathered regarding the destruction of the three World Trade Center towers. After becoming convinced something was amiss and that it was my moral obligation to do something about it, I endured months of insomnia, nightmares, and a persistent worry CIA agents would hunt me and my family down and kill us.

My husband, who for many years had studied the assassinations of the 1960s, had subsequently turned his attention to the study of 9/11. Because he's English, he didn't receive systematic American patriotic conditioning and therefore didn't experience the upheaval I encountered. He had never emotionally "attached" to the US government and was already inured to the idea of deep corruption within it. But for me it was traumatic: I had to let go of the image of my government as a benign parental figure.

This happened both overnight with the initial shock of allowing the alternative information to penetrate my defenses and over time as I continued to research and consider the implications.

What is collective trauma, and can you relate that to the JFK assassination?

We've witnessed the national, even global, outpouring of rage and grief precipitated by the murder of George Floyd by a Minneapolis police officer. The killing was filmed by a bystander and posted to Facebook. The footage of Floyd pleading for his life, then slowly dying as the officer's knee crushed his windpipe, is horrific; the fact we could viscerally witness it for ourselves, could imagine that same knee cutting off our own airways, brought millions upon millions of us collectively traumatized people together in anguish and fury.[3]

President Kennedy's murder was also filmed. We see him and his wife disembark from Air Force One. We see the couple greet the local dignitaries and be driven to the killing fields of downtown Dallas. We watch as the president dies before our eyes and his terrified wife crawls over the back of the limousine to retrieve a piece of his skull. We witness the funeral procession as a veiled Mrs. Kennedy stands bravely and her tiny son salutes the carriage bearing his father's casket. And we notice our grief is still there, our pain persists. Jack Kennedy would be 104 years old, and he has been dead going on fifty-eight years. His assassination froze him in time: he remains our golden boy who died too young but used his one thousand days in office to work ceaselessly for the cause of peace.

Our national fascination with the intricacies of the CIA/Pentagon-led plot to kill President Kennedy marks our continuing sense of unease, of unfinished business, of justice denied. It stands in for the intolerable knowledge that the coup that executed our leader was successful, that although most of the individual planners are now dead, the ungodly,

The funeral procession of President Kennedy goes into Arlington National Cemetery in Washington, DC. (Photo by National Archive/Newsmakers/Getty Images)

unelected, despotic apparatus they installed in the wake of the assassination controls our nation's affairs to this day.

So, in your opinion, the Kennedy assassination was a CIA/Pentagon-led plot?

Yes . . . and once I recovered from the initial shock of the George Floyd murder, I noticed another parallel with the JFK assassination: a gut feeling we'd been had, that a coup of sorts had unfolded under our noses. I saw a nationwide move by highly militarized law enforcement personnel to "restore order" for the benefit of the rich and powerful, to push the country even further toward the right and toward fascism by imposing martial law in the form of curfews; by beating, shooting, and gassing peaceful demonstrators; by officers obscuring their badge numbers to avoid personal accountability; and by police departments actively instigating and enabling looting and property destruction they can then blame on demonstrators.

What is cognitive dissonance, and can you relate that to the JFK assassination?

Cognitive dissonance is the inability to maintain a sense of consistency and coherence within our individual worldview. Learning that JFK was killed by people in our own government is not a stretch intellectually because the forensic and behavioral evidence is readily available, is plentiful and of high quality, and consistently points in that direction. But engaging with this evidence and allowing ourselves to contemplate its implications can feel unbearably sad and frightening. Our inability to tolerate these feelings can force us into an intellectual regression whereby we disregard the import of the facts before us and regress to a comforting yet childish and helpless "Father (the mainstream media/the government) knows best" stance.

What kinds of challenges have you encountered while doing your research?

The toughest part of researching the deep state has been a continuing sense of intellectual alienation from my friends who aren't so inclined. The more

I learn, the more challenging it becomes to maintain a sense of optimism and hold on to the idea that people are essentially good. I've encountered a deep sense of grief and loss as I've contemplated the deaths of John Kennedy, Martin Luther King, Viola Liuzzo, Robert Kennedy, Malcom X, and countless other participants in the Civil Rights Movement, as well as those killed in the 9/11 "attacks" and other pretext wars.

On the bright side, I have many clients who specifically seek me out because of my visibility as an advocate for truth and justice. These clients benefit from having a therapist who doesn't start off the therapeutic relationship by judging them for being "conspiracy theorists." And I learn a great deal from these brilliant people who aren't afraid to intellectually color outside the lines.

What have been the ripple effects of the JFK assassination, good and bad?

We can't know what the world would be like had JFK lived; my philosophy is that what happened had to happen because it *did* happen, and I have no patience with speculating about alternate realities. I *will* say the term "conspiracy theory" both gained traction after the assassination *and* was strategically and systematically discredited through the work of the CIA and its mainstream media partners. Attempting to rehabilitate the term has required much effort on the part of advocates for 9/11 truth and justice that could have been more productively employed elsewhere.

The CIA and the mainstream media have most definitely discredited any attempts to uncover real conspiracies, which of course have always existed at various levels of insidiousness throughout history. It's sad, really.

I find solace in the thought that although JFK's incipient efforts to end US military involvement in Vietnam ended with his assassination, his dogged work to bring an end to the Cold War, improve relations with Cuba and the Soviet Union, and relegate nuclear weapons to the dust heap of history have over time yet in significant ways borne fruit. His killers failed to fulfill most of their objectives.

President Kennedy during his American University speech, during which he announced that the United States, Russia, and Great Britain would begin "high-level" talks in Moscow soon in an effort to rescue a general nuclear test ban treaty. (Source: Bettmann via Getty Images)

From a psychological perspective, what do we need to understand about the JFK assassination?

We need to know we can bear the unbearable, we can join with others on the same path toward truth, we can feel the awful feelings and come out the other side, whole and undaunted. We can educate ourselves. We can overcome our individual and collective legacies of learned helplessness. Instead of being so horrified and shocked by assassinations, false flag attacks, and other crimes against democracy we perceive as discrete, one-off events, we can instead calmly collect and share information and together analyze these events as potential elements of a larger pattern. Together we can determine how best to expose and stand against the criminals in high places who organize these travesties.

How do you see the psychology of the conspirators?

To project based on my own experience: I grew up in an angry family in which the children experienced much physical and verbal violence. I carry that message in the less-evolved part of my brain, the idea that violence is the best tool to solve problems. We can know intellectually it can't, but under stress we revert to what we experienced in childhood, this time from the oppressor rather than the oppressed end. Perhaps the conspirators were similarly conditioned by family violence.

Or we can consider Hannah Arendt's theory of the banality of evil.[4] When evil is compartmentalized, it becomes easier for each actor to play his or her role; not being allowed to know all of the details and perhaps even the intended result of a given operation, s/he isn't compelled to consider the moral implications of the whole. That's apparently why the Nazi "final solution" machine was so efficient and effective.

Perhaps we should also consider the contribution of class on emotional upbringing. In RC, we give much attention to encouraging the individual's natural healing processes, but we also consider how oppression shapes each person's distresses. We believe class oppression underlies all of the other oppressions such as racism, sexism, and the oppression of young people.

I've observed a nearly perfect overlap between common behavior patterns of the wealthy ("owning") classes and individuals labeled as narcissists, among them an overt lack of sensitivity to the plight of the less fortunate, a callousness, an emotional numbness. Children of the owning classes are often conditioned by cold, critical parenting—a kind of emotional torture—that systematically installs oppressor patterns, to the point wherein owning-class children can become unable to know what they're feeling, much less intuit the feelings and needs of others. They lose sight of the value of close, loving, reciprocal relationships and make do with the lesser satisfactions of winning, of competing in a deadly serious "game" of life.

Let's look at class oppression as it relates to the JFK assassination. In the United States, the class in power is always the moneyed class, because although money isn't power, it reliably purchases power. Consider Lord Acton, who said: "Power tends to corrupt, and absolute power corrupts absolutely." People often misquote this and leave out the word "tends," which is unfortunate because that little word tells us so much: it means a person can have *some* power yet not be corrupt at all. As people with money and moneyed connections gain power, it's like the graphs we saw of the COVID-19 infection rates in the United States. The infection line was on a fairly flat, then gradually sloping, trajectory. Suddenly it became an exponential curve and shot almost vertical.

We can think of the relationship between power and corruption in the same way. You have a little bit of power, and you may or may not have abused this power, but at some point, you hit a critical power threshold and find yourself mired in a situation in which the corruption is so deeply ingrained, so incredibly intertwined with every aspect of how you conduct your life, that the corruption and the power can no longer be disentangled. Given historical precedent, the logical extension of Acton's theory is the more power a person obtains, the more corrupt that individual will be *expected* to be, and if s/he doesn't conform to expectations, there *will* be consequences.

JFK was an anomaly from that perspective, correct?
He was an unusual person in that he was born of enormous class privilege yet had difficult things happen to him when he was young—numerous life-threatening illnesses, losing his older brother, then witnessing his friends being killed and almost dying himself when the patrol torpedo boat he commanded was smashed in WWII—that mediated his privilege, made him abhor war, allowed him to see situations from others' perspectives, and forced him to stare death in the face with equanimity and even humor. He acquired the world's most powerful job, and instead of conforming to the expectation he would be corrupted by it, he refused. He instead lived out a steely determination to do right by his country, to resist the warmongers at the Pentagon and in the intelligence services.

He did it again and again, with immensely brave and lonely steps to improve relationships with the Soviet Union and with Cuba, to withdraw from Vietnam, and to prevent nuclear holocaust. It was akin to a physical law he declined to honor: with the near-absolute power of the presidency comes near-absolute corruption, by which holders of the office are expected and required to act accordingly. Kennedy refused to play by the rules of the game and to become thusly corrupted; he was in effect a traitor to his class, so—by the rules of that class—he *had* to be taken out.

Talk about government as a "parent" and how conspiracies destroy this paradigm.
Since early childhood, most of us have been forming in our heads rough emotional equivalencies of Parent, God, and National Leader—all supremely powerful and protective entities for which we've been given or have created sets of rules so we may peacefully and productively coexist and even flourish so long as we know our place in the Great Pecking Order.

Entertaining, even embracing, the idea of powerful conspiracies within the top ranks of our government pulls this comforting rug of illusion out from under us. Considering the possibility of high-level conspiracies leaves us ungrounded, fearful, and leaderless at a time when we feel a desperate need for someone smarter and more powerful than we are to tell us what's going on and to set things right.

How has the JFK assassination affected our relationship with trust?
We trust when we feel we can be ourselves, that we can act on our deepest values without fear of reprisal. The JFK assassination was a coup. It happened here, on our home turf, in broad daylight, and almost six decades later no one has been brought to account. The lesson there for every president since 1963 is: stick your neck out and lose your head. Trust must be earned, but our leaders no longer really try to earn it from us. Since Kennedy, our presidents have been a series of cautious, mostly morally vacuous men, unwilling to set aside their personal agendas and say what needs to be said, to do what needs to be done to ensure a peaceful, just country and a peaceful, just world.

Why does the JFK assassination still matter today?
It matters because the coup that began with his assassination is still in place. It is unsettling, surreal, even nauseating, to contemplate that truth, that we Americans are still under the influence of a half-century-old coup.

Justice matters, and no person should be murdered, much less with impunity. But when a national leader deliberately steps out of the figurehead role assigned to him and attempts to do something real, something brave and creative, something good, for the people of the world, and for his trouble gets destroyed in front of us, we can either cower in fear, or we can take a page from his playbook, from Mahatma Gandhi's and Martin Luther King's playbooks, and we can choose to not cooperate. We can choose to nonviolently resist, to speak truth to power, to value something greater than our own narrow self-interest.

How do we deal with this psychologically, as individuals and as a nation?

Exchanging listening time with nonjudgmental, like-minded friends is important. Releasing intense feelings in this way will get you through the initial trauma of realizing your government isn't benign and, in fact, doesn't care about you *at all*.

Join an activist group whose mission resonates with you. The peace and justice community has many jobs, many roles to fill; we need expertise in all kinds of areas, including writing, marching, lobbying, IT and A/V, strategizing, organizing, and idea-generating.

Being part of a principled movement is a powerful antidote to loneliness and learned helplessness. We know most of the people at the top levels of government and business are corrupt. Because the best predictor of future behavior is past behavior, we have their playbook. We know when a disaster such as an earthquake or pandemic occurs, well-placed opportunists will step in and figure out how to transfer even more wealth and power to the people who already have too much. We know an outspoken, uncorruptible leader in high office will be marked for destruction. But because we have the evildoers' playbook, we can begin anticipating their moves, thwarting them and have fun doing it. We can't just live in doom and gloom.

I like real estate, I like counseling. But when I was invited to be interviewed for this book, I felt a spark of excitement. Navigating the COVID-19 pandemic has been lonely and unsettling, but this project gave my brain a chance to just light up.

We can present researching the JFK assassination, false flag operations, and other horrors of the deep state like this: "This stuff is fascinating. It's so fun to learn about history." That doesn't take away from acknowledging the terrible things people have done and are doing to one another. But let's put that in its place; if we stay focused on the tragedy, we remain frozen in a state of helplessness. If we think about what we can do to prevent similar operations, we have fun. We get together with other people, we plan, educate, write, fundraise, march. We predict what's going to happen and begin taking steps to forestall it.

Is there anything else you wish to add?
In *JFK and the Unspeakable,* author James Douglass describes "the unspeakable" as a lack, an emptiness, a hollowness, a void of responsibility and accountability. President Kennedy was assassinated, the unspeakable was installed in his place, and it endures to this day.

JFK was a man of privilege and power who retained his capacity to listen to the better angels of his nature. Resisting corruption earned him powerful enemies, and I wonder to what extent he anticipated his assassination. Was he a heroic figure like Jesus or like Neo in the *Matrix* films, intentionally sacrificing himself in pursuit of a larger cause, or was he a mere mortal in denial about how much danger he was in? I'd like to think he really knew and forged ahead anyway with his plans to create a more peaceful world for his and everyone's children.

I would like to ask Jack Kennedy, "If you knew what was going to happen to you, would you do it all over again?" I think he would say yes. I think he was that kind of guy.

CHAPTER 21

DAVID DENTON

David Denton has served as a social science instructor at Olney Central College in Illinois since 1990. He participated in the Illinois Humanities Council Speakers' Bureau from 1995 to 2002, giving presentations on the Vietnam War, Lee Harvey Oswald, and the assassination of President John F. Kennedy. He also directed an oral history project exploring the *Vietnam War, 25 Years Later*. The work, funded through the Illinois Humanities Council, features interviews with 125 veterans from Illinois and across the nation. Denton became interested in the JFK assassination in the late 1980s and for the last decade has attended historical symposiums on the subject in Dallas, Texas. He has interviewed several people associated with the case and has researched hundreds of documents related to both Kennedy and Oswald. In 2001, he began teaching a course on political assassinations of the 1960s, which explores the deaths of John Kennedy, Robert Kennedy, and Martin Luther King Jr. You can find his *Essays on the Assassination of President John. F. Kennedy* on Lulu. Denton holds both a bachelor's and a master's degree from Eastern Illinois University and was the 1999 recipient of the OCC Alumnus Award.

What triggered your involvement in JFK assassination research?
Everybody has a starting point, and for me it was picking up a book in 1988 titled *Coup d'Etat in America: The CIA and the Assassination of John F. Kennedy* by Michael Canfield and Alan Weberman. I hadn't really spent

a whole lot of time looking into the assassination, but I started reading, and once I got into the basic facts of the case, it opened my eyes. The book seemed to indicate, "Wait a minute, what we've been told about the Kennedy assassination doesn't add up."

The book focused on Oswald and his background, and I began to realize there was something more to this guy than just a lone nut, and maybe a lot of things we've been told by our government and institutions may not be true. It's a disturbing point to get to, and I can remember having a sleepless night or two thinking about it. You think, "If they could get to Kennedy, they could get to whomever they want to." And "they" is anybody who had an agenda to orchestrate and cover this thing up. You start to think all things aren't what they seem to be in this country.

I grew up with a strong notion about our country and our values. We're far from perfect; our Founding Fathers talked about creating "a more perfect union," not a perfect one, but this assassination strikes at the very heart of our American institutions and our democracy. I'm not one of those people who believes conspiracy is everywhere, but when the facts of conspiracy are staring at you, you dig deeper into it. And the more you

Lee Harvey Oswald with friends in Minsk, Soviet Union. (Photo by © CORBIS/ Corbis via Getty Images)

find out, the more you realize there was something dark and sinister going on in Dallas. I felt it became my responsibility as a historian to keep digging. I just didn't stop, and that's where I've been for the past thirty years.

When did you decide to make the JFK assassination part of your curriculum?

Throughout the 1990s, I began doing speaking engagements on the Kennedy assassination. The movie *JFK* had just come out, and it generated an enormous amount of interest. I found myself speaking at high school teaching conferences to packed houses. I was still a novice in terms of what I know now, but I knew enough to start engaging and giving presentations. I was also giving presentations on the assassination at Olney Central College, where I teach, so in 2001 my dean of instruction asked, "Why don't you make a class out of this?" I thought this was pretty bold and revolutionary because, let's face it, there aren't a whole lot of people teaching a class titled *Political Assassinations of the 1960s*.

In putting together my curriculum, I focused on the three major assassinations that occurred in that decade—JFK, RFK, and MLK. I thought I'd try it for one year, and I'm still doing it twenty years later. The students recognize I have a lot of passion for what I'm talking about. I'm not saying all young people and college students are necessarily engaged in the JFK assassination these days, but when you put the information in front of them, they become fascinated with it. They've loved the class over the years, and I've felt really good about teaching it.

It's good to have a forum, especially among young people, to get them to look at the world around them, maybe a little bit differently, and critically think and examine our institutions and realize maybe everything's not what it appears to be on some levels. I think the class has been successful in that respect.

In order for people to better understand why the JFK assassination happened, can you talk about the context of those times in terms of the cultural and political landscape?

In 1963, you almost had a dualism in America. Let's start with the public in general, which was much naiver about how our institutions operated.

There was a naïveté about trusting our leaders, believing America was always going to do the right thing and trusting our leaders would uphold their offices and be trustworthy. This kind of naïveté probably encouraged some of the things that happened in the dark and without scrutiny. The national security state that developed in post-World War II America was all about secrecy, and that secrecy became justified. I tell my students that in some ways, secrecy simply means justification to lie. In the Cold War era, there was this ultimate conflict between communism and the free world, and in the eyes of many in the US military and intelligence agencies, an extreme anticommunist attitude was justified.

In this Cold War world, the CIA operated from a position where they weren't held accountable for their nefarious actions, including assassinations, coups d'état, and manipulations of foreign governments. . . and in places where it really wasn't about democracy versus communism, but about American oil and corporate interests. In places like Guatemala and Iran, the coups committed by the CIA had nothing to do with Cold War

President Kennedy talking with aides, including Defense Secretary Robert McNamara (R), during the Cuban Missile Crisis in October 1962. (Photo by © CORBIS/Corbis via Getty Images)

concerns. These were democratically elected leaders who were taken out and replaced by brutal dictatorial regimes that happened to be friendly to the United States.

We lost our way in some respects when it came to the secrecy that allowed these things to happen and the extreme anticommunist mind-set that permeated the US military and intelligence communities. Now juxtapose this against a liberal, idealistic president who saw and eventually moved toward the idea of bringing an end to the Cold War in a nonconfrontational way, and this really becomes one of the focal points that leads to the death of the president of United States in 1963.

You mentioned the CIA operating without oversight in the 1960s, but isn't this still true today?
In the 1960s and 1970s, the CIA was most definitely in the business of assassination. In 1975, the Church Committee was able to expose that the CIA had plans to assassinate Fidel Castro. One year later, Gerald Ford issued an executive order on foreign intelligence activities explicitly prohibiting US government employees from engaging in "political assassination," including killing heads of state through covert means.

Today, even if it isn't as bad as it was in the 1960s, the CIA is still all about protecting the agency, protecting the institution. Some of the recently released documents I've looked at are very revealing, but the personnel files of three particular agents—William Harvey, David Atlee Phillips, and Dave Morales—all of whom are of particular interest to JFK assassination researchers, consist of pages and pages of sanitized, blank documents. In fact, Dave Morales's entire personnel file is missing. When I looked at it, the only thing it said was "this file has been sanitized." So, you have thirty blank pages on Dave Morales; you have fifteen to twenty blank pages on William Harvey. What are they still hiding?

There's still something to find there, and we remain hopeful, but you see how US presidents keep delaying the public revealing of these sealed documents. It's like the Jim Garrison character said in *JFK*, "They'll probably move it back another fifty years." Well, that was fifty years ago, so here we are.

What have you concluded about the assassination based on your research?
At a fundamental level, the Kennedy brothers challenged the power structure in America, and they were a threat to it on so many different levels that powerful figures in the United States acted, colluded, and conspired against the president. It's as simple as that.

It's a mistake to suggest a single entity or institution was responsible for the president's death. There are too many things that occurred both before and after the assassination that can't be explained away by implicating one institution. For example, the CIA couldn't have manipulated the Secret Service. When you do the research, it's obvious the Secret Service was pulled away in certain respects from protecting the president that day. Who could have done that? If you believe the autopsy was manipulated and the evidence controlled after the assassination, you need to focus on the military and local and federal law enforcement. The CIA didn't control those things.

You have to look at it from the perspective that powerful individuals coalesced around a nexus and moved in a direction based on seeing Kennedy as a threat. Then you have to ask who benefited, who was in a position to manipulate events and who was in a position to manipulate the evidence afterward? And that's a pretty short list. So, where's the genesis of this? Where does it start?

·Everybody has an opinion about that, but you have to look at Texas itself. Who controlled things in Texas? Who controlled the police officers in Dallas? Who could manipulate the parade route in Dealey Plaza? Who could get JFK there in the first place? A lot of those answers go back to Texas and the people associated with Lyndon Johnson. Texas oil tycoons wielded great power in Texas, but why would they want Kennedy dead? Well . . . Kennedy was going to take away their oil depletion allowance, denying them of more than $100 million as a result. Some of the most extreme, anticommunist, right-wing individuals in America controlled Texas. There was definitely an agenda there.

If you want to look at the master puppeteer, you have to look at Allen Dulles. David Talbot does a great job in his book *The Devil's Chessboard*, covering these things and pinpointing where the CIA kept overstepping its power all over the world. After the Bay of Pigs, Allen Dulles and Richard

Bissell were fired from the CIA by JFK, but Dulles was very much still operating behind the scenes in 1963. He may have been removed from the agency, but he still had immense power and influence, and he's certainly suspicious in all this. And then Lyndon Johnson puts him on the Warren Commission, so Dulles is really the guy controlling the evidence after the assassination, which is very disturbing.

Cuban soldiers stand around a wagon carrying dead soldiers, probably Americans or Brigade 2506 involved in the failed Bay of Pigs Invasion of 1961. (Photo by Graf/Three Lions/ Getty Images)

In your opinion, was Lee Harvey Oswald a patsy?
Oswald has always been the most mysterious person in this case. We know a lot more about him today than we did twenty-five or thirty years ago,

and his real story begins to put him in a better light. He truly is a tragic figure. I believe Oswald, rather than someone who was necessarily part of a plot or conspiracy, saw himself as someone trying to stop the assassination of JFK. There's enough evidence that strongly indicates this. He was a low-level operative connected with US intelligence agencies. Consider his entire trip to Russia and back . . . a lone nut doesn't have the money and wherewithal to travel to these places and do the things he did.

And then there are his activities in the summer of 1963 in New Orleans. He was obviously being handled by intelligence agents. There's also strong evidence to suggest Oswald was an FBI informant. Many of the classified documents that recently came out really drill down into this. I feel Oswald was eventually brought into this plot, but I think he believed his mission was to try and stop it.

In fact, Oswald may have been the key to stopping the first major assassination attempt against JFK in Chicago. Abraham Bolden,[1] the first black Secret Service agent who was appointed by Kennedy in 1961, was assigned to the Chicago office in 1963, and he made it clear that they were able to foil the Chicago plot because of information given by an informant named Lee. And it makes sense this is what Oswald was up to. Other researchers have also suggested Oswald may have been involved in an attempt to stop the assassination.

That's the truly sad part . . . a guy who has been vilified all these years may very well have been an American hero who tried and failed to stop something he became a part of as an intelligence operative. That's how I see Oswald, as a low-level intelligence operative who was passed around by different agencies and utilized in terms of intelligence. In the summer of 1963, he was passing out leaflets for Guy Banister to ferret out communists in New Orleans. He did what he was told; he portrayed a persona. He was told to portray himself as a Marxist on TV, not knowing this would later be used against him. Oswald was a fascinating character, and a tragic one.

What have been the ripple effects of the JFK assassination?
The most negative effect is that justice was left undone. We've simply fallen short of what we want to be as an open, democratic society, particularly

in the last fifty or sixty years with our post-World War II national security state. In what's supposed to be an open democracy, it's important that truth and justice prevail. If you don't get to the bottom of these political assassinations, it's like an open wound on the American conscious, allowing more lies and deceptions to take place. It's important in a free society that we get there and have resolution.

There's also the lack of confidence American people now have in their institutions. This trust level has been in rapid decline since the Kennedy assassination and the Warren Commission Report—the fact the American public wasn't given a true account of what happened. Then Watergate came along and destroyed and decayed a lot more of that trust. You pick up a newspaper today and see that Congress has a 25 percent approval rating, and these are the individuals we elected. With the cynicism that pervades in American society today, you wish we could go back to those ideals again, to what Thomas Jefferson laid out in the Declaration of Independence. Who are we supposed to be and how have we gone astray from that? It's a big disappointment.

I always put a quote from Marcus Tullius Cicero[2] on the board in my history class, "To be ignorant of what occurred before you were born is to remain always a child." Just because the Kennedy assassination happened fifty-eight years ago and before you were born, it still plays a critical role in what's happening today. Don't accept it at face value; the truth matters.

Another product of the assassination is the CIA's creation of the term "conspiracy theorist." It has become a derisive term thanks to the mainstream media, as it labels anyone who believes in any conspiracy as a crazy fantasist. In some cases, this may be true because there's so much misinformation out there that people get led astray by unfounded theories. The problem with this is if you assume all conspiracies are baseless fantasies, then you miss the point. Sometimes people *do* conspire, and they did in Dallas.

The important thing is to look for the facts of conspiracy, and the facts of conspiracy are overwhelming in regard to the Kennedy assassination. It takes about twenty minutes to look at some of the basic facts—Ruby killing Oswald, the Magic Bullet Theory, what witnesses saw versus the official autopsy report—and realize there was a conspiracy.

I always tell my students on the first day of class, "I'm going to take about twenty minutes to go through these things, and if you still believe Oswald acted alone . . . well . . . I'm betting you don't." And inevitably they don't because they have the common sense to realize there was something sinister going on in Dallas.

What response do you get from students when you lay that information on them?
It's usually eye-opening, and they're definitely fascinated with it. A lot of times it leads to them going on the Internet, watching videos, reading more about it. I think it creates a fascination about taking a deeper look into their past. It's a hard road to get the truth out there. It's almost like a mouse going up against an elephant, but you can make people aware one person at a time. That's the attitude I and other researchers have. If I can get a few students to take a deeper look, then that's a good thing.

I live in a community of about 10,000 residents, and I've had enough presentations over the years that I've probably converted a lot of people. But what else can we do other than try to keep up the good fight? You know, truth in its highest form exists in the mind, so if nothing else, if we can't convince our institutions that something more happened in Dallas, we can still embrace a form of justice in ourselves, having the discernment and knowledge to know what really happened. At least we have that, and we can educate ourselves and educate others. That's been my goal for a long time. I think it's the best thing we can do.

Is there an emotional impact spectrum as far as the students are concerned?
Every student's different, but I get first- and second-year college students, and some of them are transitioning from that high school mentality to what it means to be part of a college environment. Some of them are still clinging to the paradigms of their parents or their friends. They don't examine things with enough depth, but some of them do gain a little more realization and self-awareness.

We're really talking about critical thinking. Whether it's the JFK assassination, the current political state in the United States, or various other controversies, can you dig down deeper? Can you understand things better? Can you take a walk in someone else's shoes and have some sort of empathy about what other folks are going through?

Those are really hard things, but whether I'm in my JFK, sociology, or history class, I always try to bring some of that out in them, to have them critically think about events that occurred in the past and how the world is today. Back to what Cicero said, don't be a child forever, learn something about the world around you, and have an idea. Be discerning.

Do you ever get any pushback from students or their parents?
I'm surprised I haven't because this is a controversial subject, but instead of pushback, I've actually gotten a lot of encouragement from students, parents, and the administration; they help me host conferences. I think they realize the material's controversial, but there's a kind of openness, and people aren't too connected to the ideology that you have to believe everything your government tells you. Let's just say they're open-minded about the idea of understanding what really happened in Dallas. I think a lot of Americans are. The resistance comes primarily from institutions that have something to protect.

Anybody who takes a critical look at the evidence and circumstances surrounding Dallas comes to the realization that the lone-nut version of history is ludicrous. My son is a high school history teacher in this area, which is pretty rural, and he also gives public presentations on the JFK assassination. He talks about the Magic Bullet Theory and shows a picture of that specific bullet, which was found in pristine condition. And he says to his audience, "This is the bullet that created seven wounds on two different people and also hit multiple dense bones in the process. As many of you are deer hunters, have you ever seen a bullet you killed a deer with that looked like that?" And they all say there's no way that could happen, and right away, with that realization alone, they come to the only conclusion they can . . . that there must have been a conspiracy.

How critical is it that younger generations understand the importance of history?
Extremely critical. I also teach sociology and the uniqueness of human beings. For instance, we talk about social reality. One of the things that

makes humans unique in this world is we don't merely react to events, but we also interpret and define them. And that definition of any situation becomes our social reality. But what happens when we don't define something properly? Do we change our minds about history?

I always tell my students history isn't etched in stone. I'll pull out my history book and remind them it still says that on November 22, 1963, a disturbed young man named Lee Harvey Oswald acted alone and killed the president of the United States. This needs to be redefined. Just because we're told something doesn't mean it's true, and what's most important is what really happened in Dallas, not the interpretation of it.

This thing we do as human beings, these interpretations we create that become our social reality . . . well . . . sometimes they need to be changed, and we need to change the social and historical reality of what happened in Dallas. And for the young folks we're talking about, they may encounter less resistance than we did, which would be great. Maybe they can finally get to the bottom of things and heal the nation.

What parting words do you share with your students on the last day of class?
Where do we go from here? My hope is that the class leads to more personal investigation on the part of the students, and more critical thinking on their part to dig into this further. And the lesson is don't simply accept everything you're told at face value, because there's so much information out there. Social networks are a cesspool of information, and so many young people are gullible about things they don't take the time to really look at. Whether it's students, the American public in general, or people around the world, they have to cut through all of that. You have to find a way to get to the facts and let the facts lead you in a rational way.

That's the best answer I can give to anything, whether it's the Kennedy assassination or something else. The same thing applies. Can you apply rational thinking and facts to your conclusions and be an informed citizen? In an open democracy, this is absolutely necessary. Democracy is messy. The Greeks created the most democratic society in the world 2,000 years ago, but special interests and corruption were still a problem for them. We have to constantly fight against that.

What is your biggest motivation, at this point, to continue your work?
Getting to a greater truth, and I say a greater truth because here's one of the biggest misperceptions about the JFK assassination. I run into this all the time and talk about it with my students . . . is when people make the statement, "We'll probably never know what happened." How many times have you heard that? "We'll probably never know what happened in Dallas." The truth of the matter is, we know a lot about what happened in Dallas. I mean, at the end of the day, we still have to develop theories and opinions that might be wrong, but the basic facts of Dallas are already there for us to see. There's enough evidence to make some historical conclusions about the JFK assassination.

I think historians run away from it. They think it's too convoluted, too controversial, but we already have a good idea about what happened. The hard part is getting our institutions to recognize these things, to get the media, the historians, and the government to recognize the truth about what happened to JFK. That's the hard part. I think we have a good piece of the story already. We want to see more, we still do, but how do we get the attention from our institutions about recognizing the truth about it?

I don't know how or when we accomplish this, but honestly, that's my primary goal moving forward, so we can pick up a history book and it doesn't say Oswald did it. How about that for starters? That's important.

I want to wish you luck because you're tackling a broad and convoluted subject, and you're trying to get a broad scope of different opinions. I don't envy you on that one because I'm sure you've got a wide array of opinions on a lot of different stuff from a lot of different people.

One of my good friends, a JFK researcher, said the term "the JFK research community" is actually an oxymoron. It's a divergent group, but I think there's commonality. We all recognize the story we were told about a lone nut isn't true. One of the things I tell my students is a lot of people have opinions and theories, and some of them might be wild, crazy, or speculative.

We speculate about what happened in Dallas, but what are we left to do but speculate? There's never been a legitimate investigation into what happened on November 22, 1963. And so, we go on and we go on in search of some higher truth. I think that's the best way I can put it.

PART 7

KEEPING THE STORY ALIVE

People tell me, "Bill, let it go. The Kennedy assassination was years ago. It was just the assassination of a president and the hijacking of our government by a totalitarian regime. Who cares? Just let it go!" And I say, "Alright then. That whole Jesus thing? Let it go! It was 2,000 years ago! Who cares?"

—Bill Hicks
American Stand-Up Comedian

CHAPTER 22

LORIEN FENTON

Lorien Fenton became actively involved in the San Francisco Bay Area JFK assassination community after almost dying from a mysterious form of pneumonia during the H1N1 scare in the summer of 2009. Her near-death experience propelled her into doing the work she loves today, which includes as a conference producer, web designer, and podcast host. Her nonprofit, Conscious Community Events, produces UFO CON, which is held annually in San Francisco. Since 2013, she has produced nine JFK assassination conferences. Fenton also has been producing and hosting her podcast, *The Fenton Perspective,* for ten years on Revolution Radio (www.freedomslips.com). The podcast focuses on topics such as UFOs, human consciousness, near-death experiences, unexplained mysteries, ghosts, and the JFK assassination.

Where were you when JFK was assassinated, and what is your memory of it?

I was six years old and in my first-grade classroom at St. Clare Parish School in Portland, Oregon. Sister Ora May was my teacher. It was right after lunch when the principal, who was also a nun, opened the door to our classroom and stepped hurriedly just beyond the entrance to loudly (unexpected for our principal to raise her voice) announce to Sister Ora May that President Kennedy had been shot. We were all instantly tasked with praying the Hail Mary and Our Lord's Prayer. In what seemed like hours, which in reality may only have been twenty or thirty minutes, the principal was back in the doorway to report, flatly, "the president is dead." She didn't say another word and stood there for what seemed like an eternity, staring at all of us and none of us, as she turned slowly and faded back into the empty hallway.

Until that point, in the brief three months I'd been in grade school, I'd never seen a glint of emotion from Sister Ora May. She was the quintessential nun—stoic, uncommunicative, stern, smileless. However, the second she heard President Kennedy was dead, she slumped into her chair—she had been standing while praying—and started crying softly. This display of emotion lasted only about thirty seconds, and the nun I knew was back in a flash. Then, we were tasked again with praying for JFK's "immortal soul."

Shortly after, our parents started showing up to take us home from school early. Many went to the church to pray. My mother and two younger sisters went into the church for a short time. The church was packed with more people than Midnight Mass at Christmas. It seemed

Lee Harvey Oswald being led by Dallas police after being apprehended inside the Texas Theatre near downtown Dallas in the early afternoon of November 22, 1963. (Source: Bettmann via Getty Images)

like all the adult women were crying silently . . . everyone was praying for JFK, Mrs. Kennedy, and their children.

I found out years later many of the parishioners held a two-day praying vigil with our school's nuns and priests until Sunday's masses began at 6:00 a.m., which were packed to the rafters. I spoke with Father Thomas—the head priest of our parish for more than thirty years—when I was around nineteen years old, some thirteen years after the assassination, about that weekend. He said there have never been as many parishioner and nonparishioners at a mass before the JFK assassination, and the only other regular Sunday mass when the church was full again like that was in 1968 after Robert Kennedy was assassinated earlier in the week.

Father Tom also told me, "I've never prayed so devoutly for a person in my entire life as I did for President Kennedy. Looking back on it now, I think I was actually praying more for our country and his office than the man himself. Regarding his death, we all knew something was very wrong, very evil." Father Tom was a very wise man.

Describe your podcast and why it's important you give JFK researchers/witnesses a forum in which to discuss their research and/or personal experiences regarding the JFK assassination?

The Fenton Perspective is an eclectic mix of topics that include UFOs, consciousness, conspiracies, corruption, near-death experiences, ghosts and all things paranormal, but most important, the JFK Assassination.

Having JFK researchers as guests is very important to me because, in my opinion, a global population has been lied to. They believe the false narrative taught to them in school and by the media . . . the carefully crafted lies that created the cover-up of the century. The researchers I interview are the only people left keeping curiosity around the assassination alive. They're our soldiers of historic truth, helping stamp out the "collective ignorance" surrounding the assassination and bring their investigations into the light.

To me, no other topic is more important to broadcast, especially now. Exposing the truth about the JFK assassination—which was the beginning of all the corruption we're experiencing today—is imperative. I give the JFK community carte blanche to be guests on my show in hopes that the podcast will spark listeners to become curious around the truth about what happened in Dallas.

These interviews give all who listen exposure to the matrix of lies and mass mind control we're subjected to today by those in power and the corporate mainstream media—and hopefully they begin to realize 11/22/63 was the day our freedoms began to erode.

Tell us how you got started as a conference organizer and how this led to you producing JFK conferences?
I became a conference producer at twenty when I was a member of several nonprofit dance organizations in Portland, Oregon, that all needed to raise money. I produced a dance training conference and found my true calling in "organizing." Later, I helped manage dance companies in which I was a member. A few years later I started my own nonprofit dance company, and that was significant because putting on a dance performance and managing tours is, on many levels, parallel to producing an educational conference.

After that, I started working at a speaker's bureau as a sales and marketing professional for bestselling authors turned keynote speakers, booking them at major conferences all over the world. Because I had produced conferences, I was a natural at selling speakers for events and getting them top dollar. Due to my success in that field, I was hired by a bestselling author, speaker, and government HR trainer to be her workshop and training producer. By 2000, I was producing several conferences a year for large nonprofits in the Bay Area.

In 2010, I was helping out with a conference and met a founding member of The Oswald Innocence Campaign, and in the summer of 2013 the founders asked if I would help produce their JFK 50th Anniversary Assassination Truth Conference in Santa Barbara, California. I agreed to do it, and that was the first of nine conferences I've produced in conjunction with several organizations in the JFK community and my own nonprofit production company, Conscious Community Events.

People ask me why I choose to produce these conferences, and the answer is simple: I want to give a voice to the "silenced" truth tellers—the researchers, authors, and witnesses who have concluded that JFK was assassinated by elements in our own government and Lee Harvey Oswald wasn't a lone-nut assassin.

Why do you say "silenced" truth tellers?
In my experience, the assassination conferences have been almost completely ignored by the mainstream media. Usually, when you hold a conference with high-caliber speakers on a subject, you're inundated with requests for press passes and inquiries about interviewing the speakers. In over a decade of "fringe" events production, I've received three interview inquiries. And in the end, those stories/interviews were edited to make the interviewees appear obsessed and/or unstable (overtly or subtlety), adding more disinformation to the cover-up. And in most cases, we're talking about extremely educated scholars and researchers who deserve to be treated with respect.

It's an amazing feeling bringing together scholars, authors, researchers, and witnesses to all share their stories and information. The content of the conferences is always profoundly educational, and there hasn't been one conference that didn't have a "wow" moment and an hour or more of information sharing I didn't know about in regard to the assassination. In this genre, after a lifetime of study, you start to think you know everything there is to know, but you don't.

Are there a lot of disagreements among the researchers, and does this hinder progress toward the truth or help keep the researchers focused?
Because of this "belief of knowing everything," there are rivalries between them, and not everyone sees eye-to-eye. When I first noticed this, I was angry. I felt there was no place for infighting among people who were all after the same thing—the truth. But as time has passed and I see rivalries pop up now and again, I'm actually glad. I've realized they relish in arguing over who the third tramp was, whether James Files[1] was the gunman behind the fatal head shot, whether Oswald was really up on the sixth floor before the shooting, and my favorite, whether Oswald was actually on the steps in front of the Texas School Book Depository when the shots were fired. These differing opinions keep researchers on their toes, and it has worked in the community's favor because debate is healthy. I wouldn't have it any other way.

What is JFKTruthTV.com?

JFKTruthTV.com is an Internet TV channel available on the web, Roku, and soon on all Internet streaming platforms (e.g., Apple TV, Amazon Fire TV, Google TV), where award-winning filmmaker Randy Benson (see Chapter 24) and I feature past JFK assassination conferences from a variety of producers and organizations, including my conferences. We will also be providing movies and podcasts. Coming in 2022, Randy and I will be hosting "made for network" interview- and newscast-style programming.

We started JFKTruthTV because the JFK community has hit a critical juncture. Many of the original researchers have died, and the ones left standing are mostly in their seventies and eighties. I'm 64 and considered one of the younger community members. Randy is in his fifties and is considered a baby within the group.

JFKTruthTV was launched to preserve the research. Our hope is the network will serve as a time capsule for future generations concerning the truth about all twentieth-century assassinations.

In your opinion, was Lee Harvey Oswald a patsy?

I believe Oswald was a patsy. If you study the assassination, you quickly realize how organized and planned-out it truly was. You also realize Oswald wasn't the only patsy being lined up to take the fall. Much research suggests there were a few "backup" patsies, not only in Dealey Plaza that day, but also in cities like Chicago and Tampa, where assassination plans had also been set in motion.

Tosh Plumlee,[2] a CIA contract pilot, said he was part of a special team sent to Dallas to "abort" an assassination attempt, and he seems a likely candidate, along with the other members of his team. Plumlee believes his team was sent to Dallas to stop any attempts on the president's life, but they failed. This may be true, but they were positioned too far away from Elm Street to make a difference on the old motorcade route, and they were never informed of the motorcade's detour onto Elm Street. Many people believe they were sent there to be the fall guys if the Oswald scenario didn't play out.

Researcher Larry Rivera (see Chapter 2) has offered very compelling evidence that Oswald wasn't even on the sixth floor of the Book

Depository at the time of shooting. Rivera actually continued the work of other researchers before him and has shown through thorough photographic analysis that Oswald was standing on the front steps of the Depository looking out toward the limousine seconds before the shots were fired. Rivera goes into meticulous detail about this in his book *The JFK Horsemen.*

Another fascinating book on this particular aspect of the assassination is *The Men on the Sixth Floor* by Glen Sample and Mark Collom. In it, the authors cover the "sixth floor timeline" in great detail, providing information that Oswald wasn't on the sixth floor at the time of the shooting. The book focuses on Malcolm Wallace, Lyndon Johnson's hatchet man, and presents solid evidence that Wallace—a much better shot than Oswald—was actually the shooter on the sixth floor of the Depository that day. It also includes interesting documents on Billy Sol Estes, a Texas con man and good friend of Lyndon Johnson. The book basically provides a clear

A camera captures the back of Jack Ruby as he shoots Lee Harvey Oswald, who is being escorted by guards during a television press conference at the Dallas police headquarters. (Photo by © CORBIS/Corbis via Getty Images)

picture of the web of scandal, corruption, and criminal activity taking place in Texas—by Lyndon Johnson and other extremely powerful good ole boys—leading up to the assassination. In essence, it reveals the Texas connection to JFK's death.

Why does the JFK assassination still matter all these years later?

JFK's assassination paralyzed the world, but mostly the American people. A palatable grief took over the country all in a matter of minutes. I remember my parents being very sad, and this sadness was mixed with what I now know was a sense of defeat. In many ways, the loss of JFK cut deeper into their souls than the loss of a close family member did. People were shocked and saddened, but they also lost faith in the country . . . lost hope in the ability for our country to do the right thing. Somehow everyone knew this was the first blow in a long line of battles for this country's sovereignty. It's like the saying goes, "If they got away with it once, they could get away with it again."

How do you explain to younger generations the magnitude of the JFK assassination?

It's hard to explain to anyone not alive at the time how this assassination changed the world. It was one death—compared to the millions of deaths during the First and Second World Wars—that effected humanity on a global scale. And it did so in hours, not weeks or months. Even goatherds in Mongolia heard about JFK's death within days. What's even more remarkable is that these goatherds had "an idea" of who he was. How does a goatherd halfway across the world in 1963 really "understand" America and the leader of that country? But even they were affected. Tribesmen in Africa were affected. Russian citizens were affected. This shows how deeply rooted the sadness was around his death.

What is your biggest motivation, at this point, to continue your work?

For me, personally, I want to expose the truth about Lee Harvey Oswald because I truly believe he was set up to be a patsy. Judyth Vary Baker, and her personal story about her relationship with Oswald (see Chapter 7), are major motivations for me. Some researchers dismiss her story because it doesn't jibe with what they think they know, but I knew she was telling the truth from the moment I heard her story.

She brings a human element to Oswald's life that "serious" JFK researchers don't handle well. I find this sad because she's the only person who was close to Oswald who has exhaustively crusaded for his exoneration. And she put it all on the line to come forward—losing her family, her job, and her friends, as well as becoming a target of those who don't want the truth about Oswald to come out.

Judyth has never given up. She continues to paint a picture of Lee Harvey Oswald that is vastly different from the picture the mainstream media has painted over the years. How can we not be motivated by Judyth's courage and not want to emulate her bravery by looking into all aspects of the JFK assassination and exonerating Oswald? Her conviction equates to motivation for me.

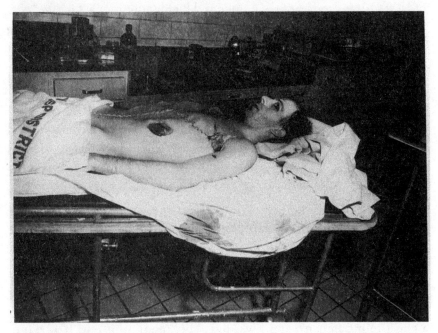

The body of Lee Harvey Oswald after his autopsy. (Photo by © CORBIS/Corbis via Getty Images)

CHAPTER 23

JEFFREY HOLMES

Jeffrey Holmes is the coowner (with his wife, Jane) of Strange True Tours of New Orleans and leads the unique and highly educational *Oswald's New Orleans Tour*, which follows in the footsteps of Lee Harvey Oswald during the summer of 1963. Jeffrey is the go-to expert in New Orleans when it comes to Oswald's local connections and his whereabouts that summer. He has conducted extensive research, including interviewing witnesses to pivotal events and those who knew Oswald personally. He has been a featured speaker at the Dallas JFK Conference on the JFK assassination and has been cited in various articles and research papers by researchers. He is also one of the top researchers on the origins of organized crime and the mafia in the Crescent City.

Why did you start the Oswald tour?
I have to go back a little bit further to when I became a ghost tour guy. After Hurricane Katrina, I met my wife, Jane, who has a history degree. She got a job working for a swamp tour company and very quickly ended up managing all their sales kiosks. They were in partnership with a ghost tour company, and I was like, "Let me try this out. It'd be fun. I can go out in the evening and make some money." So, I immediately went to work as a ghost tour guide. A few months into it, I realized the whole thing was pure nonsense. Now, New Orleans is most definitely haunted, but the stories told on the tours are loosely based on fact if

not totally made up. The average ghost tour guide simply memorizes a script.

Well, at about that time I came across a book titled *Mr. New Orleans: The Life of a Big Easy Underworld Legend,* written by Frenchie Brouillette and Matthew Randazzo V. Frenchie was a gangster here in the '50s and

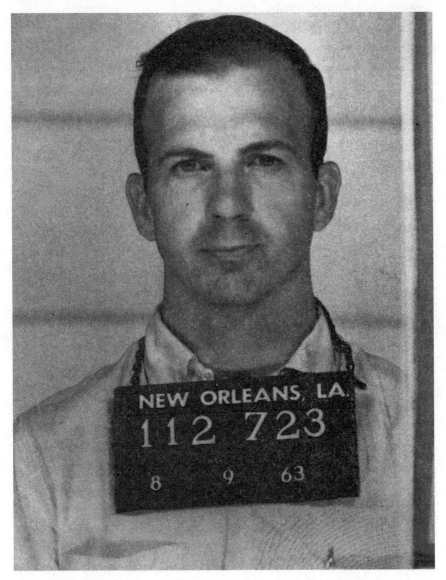

Lee Harvey Oswald's New Orleans mugshot. (Photo by © CORBIS/Corbis via Getty Images)

'60s and was taken under the wing of Carlos Marcello. He knew all the New Orleans characters. Attorney Dean Andrews[1] used to sleep on his couch when he was too wasted to go home. There's an entire chapter in the book dedicated to the JFK conspiracy. And in this chapter, Frenchie says, "Out of all my cronies in New Orleans, I'm the only person who wasn't involved in killing Kennedy."

Frenchie had an FBI file that was several hundred pages long. He was in the thick of everything mob-related and knew Oswald, Ruby, Marcello, Andrews, Clay Shaw, and Jim Garrison. One thing people have to understand about New Orleans is it's a small town, and I really try to emphasize this on the tour. If you live or work in the French Quarter, it's like being in high school. There's a bar on every corner, and we sit in every one of them and know every bartender, and we all sit and tell stories. It's a close dynamic.

So, I read the Frenchie book and was like, "Holy s*#t! This is amazing stuff." Then I came across the work of local historian Buddy Stall, who chronicled all of this really weird and unusual stuff about New Orleans, so I asked myself, "Why isn't anybody doing these types of tours?" So, Jane and I talked about it, and we started our tour company.

How did the Oswald tour develop?

We did a lot of research to develop the tours and told real stories about prostitution, cross-dressers, family intrigue, pirates, and slavery. And then a friend of mine, Mr. Lou, an old New Orleans artist who back in the '60s painted portraits for the Marcello family and played pinochle with Carlos in the bars on Bourbon Street, turned me on to the book *Dr. Mary's Monkey*, by Ed Haslam, and that just blew my freaking mind. And then more research led me to Judyth Vary Baker and her book *Me and Lee*.

I discovered Judyth was doing her first public appearance in Toronto on October 18, 2011, and I looked at my wife and said, "I gotta go." I booked a plane ticket and flew to Toronto. I was there for two nights and actually spent the day with Judyth. At the big press conference, there were experts in the audience and TV cameras and reporters, and Judyth was trying to explain the dynamics of New Orleans. Suddenly, she looked over at me and said, "Well, he can explain it. Jeffrey, come here." She brought me on camera on national Canadian television. I almost soiled my pants. Here I was this young buck just scratching the surface on this stuff.

I went back home and started including a little Oswald story in the tour, and we eventually developed a full two-hour Oswald tour. And at that point I just dove in. I found other books and research, and throughout the years, I met locals, old-timers . . . people who were waiters and bartenders back then. They told me things like they used to wait on Carlos, or they worked at Antoine's[2] and overheard weird phone calls. One girl told me on the phone, "My daddy helped fly Carlos back in." And I was like, "Let's get together for drinks."

Another great book is *Flashback* by Ron Lewis. It's out of print, so if you can find a copy it won't be cheap, maybe $50 to $100. Ron was kind of a vagabond, and he claimed to work with Oswald in New Orleans in the summer of '63. And what I've found is although all of these books— *Me and Lee, Dr. Mary's Monkey, Flashback, Mr. New Orleans*—don't perfectly match, there are significant parts that do come together. This happened more than fifty years ago, so people grow old and forget details, but the stories come together and form a nice tight little web you really can't puncture . . . not in my opinion, not in any logical sense.

The tour has just grown, and we get all kinds of people on it. Judyth started doing an Oswald conference in New Orleans a handful of years ago, and that really put me further down the rabbit hole. And there are other dynamics I mention on the tour that aren't in any of these books because of the social and political dynamics that still exist in New Orleans to this day.

When you talked to locals who knew Oswald, what did they say about him?
Most locals have scattered memories of Lee, mostly recollections of him at a bar or in school. He moved in and out of New Orleans, so he never truly had the time to become close or longtime friends with anyone. Lee grew up without a father, without any real father figure. I think that's one of the reasons he ended up in the military. He was looking for an authoritative figure. As young boys growing up, we need somebody we can look up to who can guide us and turn us into men. Lee never had that. His

dad died just before he was born, and he moved all over the place with his mom.

His childhood was very difficult and lonely. He never had a tight-knit family, which also had an effect on him. So, he was looking for guidance, looking for discipline. He was a man who truly believed in his country and believed he was doing the right thing, even though it looked like he was doing the wrong thing. He was definitely a patsy. He was being set up, and toward the end he knew it. There's so much evidence that supports this. You don't even need to go to Dallas and talk about the gun being changed or the fingerprints, or the fact there were no nitrates on his cheek or any of that stuff. You only need to focus on what happened in the summer of '63 in New Orleans.

When I started getting into this, the experts told me, "Find a particular aspect of the case and focus on it." I live here; it's my backyard. Oswald's childhood home is in my neighborhood. I can walk the dog from my house and walk past where he lived as a child. So, this is why I have an almost personal connection, because he was a New Orleans boy.

What information do you impart on your tours?
I try to make people understand how close everything is and how there are no coincidences in this story. The tour starts at 544 Camp Street in Lafayette Square, where in the movie *JFK* Jim Garrison tells his guys it's the center of US Intelligence for the entire southern United States. It's literally one square city block. When you're standing there, you can clearly see the federal building that houses the CIA, FBI, Secret Service, US Marshals Service, and even the Office of Naval Intelligence. Reily Coffee Company, where Lee worked that summer, was literally around the corner on the other side of the courthouse from the square.

I point out where Lee was and what he was doing and that everything I'm saying is based on documented fact. And at the end of the tour, I leave it up to the tour guests to come up with their own conclusions. I also give them my conclusion, which is there's no way anybody could've walked these streets, been engaged in this kind of activity, and been involved with people of this caliber in *this* city and have it *not* been something more than what it seemed.

New Orleans is small, and you don't realize this until you're standing on its street corners. Lee's office at 544 Camp Street was actually in the same building as Guy Banister's office, even though Banister had a different address. Unless you're here looking at it, you don't understand that corner buildings in New Orleans have two addresses, which doesn't happen anywhere else in the United States. So, I show people where he worked, Judyth's initials on his timecard, and the parking garage directly next door. When you're there and you see it, you just watch the epiphany; you see the wheels starting to turn and people are like, "Oh my God." The head of the House Committee on Un-American Activities, Edwin Edward Willis, could turn around in his office chair, look out his window, and see Oswald in the parking garage right next door to Reily Coffee Company. He could throw a rock and hit him. It was physically that close. You can't walk the same block in New Orleans for one week without knowing everyone on that block.

I take people to the front door of organizations and social clubs like the Pickwick Club and the Boston Club, which have been around since the end of the Civil War because their members have always been like-minded southerners and the elite of the city. And you can look out the window of these clubs and see where Oswald was passing out his leaflets on Canal Street on August 9. Old New Orleans families are very old and stick together. Their grandparents grew up together as children, and their children will grow up together, as well. It's tight-knit, and these social clubs are an extension of that.

Take Edith Stern, who owned WDSU-TV studio. She played a primary role in helping promote Oswald's image as a procommunist agitator. When Oswald was handing out pro-Castro leaflets outside Clay Shaw's International Trade Mart on August 16, WDSU-TV was there to film it, apparently having been alerted in advance. On August 17, WDSU Radio arranged for an interview with Oswald, who proclaimed his leftist views. And on August 19, WDSU again contacted Oswald and arranged for him to appear in a debate with an anti-Castro activist, and it was during this debate when Oswald proclaimed himself a "Marxist."

These WDSU interviews were all used for the INCA (Information Council of the Americas) propaganda LPs created after the JFK

assassination. INCA was a right-wing propaganda machine created by
Dr. Alton Ochsner. My point is, Stern hung out socially with people like
Clay Shaw, Ochsner, and William Reily, owner of Reily Coffee Company,
where Oswald worked. On the tour, I stand people across the street from
where this stuff happened and connect the dots, and this helps solidify the
fact there were no coincidences in the summer of '63.

Another thing I do is show tour guests historic items, such as the
INCA albums. I have six different versions. I also have old newspapers
from 1963 from the assassination, old postcards from the 1960s of the
clubs on Bourbon Street where Oswald was, where the mafia was, and
where Oswald was passing out his literature. I actually put these items in

Clay Shaw was one of many interesting characters in New Orleans who had ties
to the US intelligence community. (Source: Bettmann via Getty Images)

their hands, and this makes it real for them because they not only see it, but they can feel it, touch it, smell it. It smells old. I do this at the end of the tour, and it seals the deal.

What are your tour demographics?

I don't get your average tourist taking my tour. These people are really into it. They're researchers and individuals who've been interested in the Kennedy assassination for half their lives. It's an older crowd; I don't get too many younger folks, but on occasion I do. It's usually the guy who's on the tour because it's really his thing, and his wife is tagging along, and the couple they're vacationing with is also tagging along because they're thinking, "This sounds interesting. Let's check it out." By the end of the tour, I have skeptics and people who just didn't think any particular way about it saying, "Oh crap! There's a lot more to this than we realized."

How do tour guests react to what you're telling them?

I'll be doing the tour, and in the middle of a story, a local will pass by, stop and listen to me for a minute, then say, "I knew Carlos," or, "I knew Clay Shaw. He's right." And they turn around and walk away. My guests are stunned. It's really a validation moment. It's the closeness, the tightness of New Orleans and the French Quarter, that provides that personal interaction on a regular basis. And I can't make it up. I can't plan it. It's just the old farts rolling down the street saying, "Yeah, I remember that guy. He's right."

There's a story we tell about a famous Madam who closed up shop in the 1960s,[3] and I still have old guys walk by and say, "I knew Norma. She was a wonderful woman." And I'm like, "Yeah, I bet you did." So, afterward everyone on the tour is excited to have heard the story about Norma. It creates a sense of intimacy.

Also, the Oswald tour is personalized. It's usually me and between two and five people for two hours. Half the time the tour goes longer because everyone has their own questions they want to ask and their own knowledge they want to share, so we'll just sit in a coffee shop and talk about it. I've learned a lot from my guests because they've really studied this, and it adds to what I already know and puts other pieces of the puzzle together.

Every tour is different. I never know what's going to happen on the streets. I never know who's going to walk by and add their personal story. I did a private tour for this well-known actor, and halfway through the tour he said, "I'm trying to write a movie about Oswald. I'm a producer and here's my card." I had the whole cast of *Chicago Fire*, *New York Times* bestselling authors, and all kinds of historians.

What was one of your more interesting tours?
We did a special event with Judyth once, and it had a lot of people on it. We were standing in front of Reily Coffee Company doing our thing, and she was adding her personal stories, and when we were ready to start walking away, she said, "Oh wait. Hang on everybody." She led us around a block and a half to the back door so she could show us where she and Oswald used to make out. This was priceless.

We had a TV camera crew, an international press photographer, another handful of media, half a dozen people from the Louisiana State Museum system, another six people who were licensed tour guides, and a handful of couples who were all old New Orleanians who had their own personal input. The tour took almost four hours. It was one of the most insane tours I've ever done, and it was emotional because Judyth was sharing her personal recollections about Lee.

Have you had any epiphanies about the JFK assassination since starting your tour?
Before Hurricane Katrina, I worked at a restaurant called Old New Orleans Cookery, and the owner of the restaurant was this old curmudgeon named Michael Lala. Back in the '50s and '60s, Lala was a cameraman for WDSU. He filmed Oswald on the corner the day he was handing out those leaflets, and he told me, "I got to work that day and picked up the clipboard, and it said we needed to be on that corner at a specific time because something was going to happen." Years later, when I started the tour, I heard the date and it clicked in my head. I was like, "Holy c#*p! That event was staged."

The station knew it was going to happen before it happened, which is why it was on Lala's schedule that day. When you control the media, you control the message. The boss calls up the station and says, "You're going to have a camera set up on this corner at this time." And you say, "Yes ma'am." You don't ask questions. This goes back to Edith Stern again, who owned WDSU. She was very right wing and a member of the Pickwick Club, and she was also a financer of INCA. Welcome to the party.

What has the tour meant to you?
It has been an absolute blast because everything, every teeny tiny nugget of information fills in the entire foundation of the thing. Each is just another grain of sand, but with enough of them you have an island. I'll never know

In 1969, New Orleans District Attorney Jim Garrison arrested and charged local businessman Clay Shaw with conspiring to assassinate President Kennedy. (Source: Bettmann via Getty Images)

everything about the New Orleans connection, but I'm constantly learning something new, and that keeps me motivated because I feel like a kid at Christmas. I just discovered this, and it fits in with this, which brings the big picture a little more into focus. I don't make money doing this tour; I do it out of a passion. We make our money doing bicycle tours and telling stories about prostitutes and taking people to graveyards.

I just kind of fell into this whole thing backward. I fell into the lure of New Orleans and the incredible tapestry that represents the many layers of this city's history. Because one thing leads to another, leads to another, and leads to another. Meeting these people who have these connections has been fascinating to me, plus I'm now one or two degrees of separation from the main players. I'm some kid from a cul-de-sac in South Florida, a planned community of cookie-cutter houses, and now I'm in New Orleans, rubbing elbows and becoming ever more connected to the heart of the New Orleans connection to the JFK assassination.

There's a saying: There are two kinds of people in this world. People who talk about what they want to do and people who talk about what they've done. I'm going to be that seventy-year-old curmudgeon sitting at the bar saying, "I kissed Oswald's girlfriend." I'm not only touching history, but I'm also becoming part of it. But most important, I'm helping keep the story alive.

What have been the ripple effects of the JFK assassination?
The biggest ripple effect of all, which I think we're all aware of, is the rise of the military-industrial complex. We're in a state of perpetual war with an unseen, unknown enemy who doesn't have a physical country, so to speak. I'm a firm believer in the writings of Smedley Butler, the WWI major general who wrote the speech and short book titled *War is a Racket*. He said the war mongers were in it for GOD = Gold, Oil and Drugs, and he was absolutely right.

My wife was in the Air Force during the first Gulf War at a forward operating base. She's a combat veteran, and she saw the ungodly, unethical waste of US tax dollars for absolutely nothing. Dropping billions of dollars of bombs a day just because someone has a contract with a corporation. What's the intro to Oliver Stone's movie? The warning from

President Eisenhower about the military-industrial complex. This is the biggest thing that drives our economy: it's death. Think about all the entities the Kennedys went after—the mafia, the CIA, the Federal Reserve, the oil industry, and the military-industrial complex. At the end of the day, it's all about business. Follow the money. That day in Dallas solidified the power of these people.

What would you want younger generations to know about the Kennedy assassination?
I do get people in their thirties on the tour, and every now and then I'll get people in their twenties and teens being dragged along by Dad. And some of them are actually into it because they've watched the movie *JFK* with their dad, you know, like thirty-five times. What I try to impart to them is to question everything, to study and research for themselves. Don't believe your government and everything they tell you. Don't believe everything that every adult tells you. Fact-check, do your own research, come to your own conclusions, be your own person, have your own mind. There's so much more going on. As long as you remain glued to your big-screen TV and captivated by Kim Kardashian and her booty, these people are going to run roughshod over you.

Nowadays young people are becoming more aware. I hate using the term "woke," but we're becoming more diversified. Young people have more gay, lesbian, and transgender friends. They have more African American friends, more Middle Eastern friends, more Latino friends. My daughter had the good fortune of growing up in New Orleans, and when she was a kid, her babysitter was Danny the Tranny. They liked to play dress up and put on makeup. These young kids are realizing grandpa was probably a racist, grandpa was probably an asshole, and they know we need to move on from that old mentality.

What I try to make them understand is that in history, one thing leads to another. And once they understand that, I think it empowers them a little bit more. Look back to the 1960s. They weren't all hippies running around screwing and smoking dope. Some of these kids were out in the streets protesting for the rights we have now, especially for the younger gay and transgender kids. They don't understand what their forefathers went through and died for in some cases. So, I try and make them understand that the good old days weren't that good. We need to be aware of this so we can move forward from it.

All my tours are kind of Aesop's fables in disguise, little lessons. But that's just our personality, and we want to encourage our guests to explore further. When you come off a ghost tour, you're like, "Okay. That was fun. Let's go to Bourbon Street." When you come off our tour, you have a list of three or four books you want to read. You now have a thirst for knowledge, whatever subject it is. And once you have that thirst for knowledge, it will grow. I ended up here because of my thirst for knowledge. I just wanted to be a ghost tour guy and have fun on the streets, and then I realized the real story, the real history is so much better than anything you can make up.

These were real people, just like you and me, and that's what I try to instill in my guests, that at the end of the day, Lee was just a regular guy like you and me. He went into the military because he had no direction in his life, and he wanted to find something, a purpose, and that purpose was railroaded by very powerful, deceitful people.

In your opinion, what is the cost of conspiracy?
The cost of conspiracy is, in a sense, our life and liberty. It's our true freedom as human beings. I'm not a religious person, but I think of myself as spiritual. We're God's creations, be it an animal, dog, horse, or human being. These conspirators have destroyed love, empathy, and compassion in mankind, all for greed and power. Even today, we're 2,000 years allegedly beyond the birth of Jesus Christ, Lord and Savior of the Christian world. I'm not dissing any religion, but it's that cloud of existence they want us to believe. You have to go through the machine. You have to work. You have to be better than your neighbor. You have to have a bigger house. You have to be more powerful. You have to have a nicer car. You have to go to better parties. And all of this just takes away the essence of being human. That's what the cost of conspiracy is; it's the essence of being human.

We're destroying people we don't know halfway across the world, just for cheap plastic products at Walmart and cheap oil. Industries that can save our planet are being put by the wayside for profit. And there are animals and human beings being destroyed that will never come back again, animals alive today that my child may never see in her lifetime because we may not get to Africa or India or New Zealand to see them. And then they're just gone, and the dynamics this has on the whole ecosystem of our planet is devastating. So, I guess the cost of conspiracy isn't just the cost of being human, but it's the cost of the existence of our planet. It's a shortsighted greed factor: "I've got mine, so screw you."

I could make a lot more money if I did ghost tours, but I wouldn't be happy. I have a wonderful family. I have a daughter who's very aware and knows what's going on. And hopefully we'll be part of the next generation that can fix some of this stuff. But with every generation, it's another layer of shit, because it's a constant yin-yang against the powers that be who control it and keep us down as masses. We're almost reduced to a serfdom-type existence again. We're debt slaves. Many Americans have to show up at their crappy jobs every single day because half the country is two paychecks away from being homeless, and that's by design. I think the assassination was a very big step toward that. After WWII, the country was rebuilding. Everybody was happy and prosperous. And then, all of a sudden, here's the Korean War and then Vietnam, and "Hey, we're making some money on this war thing. Let's send some poor kids over there to shoot Asian people. We don't know any of them. We don't care. Our kids aren't going over there."

So, the cost of conspiracy is everything. Our very existence, our way of life, the way half our world is living. We haven't progressed as human beings; we're still pieces of shit.

What would you want people in the future to say about this tour?
That I reintroduced the conversation to New Orleans about the conspiracy, because nobody did anything about this whatsoever. And a lot of these families are still here. I know a guy who's a tour guide, and he's the nephew of Jada Conforto, the New Orleans stripper who was recruited by Ruby to work at his Carousel Club in Dallas and was witness to the fact Ruby and Oswald knew each other. All these people, all these families are still here. But it's never been talked about; it's always been hush-hush. I wasn't born

and raised here, but I came here, and this thing was thrown in my lap, and I was like, "What's going on here? This is a big puzzle, and I want to know what happened."

It's fascinating. Especially the death of Dr. Mary Sherman (see Chapter 6). Holy crap. Jesus, man. Where do you even start with that? And nobody knows about this. It isn't common knowledge? I've just been trying to help piece the big picture together.

CHAPTER 24

RANDOLPH BENSON

Randolph Benson is a graduate of Wake Forest University and the North Carolina School of the Arts' School of Filmmaking. His film *Man and Dog* has appeared in film festivals worldwide and has garnered numerous awards, most notably a Gold Medal in the Academy of Motion Picture Arts and Sciences' Student Academy Awards. His work has been featured on HBO, Bravo, the Independent Film Channel, numerous public television stations, Canal Plus–France, Telewizja Polska S.A.–Poland, and KBS–Korea. Benson received an Eastman Kodak Excellence in Filmmaking Award at the Cannes Film Festival and a First Appearance Award at the International Documentary Film Festival Amsterdam. His documentary film *The Searchers* premiered at the Texas Theatre in Dallas on November 21, 2016. The film explores the unique subculture of JFK researchers from the standpoint of an outsider who found himself, over time, becoming an insider. He currently teaches at the Center for Documentary Studies at Duke University.

What triggered your motivation to make *The Searchers*?
I've always been a history buff, but I guess it goes back to Oliver Stone's *JFK*. Like so many people in our generation, I learned so much about the assassination watching that film. The other thing that really piqued my interest as a documentary filmmaker was the mention in all of the interviews that Stone did of these independent researchers who were doing

the work, filing Freedom of Information Act requests to get documents. It took them years and years to get these documents. Every good project begins with a question, so my question was: Who in the hell are these people doing this? So, that's what set me on the journey to make the film.

Where did you start?

I started researching the researchers and quickly realized that in order to understand what a researcher goes through, I had to put myself in their shoes, so I started researching my family. My father was a fighter pilot during the Cold War and was stationed on the East-West German border. He was on the front line of the Cold War flying technical, nuclear-tipped fighter jets, ready to go at any moment. He would fly up and down the border, shadow a Soviet MiG, and then break off so another jet could take his place. It was this dance they did for ten years.

But when Kennedy was assassinated, my dad wasn't scrambled . . . he wasn't even told about the assassination until hours afterward. He only found out because someone came into the officer's club and asked, "Hey, have you heard?" Now my dad was a true patriot—he was in World War II when he was 17, fought in Korea, trained pilots for Vietnam, and was on the front line of the Cold War—but he knew something wasn't right because he would've been scrambled, as he said, "if a Russian farted," yet nothing happened when the president of the United States was assassinated. And he stressed that protocol at that level doesn't break down, so he always suspected something was amiss. And that's not something he wanted to entertain; he didn't want to go there, but he knew something was suspicious about the whole thing.

So, over the years, he would say something to you, or you would ask him about the assassination.

When I was a kid, my father and I watched *60 Minutes*, a CBS Special Report—all of the typical things you could watch back then that were related to the assassination, and I remember my dad said, "They killed that bastard." Of course, I was like, "What? What do you mean?" And he told me why he felt that way. When I started working on the film, he told me the full story of how they weren't scrambled that day, which totally broke high-level protocol. "This just doesn't happen, ever," he told me.

And, by "they," when he said, "They killed that bastard," who was he referring to?
He was referring to the people in his world, so the military and elements within the Pentagon . . . the Joint Chiefs of Staff or rogue elements within those Pentagon groups. They were within the world he was familiar with his whole life, which is why he was acutely aware of how "highly irregular" it was for them *not to be* scrambled at that time.

The idea that these citizen researchers were trying to find the answers really struck a chord with you, didn't it?
It sure did. I like to tell stories about people who are kind of under the radar and ignored in general society. All of my stories have been about people like that . . . and these researchers seemed like the ultimate group of people who were ignored. The work they were doing was so critically important, yet they were ignored, shunned, ridiculed ad hominem . . . just one thing after another. And that piqued my interest because if they were so wrong, why would anyone bother to spend time mocking them? I felt they were onto something, and that's why there was such a huge push by virtually every institution in the country to discredit them and shut them down.

What year did you start your film project?
The start year for my journey was when I got out of film school in 1998, when I began thinking about my first project out of school. I quickly learned I knew nothing about the Kennedy assassination, and to make a film, an honest film, about the researchers and what they went through, I had to learn everything I could about the case. So, I spent the next three years devouring everything I could get my hands on . . . reading every book and watching every film. I was obsessed for three years.

I've noticed as a result of doing research for this book that objective thinkers feel intuitively that there's something not quite right about

the official conclusions regarding the assassination, and they become obsessed with the case.

And the more you learn about it, the more you realize that a) it's endlessly fascinating, and b) there was a major injustice perpetrated, and quite simply, it just made me angry. I couldn't freaking believe we'd been lied to, and to such an extent. I felt like I needed to learn about the case, and then, once I started the film, I learned it's all about building relationships. I had to build relationships with a community of people who had been shit on by every single media figure out there, so why would they bother with someone like me? I had to do what we in the business call "porch work," and that's simply visiting people, shutting your mouth, and learning from the researchers themselves . . . and doing that over the course of years. I had to gain their trust so I could get access to the best and the brightest JFK assassination researchers out there.

I knew it was going to take time. I hoped it would be one of those one- or two-year projects, but it ended up being a fourteen-year process. It has almost defined my professional career because it took so long, but I felt I owed it to the researchers who gave me so much of their time to finish the film for them, and once you build relationships, you just can't not pursue a project. I felt I couldn't take on other projects until I finished this one, but as you know, the more you learn, the more you learn what you *don't* know, and I couldn't interview these people until I really understood what they were working on.

There are so many films out there about the Kennedy assassination that were just one- or two-year films, and you can tell. They only go so deep . . . they don't know exactly who to interview, so they just interview the famous people, the ones with more notoriety. They don't interview the older researchers or the ones doing amazing work but don't get a lot of press.

One of the things I loved about your film was I had never seen some of these particular individuals being interviewed. Getting different perspectives from them was enlightening.

I shot the first frame of the film on June 10, 2002, in Washington, DC, at American University on the anniversary of JFK's peace speech. It was an interview with John Judge,[1] who became the central character in my film. He was the narrative thread we kind of followed, and he became my research mentor. His method was sound; it was nonspeculative, and he would only follow what he could prove, what was proven in the documents. He was part of a small group responsible for helping form the Assassination Records Review Board and the JFK Records Collection Act. His Citizens for an Open Archive had already drafted the bill, the JFK Records Act, so they had it in place after the movie *JFK* come out.

He was the heart and soul of the film. When I found out he passed away, I got quite upset.

He was an amazing, amazing person, and I barely touched on all of the things he did. He was involved in the Winter Soldier Initiative after Vietnam, helping soldiers come home and tell their stories. He helped arrange to give these soldiers a safe place in which to tell their stories. He was a conscientious objector, yet he was the guy who helped returning vets get the benefits they were promised but were being denied. He's the one who went into schools and made teens aware of the options they had. He would say, "You don't necessarily have to go into the military. There are a number of grants, inexpensive schools, and jobs you can have while you're in school." He gave so much to the community at large. He was more than just a JFK researcher; he was a searcher for truth and justice in general.

Did you know what you wanted to accomplish with the film when you started, and did the finished product turn out being the same thing you envisioned up front?

It wasn't the same thing. My initial vision was to offer a simple portrait of a community of researchers. What it evolved into was the story of what they were up against, the challenges they faced, and their goals, so it became much more. I quickly realized this wasn't going to be a simple story about a subculture. I was going to have to enter realms they had been in, and in order to do that I had to face uncomfortable truths about my preconceptions about American institutions. I didn't think that was going to be part of this film. I thought it was going to be a simple story, but it quickly became a much larger story in which I had to criticize institutions I thought I could trust.

Is your father still alive?
No. He passed away in '07.

So, you started this project while he was still alive. Did he have any thoughts about you making the film?
He thought it was a mistake. He thought I'd never be able to tell the story. He thought I was entering a realm of deep conspiracy, and his thinking was twofold. He didn't want me to waste my time on something I wasn't going to be able to get to the bottom of. So, he saw it as folly, but I think he was worried that if I started asking questions, I'd enter an area of study in which I'd be ridiculed and face difficulties. And I think as a father, he didn't want me facing difficulties. He wanted me to make Hollywood films that felt good and made me a lot of money. He was a child during the Great Depression, so he wanted me to be able to make money and live an easy life.

When you say folly, not folly from the standpoint of "this is all just ridiculous," but more from the standpoint of "there's no way you're going to be able to find out what you want to find out," correct?
Correct.

Why do you think it was important for you to conduct an institutional analysis while making this film?
The main institution was the mainstream media and even independent media . . . just the media at large. I always thought the media were our Fourth Estate and should be our fourth branch of government. I always assumed I could trust the media and they were doing everything they could to hold power accountable. But I quickly learned, upon really digging into the media at that time, they had been co-opted, infiltrated, and embraced by our intelligence services at the highest levels. And it wasn't just rogue elements within these agencies, it was the entire institution of the CIA, of the NSA, of the DIA, that the media welcomed with open

arms in order to tell the "US Intelligence" side of the story. The media knew they were engaging in propaganda.

Do you think this was a by-product of the Cold War?
That's part of it, yes. This is just my opinion, but I believe people like Walter Cronkite felt the Cold War was the most important thing to fight, and that to even speculate about other assassination possibilities, to even question the intelligence agencies of the United States and the military, would give the Russians the upper hand, and I just don't think he wanted to go there.

In your film, you include footage of Cronkite and other mainstream journalists such as Dan Rather and Peter Jennings, who years after the assassination produced TV specials during which they continued to staunchly support the Warren Commission Report and portray Lee Harvey Oswald as a lone-nut assassin.
They went out of their way to deceive the American public, and they knew exactly what they were doing. They knew they weren't interviewing legitimate researchers when they did their specials. They only interviewed researchers who had been working on the case for ten years; they didn't interview people who had been working on the case for forty-plus years.

You also include video clips and soundbites from attorney Vincent Bugliosi[2] in your film.
He was in the pocket. And I think more than anyone else who was in the government's and/or the media's pocket, Bugliosi was a serious press hound. He had an ego, and he needed the press, and they needed him. I included these individuals in the documentary to show the frustrations of the citizen researchers and what they had to deal with. And I didn't have to call them out; I simply showed the footage of them saying what they said to the American people. And I think to most Americans, it's insulting.

I always felt that Walter Cronkite was a "nation first" kind of guy who felt it wouldn't be good for America if we questioned the official assassination narrative.

I agree. And it was a simple story he could sell to the American public, that they would accept, and then we could move on. I think he truly believed millions of Americans would die if we went to war with the Soviet Union, and it would destroy the country if it came out that the US government killed its own president. That would give our enemies and adversaries an upper hand beyond anything; it would put American democracy at risk.

If true, it was a coup d'état too big to fail. You had to go along with it to protect the country.
And that was difficult for me, but I knew it was more difficult for my dad and people like my dad, so that's one of the things I looked into early on. I researched the stand-down orders that occurred at the time of the assassination and shortly thereafter. There were stand-down orders throughout the military—our nuclear code books were pulled out of our long-range bombers, my dad wasn't scrambled, and there were a number of other anomalies that occurred regarding protocol at the highest levels. These serious irregularities had to happen by order, and the only people who could give those orders were the Joint Chiefs of Staff. My dad knew that. I think deep down, he knew his supreme military leaders gave those stand-down orders, and it scared the hell out of him. It sure as hell scared me when I learned that, and it also confirmed everything the researchers were saying.

What have you concluded about the actual assassination based on your research?
Well, it's interesting. When I'm at dinner parties or soirees with friends and I'm asked who killed Kennedy, the first thing I say is I don't know because it requires a much longer answer than simply stating a person. Serious researchers will ask you this question as a kind of litmus test. They asked me, "Who killed Kennedy?" and I answered, "I don't know, but it wasn't Lee Harvey Oswald." They responded, "That's the correct answer." I gained a lot of trust from simply being honest.

But based on my own research and having interviewed credible research-ers for many years, it appears the plan started with the Joint Chiefs of Staff, and then they employed their assets from the intelligence community, and it also appears that Operation Mongoose,[3] in which everything had been put into place for the assassination of foreign leaders, was turned inward. And in that regard, it was a very limited conspiracy. Very few people actually knew about it.

Harold Weisberg[4] concluded there were probably twelve people who knew exactly what was happening, and the rest were simply unknowing assets used at various levels. For example, all of the soldiers who were told to stand down, and the commander at Fort Sam Houston who complained and protested that they were being told to stand down . . . they weren't involved in the conspiracy. They were simply following orders.

And I think people like J. Edgar Hoover, LBJ, and others at high levels were accessories after the fact. I don't believe Hoover knew, and I don't believe LBJ knew an actual assassination attempt was going to occur. Earl Warren was also an accessory after the fact; LBJ strong-armed him into heading up the Warren Commission and whitewashing the whole thing.

What level of audacity would it have taken for the Joint Chiefs of Staff to sit in a room, behind closed doors, and say, "We've got to get rid of the president"?
I don't think they felt they were being audacious at all. I truly believe they felt Kennedy was a danger to the country, and they felt they didn't have time for the next election to take place to save the country. They also realized, early on, that Kennedy would be reelected, so they felt they had no choice. I believe they were doing what they could to, in their minds, preserve American democracy and protect us from the Soviet Union.

So, they were acting like Cold Warriors.
They were pure Cold Warriors. They didn't see their act as treason; they saw themselves as patriots trying to save the United States of America from someone who was selling us out, whom they perceived to be selling us out. But this is almost more insidious than if it was an evil cabal because it was institutional.

Both John Judge and Pen Jones, an early researcher who was Judge's mentor, would always say, "The shots didn't come from the grassy knoll; the shots came from the Pentagon." With that in mind, it's almost freeing because it takes the assassination out of Dealey Plaza, where a lot of researchers obsess about the shoe size of an assassin. Dealey Plaza was simply a mechanism to kill him; it's not going to tell us anything about why he was killed, which is the essential question.

In your opinion, was Lee Harvey Oswald a patsy?
Yes. One hundred percent. There are a number of things that confirm this for me. Just the facts about his physical presence on the second floor of the Texas School Book Depository at the time of the assassination means he couldn't have done it, and this has been verified in both eyewitness testimony and government documents.

He had also been in places where patsies were created. There's both testimony and documentation he was in the Office of Naval Intelligence's false defector program in North Carolina. He was trained as a false defector, and his movements in the Soviet Union strongly support this. The Soviet Union released their classified documents on Oswald in the early '90s, and they showed that his case went all the way up to Khrushchev's desk, which is shocking. The Soviets knew he was a plant, a false defector, and not a real defector, and they were extremely interested in his movements. This tells us a lot about who he was and how he was seen by the powers here in the United States, as well as in the Soviet Union.

Then he was allowed to travel back to the States, where he was given back his passport and given money to travel. This doesn't happen to defectors, especially during the Cold War. Remember that Oswald was someone who had been at Atsugi Air Base,[5] where the U-2 flights over the Soviet Union originated. Everything points to the fact he was groomed to be an agent, and he was an agent who was ultimately used as a patsy.

And he wasn't the only one who was set up as a patsy. We know there were multiple assassination attempts and/or placements around the country. The Chicago plot was revealed, the Florida plot was revealed, and there were patsies who looked like him, who had similar backgrounds, who had also been put in place. Unfortunately for Oswald, he was the one who was in place where the assassination was successful.

But to me, the biggest thing that points to him being a patsy, or him being more than just a lone-nut assassin, is the Raleigh call . . . the North

Carolina connection. This was researched and revealed by Grover Proctor, a researcher who lives in North Carolina.

For clarification, can you explain what the Raleigh call was?
Oswald made a few phone calls after he was arrested. He called his wife, he called a lawyer, and he made another call to a William Hurt in Raleigh, North Carolina. Hurt was a former Army Intelligence agent. What's interesting about this is Oswald had his contact information memorized. A William Hurt didn't appear in any of his personal papers, address book, or in anything they found on his person or in his belongings at his rooming house. To most researchers, and almost every Army researcher, it's another indication Oswald was a patsy. He was making that call to try and save his own ass. He was given a number and a name to call if he was ever compromised or arrested.

Is there anything you've learned that suggests Oswald, in the days leading up to the assassination, knew he might be in trouble?
Researchers I've spoken with have differing opinions on this. Many believe he knew something was going to take place in Dealey Plaza that day. I tend to believe these individuals because of who he was and what he knew. I also tend to follow John Judge's opinion on this because he was so reasonable and sound, and he also believed Oswald knew something was going to happen in Dealey Plaza. He believed Oswald didn't realize he was the patsy until *after* the assassination, which explains his movements back to his rooming house and then to the Texas Theatre. Judge believed Oswald was told by his "handler" to go to the Texas Theatre, but that Oswald was supposed to be assassinated there by the Dallas police.

And when that didn't happen, they had to get Jack Ruby to kill him. They used the mob, which was part of Operation Mongoose . . . the CIA and the FBI working with the mob. It's very simple, and again, a very closed conspiracy. I tend to go with the presumption of Occam's Razor, which states that all things being equal, the simplest explanation is usually the most reasonable explanation. However, when you enter this field of study, you have to reevaluate that presumption as new information is revealed. There's no way to peruse the millions of pages of documents that have been released under the JFK Records Act and *not* change your view. The new information has to be calculated, and the most plausible explanation is there was a conspiracy to kill the president of the United States, and the perpetrators didn't think it was a coup d'état, but it certainly was. It was a military coup d'état, and they used elements of our intelligence agencies, the mob, and the FBI to cover it up.

Today, people throw the term "conspiracy theorist" around both broadly and loosely. As a filmmaker, what do you say to people when they call you a conspiracy theorist for making this film?
Well, the etymology of that term didn't exist until the CIA wrote Document 1035–960,[6] which was directed at critics of the Warren Commission. The CIA told their media assets they were to label anyone who doubted the Warren Commission report as a conspiracy theorist, that being in a derogatory way. When people realize the CIA came up with this descriptive term specifically in response to Warren Commission critics, it's a shocking revelation. Labeling someone as a conspiracy theorist is just a way to dismiss them, that's all.

That's why I love how John Judge reacted to that. I have a whole section in my movie about those who label people conspiracy theorists, and people on the right *and* on the left both do it; it's not a left-right paradigm. Judge said, "I don't know where they get this pop psychology nonsense, but I don't fluff my pillow at night thinking there was a vast conspiracy that killed my president and actually sleep better because of it." His point is it doesn't give him or anyone else comfort to think it was a vast conspiracy. We would all much rather believe it was a lone nut, but the evidence simply doesn't support that.

Walt Brown[7] talks about that, too. He said he would much rather believe it was an aberration, an insane guy who slipped through the cracks and killed the president, and it couldn't be prevented because insane people exist, and sometimes they slip through the cracks. We actually saw this happen at the beginning of World War I when the Archduke Ferdinand was killed. It was a conspiracy, but it was one or two people who slipped through the cracks, and they found themselves in front of him on a road in a traffic jam, so they were able to shoot him. This *does* happen, but unfortunately this wasn't the case with the Kennedy assassination.

What do you believe have been the ripple effects of the JFK assassination?

I think John Judge summed it up perfectly when he said American democracy cannot exist until we solve the Kennedy assassination because that's when everything changed . . . that's when democracy was lost . . . and everything since has been clouded by the assassination of the duly elected president. We've seen the ripple effects in American democracy ever since, with LBJ, Nixon, and Carter, who was an intelligence agent . . . Bush I, an intelligence agent, and Bush II as an extension of Bush I . . . Clinton, who did the bidding of all of the intelligence agencies and the Pentagon.

Another ripple effect is literally history itself. The past is prologue, and we can't learn about and fix our present situation unless we understand our history. Kennedy was dedicated to leaving Vietnam. He signed an executive order to pull out by the end of 1965, with the first 1,000 US

Among the immediate ripple effects of the Kennedy assassination was the rise of the counterculture movement, an antiestablishment/antiauthority cultural phenomenon that included massive Vietnam War protests. (Photo by Garth Eliassen/Getty Images)

soldiers stationed in Vietnam withdrawn by the end of 1963. Imagine America without the Vietnam War, the divisiveness, the deaths of 58,000 Americans.

It literally defined a decade, so that's a whole decade that wouldn't have played out the way it did.
And, again, the ripple effects to the extent that in the aftermath of the Vietnam War, liberals have the false label as being antimilitary, and conservatives have the false label of being the only group that's promilitary. That's an instant divide in our country, and the Pentagon and the powers that be have fostered that division. When we're divided, it's easier to control us. It just is. A house divided, right?

Why is it so important to keep this story alive even after so many years have passed?
There are many parts to this, and I also think about this as why the Kennedy assassination matters. We have the history part I just spoke about and the fact that the past is prologue. I don't think our national honor can be restored until Lee Harvey Oswald's innocence is established and acknowledged. It's similar to the Dreyfus Affair in France in the early part of the twentieth century. Dreyfus was accused of collaborating with the enemy, and he was tried and found guilty. Then after many appeals, he was exonerated of the crime, but he was never proven innocent until documents were released in 2013. Only then did the French government admit Dreyfus was innocent of the crime of treason against the French people, and that's when the French regained their honor. I personally think it's a similar situation with Lee Harvey Oswald. We won't fully have our honor back until he's acquitted or until our government acknowledges he was innocent of the crime of killing President Kennedy.

Do you think you've done your part in keeping the story alive, or at least in trying to keep it alive?
I've done my part in trying to. I think the biggest success of my film is validating the work of the independent researcher. Anyone with an objective observer's mind who watches the film will realize this. It's also a gift to

President Richard Nixon and the Watergate scandal further eroded the trust Americans had in their federal government and institutions. (Photo by David Hume Kennerly/Getty Images)

individuals like John Judge, that I can say, "Hey, no matter what anyone else thinks, I see what you've done, and you deserve all of the credit possible." I think it's as simple as that.

What would you want younger generations to understand about the JFK assassination and the researchers you profiled?
I want younger people to question everything, and especially question the institutions they think they should trust, mainly the media. I also want them to understand that by looking at the citizen researchers in my film, they, too, can become citizen researchers. They have a place in our democracy, this country belongs to all of us, and by working together, we can achieve remarkable things. By working together, these researchers got the JFK Records Act passed, and that's the largest release of documents in the history of the world—thirteen million pages have been released. On the other hand, fifty-eight years after the assassination, upwards of 50,000 pages still haven't been released. That's the lesson I want them to learn . . . that these researchers worked together and got the biggest release of documents in the world, and they can do that, too.

What was the one quality in all of these citizen researchers that stuck out to you the most?
A profound sense of truth . . . a dedication to truth and justice. More than anything, they just wanted to learn the truth, the truth about a very important event in our history. As simple as that . . . but getting to that truth isn't quite as simple. Another really interesting thing that surprised me about these researchers is they span the political spectrum of American life. You have the most conservative people sitting next to the most liberal people, and they're getting along and working together, and the lesson we can learn from this is so important. By working together, we can re-establish American democracy where right and left can work toward a common goal. How we get to that goal differs based on your political predispositions, but Kennedy came from a time when the right and the left were friends. You simply disagreed, but you could work together and be friends and compromise.

How has your journey in making this film and learning what you've learned affected you on a personal level? And has it changed you?
Remarkably so. After all of these years, it's given me unbridled, open optimism in my fellow countrymen and in the possibilities of change, simply because of the citizen researchers doing what they've done. I believe in my country because of them. I believe in my fellow citizens because of them. I believe in the Cartesian common sense of the average person. Given the proper information, people are capable of change. Getting that information is difficult, but I've seen people change their opinions. I've seen people change and grow and become more active in public life simply because of the work of these researchers. And the lesson we can learn from Kennedy's life is that he fought for peace, and he knew he would probably be killed because of it. He had premonitions about his own death, yet he still pursued peace. And for me, it's optimism and hope . . . that's what I take away from all of these years.

REFLECTIONS

Friends, Romans, countrymen, lend me your ears;
I come to bury Caesar, not to praise him;
The evil that men do lives after them,
The good is oft interred with their bones,
So let it be with Caesar . . . The noble Brutus
Hath told you Caesar was ambitious:
If it were so, it was a grievous fault,
And grievously hath Caesar answered it . . .
Here, under leave of Brutus and the rest,
(For Brutus is an honourable man;
So are they all; all honourable men)
Come I to speak in Caesar's funeral . . .
He was my friend, faithful and just to me:
But Brutus says he was ambitious;
And Brutus is an honourable man . . .
He hath brought many captives home to Rome,
Whose ransoms did the general coffers fill:
Did this in Caesar seem ambitious?
When that the poor have cried, Caesar hath wept:
Ambition should be made of sterner stuff:
Yet Brutus says he was ambitious;
And Brutus is an honourable man.

You all did see that on the Lupercal
I thrice presented him a kingly crown,
Which he did thrice refuse: was this ambition?
Yet Brutus says he was ambitious;
And, sure, he is an honourable man.
I speak not to disprove what Brutus spoke,
But here I am to speak what I do know.
You all did love him once, not without cause:
What cause withholds you then to mourn for him?
O judgement! thou art fled to brutish beasts,
And men have lost their reason . . . Bear with me;
My heart is in the coffin there with Caesar,
And I must pause till it come back to me.

—William Shakespeare, *Julius Caesar*
Mark Antony's Eulogy

There are certain events that linger, events so impactful and emotionally charged they cast a permanent shadow over a place and its people. The assassination of Julius Caesar was one of these events, as it marked a turning point in the history of Rome. Caesar's murder on the Ides of March placed the Roman Republic at a crossroads that ultimately led to the emergence of its Imperial era, during which the "common man" lost true political power.

I've walked on the hallowed ground of Gettysburg, Pennsylvania, where close to 60,000 men became casualties during a three-day struggle in 1863. This bloody battle not only changed the course of the Civil War, but also of American history. More than 150 years later, the strong emotional toll exacted from that clash still resonates . . . the sheer terror, pain, and hopelessness felt by those soldiers have become a permanently placed dark shadow looming above the surrounding environment.

Two thousand years after the assassination of Julius Caesar, and one hundred years after the battle of Gettysburg, another enduring event occurred when President John F. Kennedy was assassinated in Dallas, Texas. At the time of the assassination, it was so much bigger than anyone realized, and it has hovered like a dark shadow and disfigured like a terrible scar, not only on the landscape of Dealey Plaza, but on the American experience, ever since. It has become an indelible imprint on the American psyche, whether we realize it or not . . . and whether we want to accept it or not.

When I started this project, my goal was to share current perspectives on the Kennedy assassination and examine its ripple effects. I wasn't sure where the journey would lead me, but a very wise man once told me, "When you're on purpose in life, the waters will part for you," so my plan was to be purposeful and authentic in the work. By moving forward with an open mind and good intentions, I knew certain synchronicities would occur that would help shape the book into what it was meant to be. I also knew it would be an emotional journey, a testament to the fact that even though the assassination occurred in 1963, its impacts are still being felt today.

What I wasn't prepared for, however, was the sheer intensity and mix of emotions—sadness, frustration, helplessness, defiance, and outrage—that still surround it. The collateral damage associated with the assassination, as well as the collateral damage associated with being part of the CIA "family," left lasting scars on many individuals, including several inter- viewees in this book.

What also moved me deeply was the level of commitment and con- viction displayed by the researchers and authors who continue to do the heavy lifting so that someday the entire truth regarding the murder of President Kennedy will come to light. The amount of pushback they endure is staggering, yet they continue to do the important work.

The biggest surprise for me, and I believe will be for many readers, was the fascinating insight provided regarding Lee Harvey Oswald. I never anticipated this book would be as much about Oswald as it would be about Kennedy. We know Oswald was murdered by Jack Ruby before he could be tried for the murder of President Kennedy, but the jury, at least as it's comprised of in this book, has reached its verdict: The overwhelm- ing majority of them believe Lee Harvey Oswald was a patsy, and some went as far as to say, with confidence, that he was a US Intelligence asset who knew about the assassination plans and attempted to warn the FBI about plots in *two* different cities—Chicago and Dallas. And emotions were high on this count; the sense of injustice perpetrated against Oswald, and the undue burden his family has had to carry ever since, is something most of the interviewees found wholly unacceptable.

I can't say with any level of certainty what Oswald's role was in the assassination, if any, because, as I tell people, I wasn't there. I wasn't on the sixth floor of the Texas School Book Depository when the shots rang out to see if Oswald, or anyone else for that matter, was perched in a sniper's nest by that window. Likewise, I wasn't on the front steps of the Depository to notice if Oswald was actually standing next to me watching the president and first lady pass by just before the shots were fired. And I wasn't behind the grassy knoll or in any other locations where I could have identified possible "other" assassins.

I don't know what to make of Oswald, but what appears most likely when using some critical-thinking skills is he was a low-level CIA asset who was also used by the FBI for intelligence operations. Further, he was in the fake-defector program run by the CIA, which explains a great deal about how he was able to be "sheep-dipped" and set up to take the fall for Kennedy's murder. And if in fact Oswald was set up by his handlers at the CIA and used as a scapegoat in the most consequential coup d'état ever perpetrated, than he most certainly needs to be exonerated of this crime before the United States can ever redeem itself and get back on track to being a beacon for freedom and democracy. One thing is certain: As Americans, we've been told little to nothing about the real Lee Harvey Oswald, regardless of whether or not he fired a gun that day, but thanks to individuals such as Judyth Vary Baker, Pat Hall, and Victoria Sulzer, we now have a much greater understanding of the man he was, albeit an incomplete picture.

One of the things that also became abundantly clear as a result of conducting these interviews is that human nature, and the negative character traits associated with being human, must be considered in determining the "why" of the Kennedy assassination. Additionally, when determining the "why" of the response to the assassination and the American public's almost zombie-like acquiescence to the "official narrative," we must explore the psychology of human behavior while considering certain factors, including personal experiences, the society in which people live, and the indoctrination to which they've been subjected. This is where Fran Shure, Lee Basham, Dorothy Lorig, and David Denton provided valuable insight in regard to the social sciences and humanities and how applying these disciplines and their tenets can explain a great deal about both the motives of the perpetrators and why it was so easy to pull the wool over the eyes of the American public.

This much is crystal clear: US intelligence agencies, especially during the 1950s and 1960s, answered to no one and sanctioned many nefarious and illegal endeavors that should have landed many of their decision makers in prison for a very long time. Some of the crimes against humanity perpetrated by these agencies rivaled the egregious crimes committed by the Nazis in the 1930s and 1940s. They also engaged in a propaganda campaign to win the minds of the American people that would have made Joseph Goebbels proud. Programs such as Operation Northwoods, MK Ultra, and Operation Mockingbird *did* exist, and they were all aimed at manipulating both the American media and the American public.

In fact, the refusal, and ultimately failure, of the Fourth Estate to do its job after the Kennedy assassination served to solidify the power of the perpetrators and cast anyone who ever questions authority in a negative light. Our Fourth Estate no longer exists; the mainstream media is controlled by the deep state and special interests, and as a result, we can no longer call ourselves a democratic system of checks and balances. The oligarchs have won, warmongering and world dominance have become our modus operandi, and American Exceptionalism has become a distant memory.

When you think about it, we've always been a country wherein an elite class rules over the masses—the few over the many as a perceived necessity in governing. Almost every top official in the United States in 1963 (and throughout our history) was socioeconomically advantaged and Ivy League educated. There were exceptions, of course, but we need only look at how the CIA recruited its members to see how the American system worked. Allen Dulles had blue blood, and he recruited men of the same social status straight out of Harvard, Yale, and other Ivy League schools. From the day they were born, these individuals were indoctrinated to believe they were superior to the masses and that one day they would rule over them. This sounds hyperbolic, but it isn't. Elitism is a belief system that supports the notion that a select group of people actually have superior intellect, special skills, notability, wealth, and power and therefore deserve influence and authority over others. It is the opposite of populism, which emphasizes the idea of "the people," as in "We the People . . . ."

Add to this elitist mentality an obsessive preoccupation with self (egomaniac); an inflated sense of self-importance, omnipotence, and entitlement (narcissist); and a lack of empathy, conscience, remorse, guilt, or shame (sociopath); and you've just described some of the personality traits of many of the major players in US Intelligence in 1963. Historically, many people in powerful positions (politicians, CEOs, barons of industry) tend to exhibit destructive mental and emotional traits. This is simply part of the human condition (recall Donald Jeffries's "Bullyocracy" social hierarchy theory), and it is something that sheds a great deal of light on the minefield President Kennedy was trying to navigate in the early 1960s.

Allen Dulles and his brother, John Foster Dulles, represented a very powerful and elite class of people who had a strong sense of entitlement as a result of their inherent influence. They were two of the most authoritative men in the world during a time when a Cold War mentality allowed many powerful people to act with impunity. The only thing in their way in 1963 was John Kennedy, an Irish Catholic president whose father was a bootlegger and who, together with his brother, Robert, was determined to shake things up in this country and change the old-school paradigms of those times in order to create a better tomorrow. This, of course, was a major threat to the real power brokers in this country who were used to getting their way in all matters. I can only imagine the egoism and arrogance (and in some cases sociopathy) coursing through the veins of individuals such as J. Edgar Hoover, Allen Dulles, Clint Murchison, George Herbert Walker Bush, William Harvey, James Angleton, Cord Meyer, Lyndon Johnson, Edward Lansdale, et al. According to their paradigm, they "deserved" to sway influence over the poor, huddled masses; after all, it was a birthright.

Each and every one of these men wielded immense power, and they didn't respond well to those who would upset their oligarchic agenda. Kennedy, for his part, wasn't perfect, but he was a threat to the status quo because he realized, as a result of the Cuban Missile Crisis and his

Allen Dulles (left) and his brother, John Foster Dulles (right), represented an extremely powerful and elite group of Americans who saw war as profit. (Source: Bettmann via Getty Images)

adversarial encounters with the Cold Warriors embedded in the halls of US politics, that a push for peaceful relationships with the Soviet Union and an end to the Cold War was the only way to prevent nuclear annihilation. Kennedy, for all intents and purposes, was in a tug-of-war with a massive freight train created by the Cold War mentality prevalent at that time. His domestic enemies were many, and I believe he became fully aware of what he was up against when he was deliberately misled by Allen Dulles in regard to the failed Bay of Pigs Invasion in 1961.

Again, I hesitate to conclude anything about the JFK assassination in regard to who planned it and who pulled the trigger(s) because I wasn't there. I wasn't invited to any clandestine meetings among the Joint Chiefs of Staff and/or rogue elements of the CIA when, and if, any mention of eliminating President Kennedy came up. I wasn't in Miami when meetings between militant Cuban exiles, mob figures, and CIA operatives such as Frank Sturgis and David Morales took place. I wasn't in New Orleans to witness the fascinating and foreboding spycraft taking place throughout that city leading up to the assassination. And I certainly wasn't lurking in the dark recesses of the minds of individuals like Allen Dulles and Lyndon Johnson, as God only knows what kind of sinful, iniquitous thoughts were swirling around in their heads.

John Kennedy and his brother, Robert, represented a refreshing change from "good old boy" politics to "a new hope" that would usher in world peace and a brighter future for all Americans. (Source: Bettmann via Getty Images)

I do, however, feel confident in proclaiming a few things. If pressed on the question of who killed John F. Kennedy, I would answer, "The Cold War killed him." And I wouldn't hesitate in saying this. Regardless of the nuances and details, there's no question the Cold War, and the times in which he governed, ultimately led to Kennedy's death. The impact of the Cold War, and the Cold Warriors it produced, cannot be overstated.

Starting before World War II even ended and Nazi war criminals could be brought to justice, the United States and United Kingdom zeroed in on a new enemy—Communism. Unfortunately, many of the elite and powerful men in this country at that time already had fascist leanings, so quickly focusing their attention on destroying Communism at all costs was something they relished. As a result, the CIA's Operation Paperclip went into effect, and thousands of Nazi war criminals were given sanctuary (in places like Argentina and the United States) courtesy of the CIA, the Vatican, and powerful American industrialists. This represents a very sad but critical moment in US history, and one that many Americans are either unaware of or are reluctant to accept as fact. The ensuing propaganda campaign against Communism was all-consuming, and the American public ravenously consumed it. For Americans, Communism was the enemy now, and nothing else mattered. Is this how Walter Cronkite must have felt when faced with the dilemma of either whitewashing the assassination or damaging the reputation of the nation he loved so much and that was committed to fighting the evil communists?

We'll most likely never know the answer to this question and many others regarding the Kennedy assassination, but thanks to the individuals who generously and graciously shared their time with me, many of whom continue to work to keep the story alive, I'm confident that one day we may know the truth about one of the worst days in American, and world, history. More important, we must learn from the Kennedy assassination and understand why it happened in order to learn from our past mistakes, hold those responsible accountable in the eyes of history, and remove that looming shadow in order to move forward as a nation and attempt to "form a more perfect union."

If I had been invited to President Kennedy's funeral and given the honor of speaking, I may have taken a line or two from Mark Antony's eulogy from William Shakespeare's *Julius Caesar*. His speech has been called a master class in irony and the way rhetoric can be used to say one thing but imply something totally different. He states in his eulogy more than once that Brutus, one of the assassins, is an "honourable man." In fact, he says, "So are they all; all honourable men." And by doing so, what Antony is actually saying to Rome's citizens is that these men, these assassins, are anything but honorable.

Perhaps I would have said:

> *But Dulles says he was ambitious;*
> *And Dulles is an honourable man . . .*
> *Here, under leave of Dulles and the rest,*
> *(For Dulles is an honourable man;*
> *So are they all; all honourable men)*
> *My heart is in the coffin there with Kennedy,*
> *And I must pause till it come back to me.*

Were those responsible for the assassination of John F. Kennedy honorable men? They may have thought they were saving the American Republic, just as the Roman conspirators believed they were saving the Roman Republic, but they were far from being honorable men. And this is something we, as Americans, must never forget. We must demand the truth about what happened on November 22, 1963. American hearts have been in that coffin with Kennedy for far too long, and the United States can't be whole again without them.

NOTES

Chapter 1

1. In 1968, a panel of four medical experts appointed by Attorney General Ramsey Clark met to examine photographs, X-rays, documents, and other autopsy evidence. The panel concluded Kennedy was struck by two bullets fired from above and behind, one traversing the base of the neck on the right without striking bone, and the other entering the skull from behind and destroying its upper right side. They also concluded the skull shot entered well above the external occipital protuberance, which was at odds with the Warren Commission's findings.

2. In a comprehensive research paper written for the Medical Research Archives in 2015 (Issue 3) titled *The John F. Kennedy Autopsy X-rays: The Saga of the Largest "Metallic Fragment,"* David Mantik concluded, "This mysterious 6.5 mm image was (secretly) added to the original X-ray via a second exposure. The alteration of the AP X-ray was likely completed after the autopsy. Its proximate purpose was to implicate Lee Harvey Oswald and his supposed 6.5 mm Mannlicher-Carcano carbine, to the exclusion of any other suspect, and thereby rule out a possible conspiracy. The ultimate purpose for such a forgery is left to the historians."

3. In 1962, William Harvey served as chief of Task Force W, the CIA's anti-Castro operation. During the Cuban Missile Crisis of October 1962, Harvey lost his job after a profane outburst against Attorney General Robert Kennedy for what he regarded as the Kennedy administration's weak Cuba policy. When Congress investigated JFK's assassination in the 1970s, the CIA pulled a 123-page file on Harvey's operational activities, but that file remains secret, according to the National Archives online database.

Chapter 2

1. The United States House of Representatives Select Committee on Assassinations (HSCA) was established in 1976 to investigate the assassinations of John F. Kennedy and Martin Luther King Jr. in 1963 and 1968, respectively. The HSCA completed its investigation in 1978 and issued its final report the following year, which concluded that Kennedy was probably assassinated as a result of a conspiracy.

2. The term "deep state" in the United States implies the existence of a premeditated effort by certain federal government employees or other persons to secretly manipulate or control the government without regard for the policies of Congress or the president of the United States. The concept of a deep state—also called a "state within a state" or a "shadow government"—was first used in reference to political conditions in countries like Turkey and post-Soviet Russia.

3. The President John F. Kennedy Assassination Records Collection Act of 1992 created the Assassination Records Review Board as an independent agency to reexamine for release the assassination-related records that federal agencies still regarded as too sensitive to open to the public. The Board finished its work on September 30, 1998, issued a final report, and transferred all its records to the National Archives and Records Administration.

4. Generally credited to Warren Commission staffer Arlen Specter, the single-bullet theory (also referred to as the magic-bullet theory) posits that a single bullet caused all the wounds to Texas Governor John Connally and the non-fatal wounds to the president, which totals up to seven entry/exit wounds in both men. Specter theorized that a three-centimeter-long (1.2") copper-jacketed lead-core bullet from a 6.5x52mm Mannlicher-Carcano rifle fired from the sixth floor of the Texas School Book Depository passed through President Kennedy's neck into Governor Connally's chest, went through his wrist, and embedded itself in Connally's thigh. If so, this bullet traversed fifteen layers of clothing, seven layers of skin, and approximately fifteen inches of muscle tissue. It also struck a necktie knot, removed four inches of rib, and shattered a radius bone.

5. Jim Garrison was the District Attorney of Orleans Parish, Louisiana, from 1962 to 1973. He is best known for his investigations into the JFK assassination and prosecution of New Orleans businessman Clay Shaw to that effect in 1969, which ended in Shaw's acquittal. He authored three books, including *On the Trail of the Assassins*, which became a prime source for Oliver Stone's film *JFK* in 1991.

6. The Zapruder film is a silent 8mm color motion picture sequence shot by Abraham Zapruder with a Bell & Howell home-movie camera as President Kennedy's motorcade passed through Dealey Plaza in Dallas, Texas, on

November 22, 1963. The sequence unexpectedly ended up capturing the president's assassination, including the fatal head shot.

7.   Since 1967, the Freedom of Information Act (FOIA) has provided the public the right to request access to records from any federal agency. It is often described as the law that keeps citizens in the know about their government. Federal agencies are required to disclose any information requested under the FOIA unless it falls under one of nine exemptions that protect interests such as personal privacy, national security, and law enforcement.

Chapter 3

1.   Charles Harrelson was an American hitman and organized crime figure who was convicted of assassinating Federal Judge John H. Wood Jr., the first federal judge to be killed in the twentieth century. While incarcerated, Harrelson admitted he had been involved in dozens of murders beginning in the early 1960s.

2.   Josefa Johnson died of a cerebral hemorrhage on December 25, 1961. Despite state law, no autopsy was conducted. Twenty-three years later, Billie Sol Estes's lawyer, Douglas Caddy, wrote to Stephen S. Trott at the US Department of Justice. In the letter, Caddy informed how *"Mr. Estes was a member of a four-member group, headed by Lyndon Johnson, which committed criminal acts in Texas in the 1960's. The other two, besides Mr. Estes and LBJ, were Cliff Carter and Mac Wallace. Mr. Estes is willing to disclose his knowledge concerning the following criminal offenses: I. Murders: 1. The killing of Henry Marshall; 2. The killing of George Krutilek; 3. The killing of Ike Rogers and his secretary; 4. The killing of Harold Orr; 5. The killing of Coleman Wade; 6. The killing of Josepha Johnson; 7. The killing of John Kinser; 8. The killing of President J.F. Kennedy. Mr. Estes is willing to testify that LBJ ordered these killings, and that he transmitted his orders through Cliff Carter and Mac Wallace, who executed the orders."*

3.   Dallas Police Officer Billy Joe "B.J." Martin said that according to his fellow motorcycle cops *"who were escorting the vice-presidential car, he [LBJ] started ducking down in the car a good 30 or 40 seconds before the first shots were fired . . . "* Martin said, in reflection upon the moments before the shooting, *"our new president is either one jumpy son of a bitch, or he knows something he's not telling about the Kennedy thing."*

4.   Allen Welsh Dulles was an American diplomat and lawyer who became the first civilian but third director of Central Intelligence. He served in the position from 1953 to 1961 and was chief spymaster during the Cold War period. He was also the first CIA Director to be fired for insubordination. President Kennedy forced his resignation because of several unlawful and reckless black operations conducted by the CIA under Dulles's direct oversight. Specifically, the president accused Dulles of lying and manipulating

him during the Bay of Pigs fiasco, during which CIA-trained Cuban exiles attempted to invade Cuba and overthrow Premier Fidel Castro. The invaders were defeated within two days.

5. James Jesus Angleton was chief of counterintelligence for the Central Intelligence Agency (CIA) from 1954 to 1974. His official position within the organization was Associate Deputy Director of Operations for Counterintelligence (ADDOCI). He wielded far-ranging power and influence during his long tenure at that position. Angleton's Special Investigation Group (SIG), which was tasked with investigating current CIA agents who were potential security risks, held a personnel file on Lee Harvey Oswald three years prior to the Kennedy assassination, thus making Oswald a compromised CIA asset.

6. Carlos Joseph Marcello was an American crime boss of the New Orleans crime family from 1947 until the late 1980s. G. Robert Blakely and other investigators have asserted that Marcello—along with Santo Trafficante Jr. and Sam Giancana—masterminded (or were at least coconspirators in) the 1963 assassination of President Kennedy in retaliation for federal prosecution that threatened their secret criminal organization's multibillion-dollar international organized crime empires.

Chapter 4

1. Earl Forrest Rose was the medical examiner for Dallas County, Texas, at the time of the assassination of President Kennedy. After being shoved by Kennedy's aides, he stepped aside and allowed Kennedy's body to be removed from Parkland Memorial Hospital without performing an autopsy. He later performed autopsies on J. D. Tippit, Lee Harvey Oswald, and Jack Ruby. In a 1992 interview, he said, "the law had been broken" and "a Texas autopsy would have assured a tight chain of custody on all the evidence."

Chapter 5

1. The Association of Former Agents of the United States Secret Service (AFAUSSS) was founded in 1971 to bring together former and current employees of the Secret Service for comradeship, networking, and support in time of need.

2. The Babushka Lady is an unknown woman present during the assassination of President Kennedy who might have photographed the events that occurred in Dealey Plaza at the time President Kennedy was shot. Her nickname arose from the headscarf she wore, which was similar to scarves worn by elderly Russian women. Beverly Oliver, a former dancer at the Colony Club in Dallas, claims to be the Babushka Lady.

Chapter 6

1.   The Manhattan Project was the code name for the American-led effort to
     develop a functional atomic weapon during World War II. It was started
     in response to fears that German scientists had been working on a weapon
     using nuclear technology since the 1930s . . . and that Adolf Hitler was
     prepared to use it.

2.   David Ferrie was an American pilot and US Intelligence asset who was
     alleged by New Orleans District Attorney Jim Garrison to have been
     involved in a conspiracy to assassinate President Kennedy. On February 22,
     1967, less than a week after the *New Orleans States-Item* broke the story of
     Garrison's investigation, Ferrie was found dead in his apartment. Garrison's
     aide, Lou Ivon, stated that Ferrie telephoned him the day after the story of
     Garrison's investigation broke and told him: *"You know what this news story
     does to me, don't you? I'm a dead man. From here on, believe me, I'm a dead
     man."*

3.   Alton Ochsner was a surgeon and medical researcher who worked at
     Tulane University and other New Orleans hospitals before he established
     The Ochsner Clinic, now known as Ochsner Medical Center. Ochsner
     was a staunch anticommunist and known FBI and CIA asset. Freedom of
     Information Act records reveal the FBI released him in 1959 to take a "sen-
     sitive position" at Tulane University to find a vaccine against SV40, presum-
     ably to prevent an epidemic in soft-tissue cancers in children exposed to
     SV40 via the polio vaccine. Numerous documents and witness statements
     suggest an additional intention was to create a cancer-causing virus for use
     in the assassination of Fidel Castro.

4.   William Guy Banister was an employee of the Federal Bureau of Investigation,
     an assistant superintendent of the New Orleans Police Department, and a
     private investigator. After his death, he gained notoriety from allegations
     made by New Orleans District Attorney Jim Garrison that he had been
     involved in the assassination of John F. Kennedy. He was an avid anti-
     communist, alleged member of the Minutemen, the John Birch Society,
     Louisiana Committee on Un-American Activities, and alleged publisher of
     the *Louisiana Intelligence Digest*.

5.   On August 13, 1946, the Hill-Burton Act was signed into law by President
     Harry S. Truman. The bill, known formally as the Hospital Survey and
     Construction Act, was a Truman initiative that provided construction
     grants and loans to build hospitals where they were needed and would be
     sustainable.

6.   An oligarchy is a form of power structure in which power rests with a small
     number of people. These people may or may not be distinguished by one
     or several characteristics, such as nobility, fame, wealth, education, or cor-
     porate, religious, political, or military control. Some contemporary authors

and political scientists have characterized current conditions in the United States as oligarchic in nature.

Chapter 7

1. On August 9, 1963, only three months before he was accused of assassinating President Kennedy, Oswald was arrested after an altercation due to handing out leaflets at the corner of Canal Street and St. Charles Avenue. Printed on Oswald's Fair Play for Cuba Committee leaflets were the words "Hands Off Cuba!"

2. Clay Shaw was a businessman and military officer from New Orleans, Louisiana, who some researchers believe had ties to the US Intelligence community. He is best known for being the only person brought to trial (by New Orleans District Attorney Jim Garrison) for involvement in the JFK assassination. Shaw was acquitted in 1969 after less than one hour of jury deliberation, but some researchers continue to speculate on his possible involvement.

3. President Kennedy was due to appear at Soldier Field, the football stadium in Chicago, on Saturday, November 2, 1963. Three days before his arrival, the FBI contacted the Secret Service office in Chicago and informed them of a plot to assassinate President Kennedy on his journey to the stadium. According to the FBI, a group of four right–wing extremists, armed with rifles, would probably attempt the assassination while the president's car was on the Northwest Expressway between O'Hare Airport and downtown Chicago. The tip-off to the FBI about this assassination plot came from an informant identified only as "Lee."

Chapter 9

1. David Atlee Phillips joined the CIA as a part-time agent in 1950 in Chile and became a full-time operative in 1954. He operated a major psychological warfare campaign in Guatemala during the US coup and its aftermath. He rose through the ranks to intelligence officer, chief of station and eventually chief of Western Hemisphere operations, serving primarily in Latin America, including Cuba, Mexico, and the Dominican Republic. Phillips has been repeatedly accused of involvement in the JFK assassination, named by both investigators and CIA family members, as well as being implicated during the mid-1970s House Select Committee on Assassinations.

2. Cord Meyer Jr. began working for the CIA around 1949 and officially joined the agency in 1951 at the invitation of Allen Dulles. He became a high-level operative and good friend of James "Jesus" Angleton, and it is believed he was the principal operative in Operation Mockingbird, the CIA initiative put in place to secretly influence domestic and foreign media. He was married to Mary Pinchot Meyer from 1945 to 1958.

3. David Sanchez Morales, a.k.a. "El Indio," worked for the CIA under the cover of Army employment. He was involved in PBSUCCESS, the CIA's 1954 overthrow of the Guatemalan government, and rose to become chief of operations at the CIA's large JMWAVE facility in Miami. In that role, he oversaw operations undertaken against the regime of Fidel Castro in Cuba. Morales was involved in other covert operations, reportedly including plots to assassinate Fidel Castro, training intelligence teams supporting the Bay of Pigs invasion of Cuba, the CIA's secret war in Laos and its controversial Operation Phoenix in Vietnam, and the hunting down of Che Guevara in Bolivia. Morales was named by E. Howard Hunt as a participant in the JFK assassination.

4. Frank Sturgis, born Frank Angelo Fiorini, was one of the five Watergate burglars whose capture led to the end of the presidency of Richard Nixon. He served in several branches of the United States military and in the Cuban Revolution of 1958 and worked as an undercover operative for the CIA. Sturgis and Miami CIA head David Morales met with E. Howard Hunt shortly before the Kennedy assassination. Eyewitness Marita Lorenz also placed Sturgis, Oswald, and several Cuban exile militants in a house in Miami shortly before the Kennedy assassination.

5. The tramps were three men photographed by several Dallas-area newspapers under police escort near the Texas School Book Depository shortly after the Kennedy assassination. The tramps, who were rounded up in the railway yards behind Dealey Plaza, are considered "suspicious characters" by many JFK researchers due to the way they were dressed and their resemblance to either known assassins or intelligence operatives.

6. The 1954 Guatemalan coup d'état, code-named Operation PBSuccess, was a covert operation carried out by the CIA that deposed the democratically elected Guatemalan President Jacobo Arbenz and ended the Guatemalan Revolution of 1944–1954. It also installed the military dictatorship of Carlos Castillo Armas, the first in a series of US-backed authoritarian rulers in Guatemala.

7. Coast to Coast is a late-night radio talk show.

8. Charles Colson was an American attorney and political advisor who served as special counsel to President Richard Nixon from 1969 to 1970. Once known as President Nixon's "hatchet man," Colson gained notoriety at the height of the Watergate scandal for being named as one of the Watergate Seven and pleaded guilty to obstruction of justice for attempting to defame Pentagon Papers defendant Daniel Ellsberg. In 1974 he served seven months in the federal Maxwell Prison in Alabama as the first member of the Nixon administration to be incarcerated for Watergate-related charges.

9. John Foster Dulles, brother of the CIA's Allen Dulles, was an American diplomat, lawyer, and Republican Party politician. He served as United States

Secretary of State under President Dwight D. Eisenhower from 1953 to 1959. Propelled by Cold War fears and delusions, John Foster and Allen launched violent campaigns against foreign leaders they saw as threats to the United States. These campaigns helped push countries from Guatemala to the Congo into long spirals of violence, led the United States into the Vietnam War, and laid the foundation for decades of hostility between the United States and countries from Cuba to Iran.

Chapter 10

1. Frank Wisner was one of the founding officers of the Central Intelligence Agency and played a major role in Agency operation throughout the 1950s. He began his intelligence career in the Office of Strategic Services in World War II. After the war, he headed the Office of Policy Coordination (OPC), one of the OSS successor organizations, from 1948 to 1950. In 1950, the OPC was placed under the CIA and renamed the Directorate of Plans. It was first headed by Allen Dulles. Wisner succeeded Dulles in 1951 when Dulles was named Director of Central Intelligence. Wisner remained as Deputy Director of Plans (DDP) until September 1958, playing an important role in the early history of the CIA. He suffered a breakdown in 1958 and retired from the Agency in 1962. He committed suicide in 1965.

2. The Battle of Leyte Gulf is considered to have been the largest naval battle of World War II and, by some criteria, the largest naval battle in history, with more than 200,000 naval personnel involved. It was fought near the Philippine islands of Leyte, Samar, and Luzon on October 23–26, 1944, between combined American and Australian forces and the Imperial Japanese Navy (IJN), as part of the invasion of Leyte, which aimed to isolate Japan from the countries it had occupied in Southeast Asia, which were a vital source of industrial and oil supplies.

3. Leo Damore's son, Nick, has never been able to find the manuscript his father was working on. The last time he saw his father was when he was ten years old, about two weeks before his father's death. They were in the garden of a friend's house when his father told him, *"If anything ever happens to me, there's a box under my bed for you."* Nick saw a metal strongbox later that evening under his father's bed but never saw the box again. Nick said his father *"was getting too close and at one point claimed to have gotten the diary that outlined the relationship between Mary Meyer and JFK. He also thought he'd found out who had killed her. . . . There were lawsuits; he thought he was being followed. Now, he's potentially going after the CIA, and that's when he starts spiraling down."*

4. Ben Bradlee married Mary Pinchot Meyer's sister, Antoinette "Tony" Pinchot Pittman, in 1957 and was also very close friends with John and Jackie Kennedy. He was one of the most prominent journalists of post-World

War II America. During his time as executive editor of the *Washington Post*, he successfully challenged the government over the right to publish the Pentagon Papers (1971) and one year later backed reporters Bob Woodward and Carl Bernstein as they probed the break-in at the Democratic National Committee Headquarters in the Watergate Hotel, which ultimately led to the resignation of President Richard Nixon in 1974.

5. President Kennedy's American University speech, titled "A Strategy of Peace," was a commencement address delivered at the American University in Washington, DC, on Monday, June 10, 1963. Widely considered one of his most powerful speeches, Kennedy not only outlined a plan to curb nuclear arms, but also "laid out a hopeful, yet realistic route for world peace at a time when the US and Soviet Union faced the potential for an escalating nuclear arms race." In the speech, Kennedy announced his agreement to negotiations "toward early agreement on a comprehensive test ban treaty" (which resulted in the Nuclear Test-Ban Treaty) and announced, for the purpose of showing "good faith and solemn convictions," his decision to unilaterally suspend all US atmospheric testing of nuclear weapons as long as all other nations would do the same. Noteworthy are his comments that the United States was seeking a goal of "complete disarmament" of nuclear weapons and his vow that America "will never start a war."

6. In his book *The Secret History of the CIA*, Joseph Trento writes: *"I asked the dying man how it all went so wrong. With no emotion in his voice, but with his hand trembling, [Spymaster James] Angleton replied: 'Fundamentally, the founding fathers of US intelligence were liars. . . . Outside of their duplicity, the only thing they had in common was a desire for absolute power. I did things that, in looking back at my life, I regret. You know, the CIA got tens of thousands of brave people killed. . . . We played with lives as if we owned them. . . . You were in a room full of people that you had to believe would deservedly end up in hell.' Angleton slowly sipped his tea and then said, 'I will see them there soon enough.'"*

Chapter 11

1. VAP-62 was a Heavy Photographic Squadron of the US Navy. Originally established as Photographic Squadron Sixty-Two (VJ-62) in April 1952, it was redesignated as Heavy Photographic Squadron (VAP-62) in July 1956. The squadron was disestablished in October 1969.

2. J. D. Tippit was an American police officer who served as an eleven-year veteran with the Dallas Police Department. About forty-five minutes after the assassination of President Kennedy, Tippit was shot and killed in a residential neighborhood in the Oak Cliff section of Dallas, Texas. Lee Harvey Oswald was charged with his murder, but many researchers dispute this, arguing that the physical evidence and witness testimony do not support that conclusion. New Orleans District Attorney Jim Garrison contended in

his book *On the Trail of the Assassins* that witness testimony and handling of evidence in the Tippit murder was flawed and that it was doubtful Oswald was the killer or even at the scene of the crime. Warren Commission attorney David Belin referred to Tippit's killing as the "Rosetta Stone to the JFK assassination."

Chapter 12

1. Since its inception in 1954 at the Bilderberg Hotel in the small Dutch town of Oosterbeek, the Bilderberg Group has been comprised of heads of international corporations, world bankers, high government officials from Europe and North America, and members of elite families such as the Rockefellers and the Rothschilds. The group comes together every spring to discuss the economic and political future of humanity and make global policy. The press has never been allowed to attend, nor have statements ever been released on the attendees' conclusions or discussions.

2. The FBI memorandum, dated November 29, 1963, is from Director J. Edgar Hoover to the State Department and is subject-headed "Assassination of President John F. Kennedy November 22, 1963." In it, Hoover reports that the Bureau had briefed "Mr. George Bush of the Central Intelligence Agency" shortly after the assassination on the reaction of Cuban exiles in Miami. A source with close connections to the intelligence community confirmed that Bush started working for the agency in 1960 or 1961, using his oil business as a cover for clandestine activities.

Chapter 13

1. Jackie Kennedy coined the phrase "Camelot" to reference her late husband's presidency. Shortly after President Kennedy was assassinated, the former first lady was talking with a journalist when she described her husband's presidency as an American Camelot, and she asked that his memory be preserved. Camelot refers to the time of King Arthur and the Knights of the Round Table and has come to refer to a place or time of idyllic happiness.

Chapter 14

1. Ruth Paine was a Russian speaker and friend of Marina Oswald who was living with her at the time of the JFK assassination. There were more than 500 witnesses for the Warren Commission, and the average number of questions asked for each witness was less than 300. Paine, on the other hand, answered more than 5,000 questions for the Commission. Over the years, researchers have speculated, but have not definitively proven, that Paine worked for the CIA.

Chapter 15

1. Thomas Hayden was an American social and political activist, author, and politician. Hayden was best known for his role as an antiwar, civil-rights, and intellectual activist in the 1960s, authoring the Port Huron Statement and standing trial in the Chicago Seven case. He was the director of the Peace and Justice Resource Center in Los Angeles County when he died in 2000.

2. Mike Lofgren is an American author and a former Republican US Congressional aide. He retired in May 2011 after twenty-eight years as a Congressional staff member. His writings, critical of politics in the United States, particularly the Republican Party, were published after his retirement and garnered widespread attention.

3. The Project for the New American Century (PNAC) was established in 1997 by a number of leading neoconservative writers and pundits to advocate aggressive US foreign policies and "rally support for American global leadership." One of the group's founding documents claimed, "a Reaganite policy of military strength and moral clarity may not be fashionable today. But it is necessary if the United States is to build on the successes of this past century and to ensure our security and our greatness in the next."

4. Michael Glennon is professor of international law at The Fletcher School of Law and Diplomacy at Tufts University. He is the author of *National Security and Double Government* and has served as a consultant to various congressional committees, the US State Department, and the International Atomic Energy Agency. He is a member of the American Law Institute, the Council on Foreign Relations, and the Board of Editors of the American Journal of International Law. He has testified before the International Court of Justice and congressional committees.

5. In *Oswald, Mexico and Deep Politics*, Peter Dale Scott takes a comprehensive look into the mysterious trip of Oswald, or someone using his name, to Mexico City in the fall of 1963. He looked at whether this trip was a key aspect of the framing of Oswald, an approved intelligence operation, or both. We now know that allegations of communist conspiracy in the wake of the JFK assassination, emanating mostly from Mexico City, caused Lyndon Johnson to put together a "blue ribbon commission" to investigate what happened in Dallas. Scott asks: Why would LBJ want the Warren Commission to rush to a conclusion, considering the far-reaching political ramifications of the commission's public findings? Scott's research suggests the evidence from Mexico City was part of the frame-up of Oswald.

Chapter 16

1. National Security Action Memorandum Number 263 (NSAM-263) was a national security directive approved on October 11, 1963, by President

Kennedy. The NSAM approved recommendations by Secretary of Defense Robert McNamara and chairman of the Joint Chiefs of Staff General Maxwell Taylor. McNamara's and Taylor's recommendations included an appraisal that "great progress" was being made in the Vietnam War against Viet Cong insurgents, that 1,000 military personnel could be withdrawn from South Vietnam by the end of 1963, and that a "major part of the US military task can be completed by the end of 1965."

2. McGeorge Bundy served as United States National Security Advisor to Presidents John F. Kennedy and Lyndon B. Johnson. Bundy, a Skull and Bones member at Yale, was a longtime CIA advisor and Council on Foreign Relations member who wrote NSAM 273 on the night of November 21, 1963, just hours before President Kennedy was assassinated. His brother, William Bundy, who was an analyst with the CIA, wrote the Gulf of Tonkin Joint Resolution, which Johnson used to escalate the Vietnam War without a required declaration of war.

3. President Kennedy was determined to improve relations with Latin America through peaceful economic cooperation and development, which would also inhibit the rise of communist-leaning insurgents such as Cuba's Fidel Castro. Kennedy proposed, through the Agency for International Development and the Alliance for Progress, both launched in 1961, to loan more than $20 billion to Latin American nations, which would promote democracy and undertake meaningful social reforms, especially in making land ownership possible for greater numbers of its people. At the time, it was the largest US aid program created for the developing world.

Chapter 17

1. The United States President's Commission on CIA Activities within the United States was set up under President Gerald Ford in 1975 to investigate the activities of the Central Intelligence Agency and other intelligence agencies within the United States. The commission was led by the vice president, Nelson Rockefeller, and is sometimes referred to as the Rockefeller Commission.

2. The Church Committee (formally the United States Senate Select Committee to Study Governmental Operations with Respect to Intelligence Activities) was a US Senate select committee in 1975 that investigated abuses by the Central Intelligence Agency, National Security Agency, Federal Bureau of Investigation, and Internal Revenue Service. It was chaired by Idaho Senator Frank Church.

3. The anti-Castro group Directorio Revolucionario Estudantil (DRE) commonly known as the Cuban Student Directorate, was an instrument of the CIA and was known inside the agency by the code name AMSPELL. The group's leaders met regularly in 1963 with George Joannides, the CIA's chief

of the Psychological Warfare branch of the agency's JMWAVE in Miami. Joannides gave them $25,000 a month to, among other things, publicize Lee Harvey Oswald's pro-Castro activities leading up the Kennedy assassination and link him to Cuba after the assassination.

4.   George Joannides was an undercover CIA officer based in Miami and New Orleans in 1963. His actions provide compelling evidence that certain Agency personnel manipulated Lee Harvey Oswald for propaganda purposes before and after President Kennedy was assassinated in Dallas on November 22, 1963. Declassified CIA records show that Joannides obstructed two official JFK investigations by not disclosing what he knew about contacts between his Cuban agents and Oswald. Most records of his activities in the summer of 1963 are still classified.

5.   The purported failure of the LIONION installation to capture a picture of Oswald was a matter of concern and some disbelief in the House Select Committee on Assassination's investigation.

6.   In the early hours of the morning of November 23, 1963, FBI agents in Dallas determined that an imposter was using Oswald's name in a taped phone call to the Soviet Embassy at the time of this visit.

Chapter 18

1.   The Milgram experiment(s) on obedience to authority figures was a series of social psychology experiments conducted by Yale University psychologist Stanley Milgram. They measured the willingness of study participants, men twenty to fifty years old from a diverse range of occupations with varying levels of education, to obey an authority figure who instructed them to perform acts conflicting with their personal conscience. Participants were led to believe they were assisting an unrelated experiment, in which they had to administer electric shocks to a "learner." These fake electric shocks gradually increased to levels that would've been fatal had they been real.

2.   Philip Zimbardo's Stanford Prison Experiment was conducted in the basement of the Stanford University psychology department in 1971. The participants in the study were twenty-four male college students who were randomly assigned to act either as "guards" or "prisoners" in the mock prison. The study was initially slated to last two weeks, but it had to be terminated after just six days because of the extreme reactions and behaviors of the participants. The guards began displaying cruel and sadistic behavior toward the prisoners, while the prisoners became depressed and hopeless.

3.   Elizabeth Noelle-Neumann developed the spiral of science theory in the field of mass communication and political science. The main ideology behind the theory is that most individuals have a fear of isolation. This means they are afraid they may be neglected or rejected by the social group or the society as a result of their opinion, especially in a controversial matter.

This fear often results in the individuals remaining silent and not airing out their views.

4. Irving Janis developed his theory of "groupthink" in 1972. Groupthink is a psychological phenomenon that occurs within a group of people in which the desire for harmony or conformity in the group results in an irrational or dysfunctional decision-making outcome. Cohesiveness, or the desire for cohesiveness, in a group may produce a tendency among its members to agree at all costs. This causes the group to minimize conflict and reach a consensus decision without critical evaluation.

5. Operation Mockingbird was a large-scale program of the CIA that began in the early years of the Cold War and attempted to manipulate news media for propaganda purposes. As part of this program, the CIA recruited leading American journalists into a propaganda network and influenced the operations of front groups. CIA support of front groups was exposed when a 1967 *Ramparts* magazine article reported that the National Student Association received funding from the CIA. In 1975, the Church and Pike Congressional investigations revealed Agency connections with journalists and civic groups.

6. The Church (see Chapter 17) and Pike Committees were companion intelligence committees in the US Senate and House of Representatives, respectively, that investigated US intelligence agencies in the mid-1970s, including the CIA, FBI, and NSA. They also investigated misuse of the IRS auditing function by officials during the Nixon administration. People tend to refer to the Church Committee—headed by Senator Frank Church—when mentioning these investigations, but the Pike Committee—headed by Democratic Representative Otis Pike—was jointly engaged in these investigations.

Chapter 19

1. The Oklahoma City bombing was a domestic terrorist truck bombing of the Alfred P. Murrah Federal Building in Oklahoma City, Oklahoma, on Wednesday, April 19, 1995. Perpetrated by two antigovernment extremists with white supremacist terrorist sympathies, Timothy McVeigh and Terry Nichols, the bombing occurred at 9:02 a.m. and killed at least 168 people, injured more than 680 others, and destroyed more than one-third of the building, which had to be demolished.

2. The Mordorian Empire is the vast, evil empire created by J.R.R. Tolkien in *Lord of the Rings*.

3. Pax Americana is a term applied to the historical concept of relative peace in the Western Hemisphere and later the Western world resulting from the preponderance of power enjoyed by the United States beginning around the

start of the twentieth century. It is primarily used in its modern connotations to refer to the peace established after the end of WWII in 1945.

Chapter 20

1. Learned helplessness occurs when an individual continuously faces a negative, uncontrollable situation and stops trying to change their circumstances, even when they have the ability to do so. The term was coined in 1967 by the American psychologists Martin Seligman and Steven Maier.

2. Jean Liedloff came into contact with the Ye'kuana (or Yequana) in the 1950s while working as a photographer for Italian diamond hunters, and in subsequent personal visits. She based her book, *The Continuum Concept: In Search of Happiness Lost,* on their way of life, particularly the upbringing of their children. She wrote the book to describe her new understanding of how we have lost much of our natural well-being, and to show us practical ways to regain it for our children and for ourselves.

3. Stanford University psychologists found that anger and sadness soared following George Floyd's death, particularly among Black Americans. They also found that when compared to other states, depression and anxiety were higher in Minneapolis, Minnesota, where Floyd's murder occurred. This finding is consistent with previous scholarship that showed location matters and the traumatic impact of racial violence and police brutality is larger in the communities in which they occur.

4. Holocaust survivor Hannah Arendt coined the term "banality of evil" while covering the 1961 trial of Adolf Eichmann, a Nazi official charged with the orderly extermination of Europe's Jews. In a series of articles for the *New Yorker* that later became the book *Eichmann in Jerusalem: A Report on the Banality of Evil,* Arendt tried to tackle a string of questions not necessarily answered by the trial itself, including: Where does evil come from? Why do people commit evil acts? How are those people different from the rest of us? She concluded people who do evil are not necessarily monsters and that sometimes they're just bureaucrats. She also concluded the Eichmann she observed on trial was neither brilliant nor a sociopath.

Chapter 21

1. In 1961 President Kennedy appointed Abraham Bolden as part of the Secret Service White House detail. Bolden spent three months working for Kennedy, and, after complaining about the "separate housing facilities for black agents on southern trips" and the "general laxity and the heavy drinking among the agents who were assigned to protect the President," he was reassigned to the Chicago Secret Service office to conduct routine anti-counterfeiting duties. Bolden claimed that in October 1963, the Chicago

Secret Service office received a teletype from the FBI warning that an attempt would be made to kill President Kennedy—by a four-man Cuban hit squad ("dissident Cuban group") armed with high-powered rifles—when he visited the city on November 2. Bolden later discovered this information was being kept from the Warren Commission. When he complained about this he was warned "to keep his mouth shut." Bolden decided to travel to Washington, where he telephoned Warren Commission Counsel J. Lee Rankin. Bolden was arrested and taken back to Chicago, where he was charged with discussing a bribe with two known counterfeiters. He was eventually found guilty of accepting a bribe and spent six years in prison. When he tried to draw attention to his case, he was placed in solitary confinement. Sam DeStefano, a Chicago mobster, was one of the men who accused Bolden of this crime. DeStefano, who was close to mobsters Sam Giancana and Charles Nicoletti, as well as Chicago police officer (and mob asset) Richard Cain, was murdered in 1973 when he was shot twice at point-blank range with a shotgun. That same year, Cain was murdered when he was shot through the bottom of his chin with a sawed-off shotgun. On June 19, 1975, shortly before he was scheduled to appear before the Church Committee, Sam Giancana was murdered in his basement kitchen after being shot in the head and neck seven times. On March 29, 1977, shortly before he was scheduled to testify before the House Select Committee on Assassinations, Charles Nicoletti was murdered in his car after being shot in the head three times.

2. Marcus Tullius Cicero was a Roman statesman, lawyer, scholar, philosopher, and academic skeptic who tried to uphold optimate principles during the political crisis that led to the establishment of the Roman Empire. His extensive writings include treatises on rhetoric, philosophy, and politics, and he is considered one of Rome's greatest orators and prose stylists.

Chapter 22

1. James Files, also known as James Sutton, served a fifty-year sentence for the 1991 attempted murders of two police officers. In 1994, he gave interviews stating he was the "grassy knoll shooter" in the assassination of President Kennedy. Files has subsequently been interviewed by others and discussed in multiple books pertaining to the assassination and related theories.

2. William Robert "Tosh" Plumlee was a CIA contract pilot who claimed that in November 1963, he was a copilot on a top-secret DC-3 flight supported by the CIA to try to stop the JFK assassination. He said the flight originated in Florida, stopped in New Orleans (where some passengers left and others came aboard), then flew on to Houston and then Dallas on the morning of November 22, 1963. He stated that among the passengers on the plane who got off in Dallas was CIA-affiliated, mob-connected Johnny Roselli. He also testified in 2004 that *"When I later learned that Oswald had been arrested as*

the lone assassin, I remembered having met him on a number of previous occasions which were connected with intelligence training matters."

Chapter 23

1. Dean Andrews was an attorney in New Orleans, Louisiana. During the trial of Clay Shaw, he was questioned by New Orleans District Attorney Jim Garrison regarding his Warren Commission testimony in which he had mentioned a man named Clay Bertrand having called him shortly after the Kennedy assassination asking him to represent Lee Harvey Oswald in Dallas, Texas. In August 1967, Andrews was convicted on three counts of perjury for lying to a grand jury in his previous testimony.
2. Established in 1840 and located in the French Quarter of New Orleans, Antoine's is the country's oldest family-run restaurant.
3. Norma Wallace, known as The Last Madam in New Orleans, ran several "bordellos" in New Orleans, but her best-known house was at 1026 Conti Street in the French Quarter, which she purchased in June 1938. Norma was known as a strict madam, running a discreet, lavish, and politically protected house of prostitution. During her reign from the 1920s through the 1960s, Norma's brothel and the ladies she employed entertained a stream of governors, gangsters, and movie stars.

Chapter 24

1. John Patrick Judge was an internationally acclaimed researcher, writer, and speaker, as well as a lifelong antimilitarist, antiracist activist, and community organizer. His primary areas of research were the assassinations of President John Kennedy, Robert Kennedy, Malcolm X, and Dr. Martin Luther King Jr. He was a key public proponent behind the creation of the Assassination Records Review Board. Beginning with the Vietnam War, Judge was not only an antiwar activist, but also a supporter of active-duty soldiers and veterans.
2. Vincent Bugliosi was an American attorney and author. He was best known for prosecuting Charles Manson and other defendants accused of the Tate-LaBianca murders of August 9–10, 1969. Bugliosi cowrote the book *Helter Skelter* (1974) about the investigation, arrest, and prosecution of Charles Manson and the Manson Family. He later wrote *Reclaiming History: The Assassination of President John F. Kennedy* (2007), in which he challenged conspiracy theories and explored the events surrounding the assassination.
3. The Cuban Project, also known as Operation Mongoose, was an extensive campaign of terrorist attacks against civilians, as well as covert operations, carried out by the CIA in Cuba. It was officially authorized on November 30, 1961, by President Kennedy after the failed Bay of Pigs Invasion. The

operation was run out of JM/WAVE, a major secret US covert operations and intelligence-gathering station established a year earlier in Miami and led by United States Air Force General Edward Lansdale on the military side and William Harvey at the CIA.

4. Harold Weisberg served as an Office of Strategic Services officer during World War II, a US Senate staff member and investigative reporter, an investigator for the Senate Committee on Civil Liberties, and a US State Department intelligence analyst who devoted forty years of his life to researching and writing about the assassinations of John Kennedy and Martin Luther King Jr. Weisberg was a strong critic of the Warren Commission Report and is best known for his seminal work, *Whitewash*, of which he said: *"In this book, I establish that the inquiry into the assassination was a whitewash, using as proof only what the Commission avoided, ignored, misrepresented and suppressed of its own evidence."* In 1992, Weisberg decided to leave his files to Hood College, where the documents were scanned and digitized at jfk.hood.edu.

5. Naval Air Facility Atsugi is a naval air base located in the cities of Yamato and Ayase in Kanagawa Prefecture, Japan. One of the aircraft based at Atsugi at least since 1957 was the U-2 spy plane. This plane was piloted by Gary Powers, which provoked an international incident when it was downed over the Soviet Union. Lee Harvey Oswald was based at Atsugi during his time in the United States Marines He was a radar operator assigned to Marine Air Control Squadron 1 and was stationed there from September 1957 to November 1958.

6. Due to the amount of public skepticism toward the Warren Commission's findings on the assassination of President Kennedy, the CIA sent a detailed directive (Document 1035–960 titled Countering Criticism of the Warren Report) to all of its bureaus. The document was released in response to a 1976 FOIA request by the *New York Times*. The directive is significant in that it played a definitive role in making the term "conspiracy theory" a weapon against any individual or group calling the government's increasingly clandestine programs and activities into question. It lays out a detailed series of actions and techniques for "countering and discrediting the claims of the conspiracy theorists, so as to inhibit the circulation of such claims in other countries."

7. Walt Brown has a PhD in history from the University of Notre Dame and teaches history at Ramapo College in New Jersey. Brown, a former special agent of the Justice Department, is a longtime researcher of the Warren Commission and the Kennedy assassination. He is also the editor of JFK/ Deep Politics and the author of several books on the subject including: *The People V. Lee Harvey Oswald* (1992), *Treachery in Dallas* (1995), *Referenced Index Guide to the Warren Commission* (1995), *JFK Assassination Quizbook* (1995), and *The Warren Commission* (1996).

INDEX

Note: Illustrations are indicated by page numbers in *italics*.